THE AUTOBIOGRAPHY OF
MARK VAN DOREN

THE AUTOBIOGRAPHY OF

Mark Van Doren, *1894*

HARCOURT, BRACE AND COMPANY • NEW YORK

c.12.58

Library of Congress Catalog Card Number: 58–10897

Printed in the United States of America

Thanks are due to Mrs. Herbert Gorman for permission to quote the letter from Herbert Gorman; the Illinois State Historical Library for permission to quote portions of "John Richman, a Typical Backwoodsman" by Dr. H. Rutherford; and *The Nation* for permission to quote portions of Allen Tate's review of *A Winter Diary*.

To
Dorothy

Lady, excellently brief
(Let me be too),
The sweet things you say
Are salt also,
For true

Contents

THE AUTOBIOGRAPHY OF
MARK VAN DOREN

Hope

1894–1900

MY father's farm lay a mile west of Hope, Illinois, an all but invisible village halfway between Danville and Urbana. A branch line of the Big Four railroad, and later an electric line which we called "the interurban," connected those two towns and ran through such smaller places as Muncie, Fithian, and Ogden; but Hope, a few miles to their north, was seldom seen by strangers during the six years between 1894 when I was born and 1900 when we moved to Urbana. Nor is it different now. Hope is hard to find in any atlas, though it still exists as Faith and Charity, its sister villages named a century ago, do not.

I was an affectionate child in an affectionate family, so that I have no unhappy memories of that time; or if I do have some, as presently shall appear, they are of such miseries as I soon could even boast about, since they made me the center of attention and in certain cases got built into little stories of which I was the hero. The earliest story of this sort that I remember had in fact two heroes, for it involved my brother Frank, two years older than I and my constant playmate in the long yard, with sheep in it and many trees, which ran down from the big white house to the road. We played here in every season of the year. There were ash and walnut groves behind the house, planted there by a former owner of the farm, and their straight rows fascinated us whenever we wandered among them; to me those groves are still ideal places, the very type of what all groves should be, and I do not forget my shock at

3

hearing, long after we moved away, that a subsequent owner had cut them down. But perhaps for the very reason that they were mysterious and wonderful we spent less time in them than we spent in the front yard, where our big brothers Carl and Guy, busy in more important ways, knew as little as our parents did of what we might be up to.

The circumstance that dates the tale in question is my inability to talk plain. Not that it does so precisely, because I was slow to speak and stammered till I was twenty. Perhaps I was three, perhaps I was four, when on this day Frank and I decided we would haul coal in our wagon, a red wagon with horses painted on its side. We had got one or two lumps loaded, and were pulling them past the house, when it occurred to us that we were hired men with a real wagon and team. My father was away as he so often was, being the only doctor for miles around, and my mother had gone somewhere too in the buggy which she drove with an expertness I admired. Our grown cousin, Inez Collison, was here from Potomac to take care of us. She was indoors at the moment, so that we thought we were alone as we shouted and swore at our imaginary plugs. At least I swore. "By Dod," I said, "Dod dam"; and more to the same effect. Frank laughed. But Inez, appearing suddenly at an open window above our heads, did not laugh. Instead she shamed us; and worse yet, she announced that when Mother came home that evening she would tell her what we had done. Instantly contrite, we had then to wait upon our punishment: perhaps a switching, perhaps only a scolding, but either was serious. I do not recall how we got through the day. I can still see, however, the buggy as it came up to the barn, with Mother in it counting on us to carry whatever she had brought, or perhaps to help her at the harness. We helped so vigorously, and escorted her into the house so piously, that she may have suspected something even then. I still do not know why nothing happened. For nothing did. Inez either told her or did not; and if she told her, our avenging goddess—who was also a wise and fond parent—may have thought we had sufficiently punished ourselves. The secret of course was ours alone, to be kept alive for months and even years by mutual reminders of a possibility that had never come to pass. We certainly did not tell our mother then; but after more than fifty years I used the incident, with some change of names, in a story called "God Has No Wife."

My mother, passionately devoted to us all, and positive that each of us excelled in something, did nothing to cure my vanity when she asked me, as she often did, "Who is Mama's prettiest boy?" She expected me to say, and invariably I did, "I am." This was because I agreed with her that the long curls she trained to fall about my neck were beautiful beyond compare. The skirts I wore were customary for boys in that generation, but not of course the curls; they were supposed to be unique. There came a time, but this was not until I had started to school, when my being mistaken for a girl, or teased because I dressed like one, no longer gave me pleasure. My mother came home one day and found me hiding under a bed, stricken by what I had done. I had used her scissors to remove, down to my very scalp, the longest of the curls. She wept, and I wept; but then she sensibly removed the rest (and kept them in a shoe box till she died). Years later she admitted that she had wanted me to be a girl in the beginning; now she must have said to herself that having proved myself otherwise I was to be free of further interference. I was not in fact her best-looking child. Carl was, or Guy, or Frank, or in his own time Paul. Nor would she have been happy had she known how often I played up to Frank's admiration for my profanity. I was vain of that too: I loved language, even bad language, and showed off such childish skill in it as I possessed. Doubtless bad talk was one of the ways I took to prove myself a boy.

I was a happy child; I was pleased with myself, and enjoyed almost everything that went on. It was exciting, for example, to become a reader at four. My mother taught me at that age because I was to go to school the next year: earlier than the average, but Frank was to be held back so that we could go together, he at seven and I at five. It was a mile to Hope, and some days the walking would be hard. So both of us were set to learning our letters, and the syllables they composed: a-b, ab, a-c, ac, a-d, ad. I do not remember moving on from this point to words and sentences, but of course I did, and in due time was making my own way through a bound volume of *Our Little Ones,* a children's magazine of which my mother had assembled ten issues for 1890 and 1891, sewing them with strong thread and covering them with heavy oilcloth, the rough side out. The resulting book survives to this day; somehow it descended to me, and it is one of my treasures. We were a reading family; my parents believed in books, and had many in the house; Carl's teacher had given him at nine, the year I was born, no less a prize than Green's *History of the English People* in four volumes; but nothing interested me so much at the moment as this collection of illustrated poems and stories about children who were either good or bad—and if bad, they were sorry. I knew nothing then of Carl's remarkable prize, which had a great deal to do with his becoming what he was when he grew up, a professional reader and writer. I was more interested in hearing my mother laugh as she told how Guy, who was four when the oilcloth book came into being, had mistaken a line in one of the poems. It was supposed to read: " 'Ho-ho!' and 'Ha-ha!' laughed the two little mice." But Guy had said: " 'Ho-ho!' and 'Ha-ha!' laughed the little two mice." And this was a delicious joke, in harmony with the picture above the poem: the brother mouse wore a striped cap, a white shirt, and pants with large buttons; the sister mouse, whose hand he held, had on a sunbonnet and a print dress.

Across the page was an overturned wheelbarrow with two plump legs sticking out behind it. These belonged to a little girl named Helen who had been helping her papa garden, but then had climbed into his wheelbarrow so that she could bark back at a fierce dog that, chained to his kennel, was threatening her over a low stone wall. There was an apple tree in a second picture, and beehives and hollyhocks; and the child, dressed in a long embroidered cloak, had an embroidered cap tied under her chin. I remember the details so well that I scarcely need to look them up. These were my first pictures, as these were my first poems and stories. They went together perfectly in my mind, where they glorified, with just a touch of alien elegance, the reality I relished all about me. I cared less for the fairy-tale themes that occasionally intruded; the angels and the sylphs were unconvincing. No, the stories must be about children and their parents and grandparents; or about animals, which interested me profoundly. There was the horse that punished a boy for tormenting a goat by picking him up with his teeth and throwing him over a hedge. There was Lucy, who when her mother died came to live with her grandmother, and whose father, because he heard she had been brave at the dentist's, sent her a puppy in a Gladstone bag. There was Percy, who went to Egypt and rode on a donkey. There was Gertrude, who lived in Florida and led on a leash a razorback pig whom she expected to eat the snakes in her way. But my favorite stories had to do with cats: the huge white one that left her kitten in Tom's sealskin cap; the minister's, named Deborah, who walked eleven miles through the snow carrying her six kittens in her mouth—five and a half round trips to put them where they ought to be; and best of all the tortoise-shell, old Sally, who saved Baby Winfred's life by running to Grandpa's store with a message for the doctor tied about her neck.

The reality around me was both like and unlike this precious book. It was less pretty and smooth, and yet strict parallels appeared, as when for example, I do not know in what year, a cow chased me across the barnyard and would have had me on her horns had not my father run to close a gate between us. This was like the story of Pollie, to whom exactly the same thing happened; but there was a sequel that would have been out of key with the book. The next day my father shut the cow into a stall and sawed off her horns; I wit-

7

nessed the operation, and learned for the first time that horns are full of blood. Nor was there any animal in *Our Little Ones* as interesting as Dick, an Indian pony who had been bought for Carl but whom we all seemed to own. Dick was fatter than "Indian" suggests; indeed his back was so broad that several boys could sit on him at once. We adored him in our several ways. Carl was old enough to race him; he was very fast for short distances; but Frank and I preferred to fondle him and poke about at the mule's pace he fancied more. He was lazy, we said, and we liked him so. He was a bay, with beautiful eyes separated by a white band down his forehead and nose. He could be stubborn; my father, who needed him one day and tried to catch him in a five-acre field east of the house, gave up at last and called him "ornery." My father carried a bridle in one hand and an ear of corn in the other; and dozens of times he thought Dick, coaxed by the corn, would either come to him or stand still to be taken; but each time, even though his nostrils were blowing at the grain, he swung his head away and started running at the last possible moment, only to stop in another corner and wait for the farce to be repeated. He was fast enough on these occasions, though with Frank and me he could be slower than sorghum, and sometimes, when he saw no sense in pretending any longer, as stationary as a stump.

I have wondered since how we ever got him to go as far as Potomac, where our maternal grandparents lived. I did not know then that Grandpa Butz had formerly lived in Hope, and in fact had all but created it out of prairie wilderness, or that Grandma Butz was still a legend there for her noble silence and good works. To Frank and me they were simply old people in another town, whither in the spring of 1899 we were driving Dick in a black and red cart with seats along its sides. Nor did we guess why we were going. Paul was about to be born, and it was thought better to have us out of the house. I have no memory of reaching Potomac; the most I can see is the double row of maple trees (Grandpa had set them out) that lined the road north of Hope; we went between those trees, then turned east and north a number of times till we were there. It is difficult to believe now that we were sent by ourselves, or that we could find the way. Perhaps an older person did go with us, though I have no memory of that. But I remember coming home and finding Paul in bed beside my mother. He was the last of us to be born, and even I could henceforth patronize him as "the baby."

If I understood little of my grandparents' past, and if my recollections of them really date from another time altogether, that of my boyhood in Urbana, the same thing is true in even greater degree of our relatives the Knights, in Muncie to the south. It must have seemed academic to me, if I knew it at all, that my great-aunt Frances Knight, whom we called Aunt Frant, was the sister of Grandma Butz, and that there were other sisters and brothers whom I was only gradually to identify. They were Tillotsons, and of those there were almost as many as Abraham had descendants. Indeed there were Abrahams among them; my grandmother's name was Rebecca; she had married Jeremiah Butz; and on my father's side too there was at least one Uncle Isaac as well as a great-grandfather Abraham. But these things were not for children to comprehend, immense though their importance might be. It was enough for me that the farm near Muncie where the Knights took so much pleasure in living was a delightful place to go—there was a stream to ford before we got there—and that one of their daughters, Laura, came up sometimes to play with Frank and me. She was joined on certain days by Gladys Henry, whose mother, our Aunt Mary, was another sister of Grandma Butz. The four of us liked particularly to play "doctor." One of us, elected to be sick, would lie down and look pathetic while the other three brought powders—cocoa mixed with sugar—to pour down his throat.

Perhaps there would be a fifth child in the party: Lorraine Thomas, whose mother we called Aunt Molly and whose father was Uncle Fred, although no blood relation existed between our families. The Thomases were simply good friends of my parents—such good friends, and of such old standing, that the titles added themselves naturally to their names. They lived in Hope, where Uncle Fred kept one of the two stores. The other store, kept by Ezra Harrison, ought perhaps to be the one I remember best because it was there that I was taken one day to see the first talking-machine ever to reach Hope; but I have no other recollection of the place, and after all it was only a machine that I saw. At Thomas's store, and in the house close by, there were people whom I loved because of their warm hearts and, now that I think of it, their large, round, dark eyes. The whole family was thus distinguished: not only Lorraine and her parents, but the older children Otie and Reid, particular friends of Carl and Guy. After we moved to Urbana I was to hear with horror how Reid had died of a laryngeal spasm; in the words of the story in *Our Little Ones* about the cat that went for the doctor, "the dreaded croup had come," and Reid was alone with it too long. But in those days, when death was something I seldom thought of, or thought of only as happening to people I did not know, Uncle Fred's store was important to me chiefly for its tall glass jars of candy—licorice, peppermint, horehound—from which he would solemnly lift the tops so that Frank and I could reach in for as much as we wanted, and to which Lorraine, the lucky girl, had access at any time. Perhaps it is not strange, however, that my sharpest memory of Lorraine has to do with a visit she and Aunt Molly made to us in Urbana shortly after we had gone there. They were to stay all night, and Lorraine and I decided we would sleep together; but our mothers said No, we were too big for that, as I for one must indeed have been, since in some queer way I understood what they meant.

The day came, in September of 1899, when Frank and I went off for our first taste of school. I suppose Carl and Guy walked with us, or it may even be that we were driven to Hope in honor of so special an occasion. But the only moment now surviving in my mind is the moment when Mr. Smith, the teacher, rang his bell and we were expected to rush in. I was busy at the pump in one corner of the yard, doubtless trying in vain to cure the terrible thirst that comes with fear. Frank had filled a cup for me to drink, and now at the sound of the bell he left me with it, supposing I would follow. But I had decided I would never go to school. I had wanted to, the worst way, until this moment. I had talked of it all summer, and I really did want to enter that small white building I had passed so many times. I simply lacked the courage. What I was afraid of I am unable to imagine, nor did I know then, I assume, with any clarity. Certainly it was not Mr. Smith, a benevolent and pleasant man, and a friend of our family. But my terror was genuine, so I held my ground. Then the door opened and Mr. Smith came out to get me. He did not argue or explain. He merely picked me up and carried me in—a sacrifice on his part, for I kicked his shins all the way, and bawled and blubbered so that he must have wondered whether such a disturbance might wreck the day. Frank, he has told me since, felt both sympathy and shame, and there was much talk of the entire business that night at home, when my mother made it clear that she was "mortified." Even so soon, however, I had accepted school; and none of the pupils could have enjoyed more than I did the term that started so unpromisingly. Mr. Smith was a good teacher. I know he was, for I can still see the ruler he sawed into twelve equal parts, each with a number on it, so that we could witness the mysteries of addition and subtraction—even multiplication and division—before our very eyes, not to say at the tips of our fingers.

My first year of school was to be our last year in the country, and I am grateful that the two things coincided. The oldest pupils reciting in the same room with the youngest, and to the same person, who meanwhile had of course to keep the others reasonably silent—this was a spectacle I never saw again. It had its merits. Yet I remember too how interesting it was to walk with Frank the mile to Hope and back, along a road that was dusty that fall and again in late spring but for several months in between was either black with mud or white with snow or frozen into iron ruts, and on the very coldest days might be colder still from wind that nipped our cheeks and ears and found its way inside clothes that my mother, a loving seamstress, had made as warm as she could. The lunches we took, packed into a tin box by the same hand, turned out on such days, when we opened them in the coatroom, to be quite suitable for the Eskimos we may have thought we were. The butter and the thick bread both were icy hard, and the boiled eggs, so good with pepper and salt, could have passed until we cracked them for brown rocks.

II

I have said that my mother made our clothes, but one of the earliest memories I have of my father concerns a garment that was bought—or rather, two garments, since Frank shared this experience with me as he did every other. Whenever it was, we had of course graduated from wearing skirts; for the garments in question were corduroy pants, short pants, to the knees only. And my father was to buy them at some town, I think Fithian, where he had driven on a professional call. Or perhaps he had ridden, depending on the state of the roads. He owned a spirited big team of grays, Prince and Billy, whom he hitched together when he could; but if the mud was deep, and there was danger of a buggy foundering, he might mount either of these handsome beasts and go off with his medicine case bouncing in one of the two saddlebags that hung down the side. I have wondered since if this did not account for the particularly powerful smell the case had; occasionally some of the corks must have loosened, and the contents spilled. As soon as he came into a room you knew what he carried; and when he opened the black leather box—ah, the pungent mixture, compounded of chloroform, paregoric, nux vomica, and I know not what else, that had no counterpart elsewhere in the life my senses lived.

But this day, or rather this night, it was my sense of hearing that was most awake. I was lying with Frank in our walnut bed upstairs, a boy's-size bed, with spindles all around it, and both of us were holding our breath lest we miss the first sound of my father at the gate. When we did hear the horse or horses there we jumped out and ran to the window to hear more. But to our sorrow the sound retreated: my father had turned about and gone away again. Unable to understand why this should be, and unable to bear it too, for we had set all our fancy to work upon the figure we would cut in our new trousers, we fell asleep and did not know until morning what had happened. My father, with many other things to think about, for he was both a doctor and a farmer, had forgotten to make the purchase; then at the gate he remembered; and, tired as he surely was, though like Carl I have no distinct memory of his ever looking or sounding tired, he went all the way back so that Frank and I would not be disappointed. I cannot swear to this, but I suspect that our pleasure in the pants was greater next day than our gratitude to him; though for him the one thing might have been identical with the other, and in any case we could scarcely have been expected to realize at such an age that our father was one of the best men in the world. He made no point of his goodness, which we therefore took for granted.

He never punished any of us, my mother used to say, because he was away from home so much, often on calls which kept him overnight, that when he did show up again our being still alive, still there, was more important to him than anything else, and he would no more have thought even of scolding us than he would have confessed that while he was gone his chief thought had been of "you wretched boys," as he preferred to say. He loved to call things by the wrong names—or, it may be, the right ones, fantastically the right ones. Either extreme is poetry, of which he had the secret without knowing that he did. It was natural for him to name two lively rams on the place Belshazzar and Nebuchadnezzar. My mother must not have reckoned on his weakness for language when she determined that none of her sons should ever be nicknamed. She gave them all names of one syllable, supposing that this would settle the matter. But he could not leave it there. Frank became Fritz Augustus—just why, I never inquired—and I was either Marcus Aurelius or Marco Bozzaris. Guy was Guy Bob, and Carl was Carlo. And Paul, when it came time for him to share in the illicit luxuriance, was no other than Wallace P. Poggin—again, I have no faint idea why. My father never discussed his inspirations, any more than he analyzed his spoonerisms, or even admitted that they had fallen from his mouth. He would cough, and appear to apologize by saying: "I have a little throakling in my tit." Of course we liked this, as we liked him, without saying in so many words that he had humor. Other men we knew—uncles, cousins, old men, young men— had reputations for being funny. His reputation was for being kind and wise. Perhaps he never played with syllables except at home. And as for my mother's fear that he would spoil us, there was nothing in that, as I suspect she knew. Pure love never spoiled anybody. If we were spoiled, and I think I may have been, neither of my parents was to blame.

Photographs taken of them soon after they were married tell the story in each case: in my mother's case, of a handsome, proud young woman—and was she not the daughter of Jerry Butz, the patriarch who founded Hope?—with nevertheless a sweetness about the eyes, and a capacity for limitless devotion to the persons she would love; and in my father's case, of a spare, dark, also handsome, also proud young man whose intense gaze communicates to me not only his ambition—to be a good doctor, to have a fine farm, and perhaps to be rich—but, buried somehow within this ambition, a powerful, a subtle, a delicate concern with whatever it is that we mean when we say human life, and a capacity for honoring that life whenever it is most gentle and courageous. The intensity of the gaze is what no one could miss, though someone might remain unaware that it forgave as much as it demanded, and would undertake if necessary to bear what cannot be borne. These two bestowed upon their five sons an equal love in which there was no least hint of favoritism; which may explain, if anything needs to, the lifelong attachment of those five to one another. Carl remarked in his *Three Worlds* that any of his brothers would be his choice for a companion, if he could have but one, on a desert island; the only difficulty, he added, would be in deciding which brother went along. I can say the same thing, even though Carl's death puts him beyond the reach of any such decision. Then I can add that his own example was potent in establishing the affection he described. He himself had it in the abundance that was characteristic of him at every turn. Without this abundance in Carl, nothing might have become what it did become.

My father was angry at the cow that tried to kill me, and sawed off more of her horns than was necessary, but in general he was fond of the animals who lived with us and he saw to it that they were not mistreated. The most he felt against Dick when that little devil would not be caught was frustration: a natural impatience with an adversary who had put him out of breath, but who because he could do that was admirable too. I am glad I can remember some of the horses he had, and can see my father in relation to them. A man and a horse are among other things a pair of wills; we transfer the image when we say of a car that it is stubborn and refuses to start, or that it is lively and responds to our touch, but the two things are not the same. The horse does have a will, as he has good nature (or bad) and can truly take delight in going with us where we go. My father enjoyed his trips with Prince and Billy in all kinds of weather; he considered them great friends, and in later years, after he had sold them, was cast down by the news that their present owner had beaten them about the ears and even about their beautiful eyes (nothing in nature is more beautiful than the eye of a horse). I heard him lament this with my mother, and gathered that he considered it his own fault for ever selling them. But while he had them he made the most of their power and beauty, as I said in "The Little Doctor," written after his death:

> The little doctor with the black
> Ambitious eyes had giant horses;
> High the reins and loud the splash
> Along those muddy country courses.
>
> Black the harness, black the eyes,
> And black the phaeton's new fringes.
> Dappled, though, the necks and flanks,
> And foaming white the fetlocks' plunges. . . .
>
> Yet the straps outsang the wind,
> And yet the hoof-spray drowned the grasses.
> So in that lost, that country time
> The little doctor ever presses.
>
> On and on, a dateless day,
> Down sunken roads where death has prospered,
> Black-eyed breezes still can blow,
> And private glories still be whispered.

I call him "the little doctor" because that is what the neighbors called him when he first came to Hope. I never actually thought of him as little, and during the forty years I knew him I believe nobody else did. But he was of only medium height, and in that early time he was very slender—I seem to have heard that at twenty-one he weighed no more than a hundred pounds, though this scarcely seems possible. His ambition then was the only thing he possessed: the ambition, for example, which drove him as a boy to do the work of three men on his father's farm up north in Illinois so that he could at last walk to Chicago with enough money to pay off the mortgage. His father, William Henry Van Doren, whom I never saw more than once or twice, was a farmer, blacksmith, and preacher combined, and, I gather, not much of a businessman, though he was excellent in his own formidable fashion. My father had gone subsequently to a small medical college in Chicago, and after a year or two of apprenticeship with his half-brother Silas had settled upon Hope as the place where he might find a wife and make his fortune.

I once asked my mother how he found *her,* and was given the modest answer that he enjoyed coming to their house "to hear Pa talk." This would be Grandpa Butz, who was certainly a talker. But the young physician must have listened to Dora, my mother, at least half of the time, and looked at her and loved her. Only, by the code of her generation, she could not tell me so. It was the same code that prohibited her from ever calling him Charlie, or even Charles, in the hearing of any other person, her sons included. He was Papa before us, and Doctor before other people. A child's hunger for signs of affection between his parents is never, I suppose, completely satisfied. There seem to be more arguments than endearments. In my own case I had slowly to understand how hard both my father and my mother worked, how many problems harassed them, and how easily their strong wills could conflict. Also, I had to understand the code. I took on faith the fact of their regard for each other; and learned most about it after he was dead.

My pride in being hailed as "Little Doc" by men I met in Hope was greater than they could have known. To be identified with my father, as it seemed to me I then was, gave me inexpressible pleasure. And I suppose I said to myself that some day I would be a doctor too. But none of us ever followed him into the profession. People remarked about this, saying it was strange, nor can I explain it otherwise than Carl did: my father never hinted that he wanted us to do so. Possibly he did hope that one of us would, but his leniency, which left us so free in little matters, extended to this great matter as well, and no scruple could have been deeper in him than the scruple against urging us to be like him. We are like him anyway, we happily discover now and then. And for my own part it was enough that he read my early poems, the ones I wrote before he died, and was glad I had written them. He said he found

17

some of them true to his own experience; which was by no means odd, for they were about things he had told me. He learned by heart the short one, "Driver Lost," which represents a horse bringing its driver home after he has fallen asleep over the reins. This time it is not Prince or Billy but a mare without a name; but the thing did happen many nights, and my father used to chuckle as he pointed out that no car would have done it.

> She points an ear at every turn
> Before a hoof arrives.
> What hand is here from which to learn?
> Who is it sits and drives?

My father's controlling desire as a doctor was that his patients be comfortable. He wanted them to feel better, and the thing I have heard most often from those he visited is that they did so as soon as he entered the house. His theory, he once told me, was to "treat the symptoms" and trust the disease to become discouraged and go away, having no longer any power to express itself. Doctors since have agreed that this is not altogether a bad theory, though of course it has its limitations. My father had gone to an "eclectic" medical college, which is to say that it was neither homeopathic nor allopathic but aimed to combine the best features of both. I cannot judge the merits of the argument, but of one thing I am certain: he stuck to his desire that the people in his charge be as clean and warm and rested and relaxed as he could make them, even if this meant that he did the duties of a practical nurse. It was not unusual for him to scrub a kitchen floor if the woman of the house was ill; to boil water in quantity; to wash dishes; to dust and air sick chambers if no one else had done it. He would stay all night to do this, and remain half of the next day to make sure the patient responded.

Not that he was a nurse and nothing else. He was of course a doctor, and he kept up with whatever new medicines and therapies came along. His final desire was that the patient live; I have been told that nobody felt sorrier when one died. The new discovery I heard him talk most about, later on in Urbana, was an antitoxin for diphtheria. He spoke once with tears in his eyes of the miracle he had just come from seeing performed: he had given an extreme dose of the antitoxin, and had watched the phlegm melt in a child's throat minute by minute until the danger of strangulation was past. He was remembering, surely, the epidemics of diphtheria that had ravaged families at Hope; of typhoid fever, too, which he also lived to see subdued.

I have forgotten just which dire disease a patient of his at Hope, a man smaller and older than my father, was dying with one November night when suddenly he said: "Doc, I'm burning up. Will you do me a favor?" "Maybe. What is it?" "Now, Doc, you don't expect me to be alive tomorrow morning, do you?" With reluctance my father admitted this. "Well then, why can't I be comfortable tonight?" "I wish you could. What do you want?" "Take me out and put me in the rainbarrel." Such a barrel stood at the corner of the house, and the water in it was good and cold. "That would kill you." "But you say I'm dead anyway. Please, Doc!" And so, unable to meet the argument, my father did. He got the poor man outdoors, ducked him as he desired—and by morning saw him on the way to recovery. There was no story he liked to tell better than this one. He would laugh until he grew quite inarticulate, trying to reproduce the old man's whine: "You say I'm dead anyway. Please, Doc!" This was indeed a case of treating the symptom. The cure was cold. So a theory had been vindicated. Also, a patient had been saved. But furthermore, it was a story, and my father liked few things better than stories.

It was my good luck not many years ago to come upon the ledger he kept at Hope between 1893 and 1900: his last ledger there, and for all he knew the last one he would ever keep, since he had thoughts when he went to Urbana of retiring from practice. He did not retire, but that is another story. The ledger, tall and tattered, records for each family of patients the services rendered and the payments received. A call at the office, a room in our house, was normally $1. Medicine was anywhere from fifty cents to $1.50. Visits were $2 or $3 or $3.50, depending no doubt on the distance traveled and the time spent—or, as my father liked to say, but only of course to us, the "timothy time." For the delivery of a child, always indicated by "obstet," the fee was $10, though in a few cases it was $8. Payment was by cash, but occasionally it was by note, and not infrequently it was in goods: wood, work, fence posts, sheep, hogs, calves, hay, hauling, plowing, lumber, wheat, fodder, molasses, syrup, oats, or timothy seed. I find one dog ($1.50), and—this puzzles me—one needle ($.25). The needle, if it was not for my mother, may have been a big one for sewing wool sacks; sheep were sheared by experts imported for the purpose (some of them were brutes, they stabbed their victims to make them lie still, and my father hated that); then the wool was tramped into long heavy sacks and shipped away. The goods thus taken in exchange were clearly farmer's goods: a reminder that my father was always deeply interested in the three hundred acres we lived on, which he hired a man to manage but which he never forgot. This interest was to grow until it became a passion. But even then, when he had as many as three farms, he perversely called them "frames."

The ledger, since its entries are of the utmost brevity, conveys no notion, nor was it intended to, of the widespread good my father did as a country doctor, or of the heroism involved in trips by night or day that would try the hardiest man. Neither does it contain any reference to the loving regard in which he was held by people as far away as ten miles in every direction. He must have known that this existed, for as he liked to praise others he liked, I think, to be praised; I am sure he listened to many a speech he pretended to believe was meant for someone else. But there came a day, just before we set off for Urbana, when those people made their feeling clear beyond any doubt.

A man came that morning with what he said was a toothache. My father put him in the chair he used for such emergencies and told him to open his mouth. "There," the man said, "—no, there, that's the one that hurts—but wait a minute, Doc, don't pull it yet, for I think maybe—can't you tell by looking? It's farther back, I guess. But you can tell, can't you? It must *look* bad, the way it feels, or last night it did." My father looked and tested and tapped. "I can't see anything the matter." "Can't you? Well then, look through that window." "What?" "The window—look out there." And what my father saw was all the buggies in the world coming over the rise from Hope. The patient's job had been to keep him from seeing them until now. But here they were, and they brought more people than had been together on that part of the earth since anybody could remember. They were coming to tell the doctor and his family good-by. And they carried with them what they would eat or drink. I was young enough so that certain items impressed me to the exclusion of the rest. For the first and last time in my life I saw lemonade in tubs. And watermelons by the wagonload, sideboards and all.

So then we went to Urbana.

Urbana

1900–1915

M Y fifteen years in Urbana, even though they lasted till I came of age, are like the six years at Hope in that they constitute a single memory. It has parts, to be sure, but they do not easily separate themselves from one another, at least as pieces of time. Time for a child does not pass so much as spread —in all directions, slowly, out and out, while he remains at the center, some days conscious, most days unconscious, of what goes on. And I was still a child, pleased with the people and things I saw, pleased with the town we lived in, pleased with myself in so far as I then knew who that was. Not that the knowledge was something I searched for. There was no call to dwell upon the subject. The distinction between myself and the world around me was happily unclear. I relished both with a kind of excitement which I assumed every other person felt too. Perhaps he did.

The first year we lived on High Street, at an intersection illuminated by an arc light, a sputtering mechanism that cast a huge cone in whose brilliance Frank and I played with neighbor children until we were called home to bed. The hiss of the carbons burning was matched on warm nights by the buzz of innumerable insects—bugs, we called them, and some of them, as they bumped against the globe, sounded like rocks thrown at it by boys. Occasionally one of us did damage the light; but on the whole we respected it for the pleasure it gave us and were content to run in and out of the great circle it made on the ground. The grown people who walked across the intersection, or drove in their buggies while we scattered to the curb, we gave no thought to and rarely even looked at. We had our own games and our own concerns; we could play marbles in this artificial day; we could match buckeyes; we could wrestle or play tag; and we could tease the girls. Some of our best friends were girls. Across High Street there were Miriam and Beth Knowlton, daughters of the Mr. Knowlton who with Mr. Bennett ran the principal drugstore in town; and next door to us on the left lived Laura Whitmire. These three we were to know through school and college better than we knew most other people in Urbana, in spite of the fact that within a year we ceased to be their close neighbors.

My father did not retire from practice after all. His old patients at Hope kept calling him back there, and he found new patients in Urbana. He soon opened an office downtown, where of course we loved to go and look at the medicine bottles on the shelves behind a wood and glass partition. My mother had not only the family to cook and care for but the town to make herself at home in. A collection of ten thousand people was naturally not what she had known at Hope, and there were problems. Of these I recognized only the simplest ones, as when for example a boy named Eddie Shell came one afternoon to play with Frank and me, and at the hour for going home did not know how to do so. This is a malady that afflicts all children, but my mother was not sure how she should handle it in Eddie's case. She consulted us secretly as to whether he should be asked to stay for supper; we thought not, so she hinted to him that his mother might be expecting him. He was so slow in acting upon the hint that we were all in despair and began to feel guilty because we had not pressed him to stay. What I remember now is Eddie standing at last on the other side of the screen door and trying to say good-by as if he meant it. My mother said warmly: "Well, Eddie, come and see us again." Whereupon he opened the door and walked in.

Now this was funny, whereas my mother's mistake about the

sweaters was not. I say mistake, but she had actually done Frank and me a great kindness. Hearing us talk about our need of sweaters as the fall grew colder, she decided to indulge us; also, to surprise us, for one day she came home with a bundle which she asked us to open; and there our sweaters were. Only, they were not the sleek blue jerseys, with turtle necks, that all the other boys wore and that we had dreamed of wearing too. They were gray wool, and thick. I am afraid we did not spare her feelings. These, we said, would never do. I know she was disappointed, though with good grace she took us downtown the next day and exchanged the garments. She had not reckoned with the fact that boys in town have fashions; even little boys, whose health and comfort might be thought of as coming first. She had not even dreamed of a fashion in sweaters.

She had been busy for one thing helping my father plan the new house we would have next year on Oregon Street. When we moved into it at last, a little before it was finished, I confess I felt proud of what in my mind was its imposing size. It was brick; it stood up off the street, so that several cement steps had to be climbed before other cement steps ascended to the wide front porch; it was square, and it was high, with enough rooms under the slate roof—these had dormers and casement windows—for the five boys to sleep and do their studies there, Carl in one room by himself, Guy in another, and Frank and I together in a third; Paul, still only two, would live downstairs a while longer. Our studies were what my father and mother had brought us to Urbana for. There were better schools here, and on the west side of town, with Champaign beyond, there was the University of Illinois to which we all would go. Meanwhile Carl was in high school and Guy was preparing to follow him.

Frank and I, who had started at the Leal School, continued there through the eighth grade. It was the public grammar school of the town, at least for our district, and we were glad that our having moved away from High Street did not separate us from the first friends we had made. We still walked in the same halls with the Knowlton girls and Laura Whitmire, not to speak of Eddie Shell; and through the circumstance of our skipping the fourth grade—we did so by a happy coincidence together—we found ourselves in the very classes we most wanted to be in. By nine I had fallen in love with Beth, as Frank had with Laura. We sent them valentines, and at parties were paired off with them in everybody else's understanding. The fact that both of us were shy, and that in my case at any rate being in love with Beth meant that I spoke to her less often than I did to any other girl, and trembled whenever by some accident I so much as touched her hand, did not mitigate our devotion. I remember how astonished my father was in one of those early Februaries when I asked him for a quarter to buy a valentine—of course for Beth, but I did not say her name. Valentines were ordinarily a nickel or a dime, and he must have thought that good enough. Nevertheless he reached slowly down into his pocket for the larger coin—I can still see him doing it—and off I went, probably to Knowlton and Bennett's, for the big box in which a heart-shaped heap of curlicues reposed. I delivered it by ringing the Knowltons' bell and running away. My valentine from Beth, sent properly through the mail, was smaller and simpler. Neither was signed, and neither was acknowledged. Beth was shy too, and always, until her death years later, serene and gentle; soft-voiced, and kind as older people can be kind.

She was more like Frank because of this than she was like me. Frank, who by skipping the fourth grade resumed his normal place in the school procession, had a brother on his hands who was two years ahead of that procession, and therefore two years younger than most of the boys he got to know. But he never permitted them to leave me out of whatever juvenile enterprises we undertook. For them the two years were crucial; to him they did not exist, and I can still hear him saying, when they made as if to elude me, "Wait for Mark." For my own part I thought I belonged there. I considered my-

26

self very knowing and smart, and liked to talk bigger than I was. If this embarrassed Frank, he never said so.

Those school years passed as one; or so it now seems. Teachers who were undoubtedly different from one another become in my memory a composite person whom it was my perpetual desire to please. Miss Fenner, Miss Lloyd, Miss Radebaugh, Mr. Lawrence and the rest—I would walk beside my father, holding his hand perhaps, and tell him how wonderful each one of them was. He always listened, and seemed glad that I approved of them; though my adjectives could have conveyed to him little of their true characters, assuming that I knew those characters at all. To me a teacher, purely by virtue of his profession, was wonderful to begin with and could not lose distinction by anything he did or said. If I was a docile child, which is to say a child who wanted to be taught, the chief reason could have been the necessity I felt that my teachers should like me. And since among other things this meant my doing my work as well as possible, I did do it as well as possible; and so I learned. The admission sounds smug, but I must make it because it is true.

It is also true that I played hard outdoors on the cinder area during recess, and often returned to class with my hands so black that I would be sent to wash them. And once a thing happened that no teacher ever knew, nor I think anybody else until this moment. I cannot recall the room in which it happened, nor the time of day, nor how it chanced that I was alone in that room with a dozen or more girls; nor, certainly, what set the explosion off. For it was something like that; or else it was such a madness as the Greeks—but I learned this only later—could imagine in their women when Dionysus was about. At any rate, suddenly I was on the floor in a corner of the room, protecting myself as well as I could from twelve pairs of hands that tore at my hair as twelve pairs of lips endeavored, to the accompaniment of what seemed to me a crazy kind of laughter, half hostile and half fond, to cover me with kisses. I was terrified. I did not enjoy it. Then just as suddenly it ceased, and the girls went away, perhaps to the other end of the room, perhaps outdoors, I have no notion where. And nothing was ever said of what had occurred. I failed to understand it then; I fail even more to understand it now. Yet it is easier now than it was then to believe that my very smugness, my tendency to pose as teacher's pet, could have been the cause. At the time it pleased me to think that my curly hair had something to do with it, and nameless other glories I am afraid I still imputed to my person.

II

Nothing else like that happened in school, and as a matter of fact most of my recollections of Urbana have nothing to do with school. Our barn, east of the house, was at least as interesting because it always had a horse in it. Automobiles were soon to make their appearance on the streets and roads, but it was not until 1908 that we had one. Meanwhile we had Marguerite, a mare of uncertain age and temper whom nevertheless we treated like one of the family. "Marguerite, you are so sweet"—my father would greet her thus as he went in to feed her or to hitch her up. She was not especially responsive to such talk; the horse that succeeded her, a male, was more so, for he would put out his nose to be petted; but Marguerite, a dark red creature with streaks of gray down her lean, rather nervous sides, did have a character and none of us has forgotten her. She meant more to me than the billy goat Frank and I had for a year; we built with our own hands a house for him to stay in, but he soon proved a nuisance and a bore and was sold back to the man we got him from.

In summer there was always an ice wagon that came down the street dripping cold water from each of its rear corners. Frank and I liked to follow it in the hope that a small piece of ice would jostle out too so that we could pick it up and suck it until it was gone. If none did, we climbed in and stole one

when the driver was not looking. Not that he cared, but the
ice tasted better if we had not asked for it, and better than any
part of the large cake my mother would buy from this same
man when he reached our house. Nor was ice the only thing
we stole. We did not make a practice, as some boys did, of
taking freezer-fulls of ice cream off back porches while parties
went on indoors; but we were known to do it, and I fear that
we never sufficiently measured the misdeed until my mother
one night was the victim of it; then our anger against the
unknown thieves was all the more righteous for being as it
were informed.

There was less sense, though no more sin, in our taking
lumber from new houses that were being built. At least we
ate the ice cream; but we had only the vaguest plans for using
the two-by-fours we marched off with at night and hid somewhere in my father's barn. I cannot imagine anyone who
would have been more horrified than he if he had known we
did this; but he never knew, and of course we did not do it
long. We may indeed have done it only once, Frank at one end
of a plank and I at the other, on some dark night when nobody
could have seen us had he tried. But that one time would be
enough to fix the memory, with its attendant modicum of
guilt, in minds that had no special notion then of a wrong
being done. For us there was little if any difference between
such a theft and the pranks we played at Halloween: up-
rooting cabbages from gardens and throwing them against
front doors, ripping pickets from fences, and writing with
soap on windows near the street. Possibly, now that I think of
it, the worst thing about the lumber-stealing was not its sense-
lessness, for we never built anything with the boards, but the
ingratitude we therein showed the carpenters who by day
cheerfully let us watch them at work and even gave us strips of
wood they had sawed off and would have no further need for.
We rejoiced over these; and then sneaked back by dark for
more. Of the owner of the house, the man who was paying for
the lumber, I am sure we never thought at all. In our own

generation we were juvenile delinquents; we did what we did for no reason that an adult could possibly imagine, or that we ourselves could have stated had we been caught.

Half a block from our house was a little stream, called the Boneyard, which ran south among the vacant lots that waited to become what is now the most impressive part of Urbana. We lived then on the edge of town, yet even so the Boneyard —it was really a branch of a larger stream that bore the same name, but for years I did not know this—was covered over a certain distance by a cement arch that supported the Oregon Street bridge and then continued as a tunnel where Frank and I, exaggerating its length, liked to imagine ourselves lost. For us it equaled in interest the sewers of Paris; though all we could do in it was wade in summer and slide in winter, some days on sleds we pulled through, rounding its one curve to see light again at the far end.

We spent less time down there, however, as we grew up and became addicted to baseball. We played the game with other boys, usually in the form known as "rounders," which did not require two full teams, but I remember best the endless hours, on Saturdays and on weekdays after school, we devoted to throwing the ball back and forth merely between us two, taking turns at being pitcher or catcher, and talking tough as we fancied the professionals did. We studied curves and we had our signals; we called out "Attaboy!" Yet the true secret pleasure of the sport was something that neither one of us at that time ever tried to express in words. I was to make the attempt in "The Moments He Remembers," which imagines an old man reconstructing his boyhood in terms of the smells that his nose if not his brain recalls:

> The hour at sunset when the ball and glove,
> Hot with the play, exhaled a leather love,
>
> And his left hand, withdrawn to wipe his eyes,
> Sweetened the whole air with musk surprise.

The only other boy we admitted to this fellowship was Herman Jacobsen—"Jake," of course—my own constant companion (never forgetting Frank) for a number of years. So constantly were Jake and I together, in fact, that whenever one of us wanted to be alone he did not know how to say so. I am sure I went to his house on Illinois Street oftener than even his great loyalty could bear; though I cannot remember that he ever did to me what I once did to him. He whistled that night as usual to announce his approach—both of us could split the air by a sound we had taught each other how to make with our lips and teeth, and I can still stop a taxi dead in New York with this very sound—but for some reason I did not rejoice. I had some business of my own indoors. Nevertheless I appeared on the porch as he expected; and then jumped down on him as if he were my enemy, not my friend. We rolled on the grass, we panted and swore; and then as suddenly I desisted, for I was glad to see him after all; and if he thought an explanation was in order he never demanded it. Nor could I have given it at that age when most such things, if they cannot be understood, must be forgotten.

Time went by in further curious ways. We had an excellent friend, Chancy Finfrock, in whose back yard on Elm Street we were overheard one day by his small, frail mother planning a system of tunnels that we would dig between her house and the alley behind it. We were quite serious about this. The tunnels were to begin as trenches, deep enough to walk in and extending in all directions, but were to end by being covered over with boards and sod so that nobody could suspect their existence. If we had ever started the operation we would have given it up soon enough because it ceased to entertain us, or because it was too hard; but Finnie's mother, all at once less small and frail, saw to it that we did not start.

But there were tamer diversions. Frank and I made money by working. Two ladies in the neighborhood, members of the faculty at the university, proposed to us that we deliver their laundry to the house in Champaign where it was done, and of course bring back with us the clean linen of the previous week. Frank rigged up for the purpose a cart with high iron wheels,

and I can still hear the clatter of those wheels on the two miles
of pavement or sidewalk we traversed each trip. We often went
at dusk, before or after supper; if before, we sometimes
returned so late that the family had got up from the table and
we were scolded as truants, until we explained that we had
been serving Miss Simpson and Miss Bevier and then the
family, remembering, apologized. There were enough of us
so that this sort of misunderstanding could easily occur; not
that it mattered in our case, for, conscious of virtue, we enjoyed the apology. Also, we mowed lawns, our own and others,
with a Pennsylvania mower we paid for twice over. And I
was permitted to help Frank in a partnership he formed with
Fiske Miles, a preacher's son who lived a little south of town.
They ground horse-radish, bottled it, and sold it to the neighbors as the pure article which indeed it was; had it been
adulterated, my eyes would not have smarted so much as I
took my turn at filling the tall containers labeled "Van Doren
and Miles: Buy the Large Bottle." Then, naturally, we labored
beside my mother in the house. We washed and dried dishes;
we shook rugs; and on Saturday mornings we helped her in
the basement with the large week's washing she insisted on
doing herself. We emptied tubs, we turned the wringer, and
we carried wet clothes up to the line. We did none of these
things blithely, but there was never any doubt in anybody's
mind that we must do them.

Frank and I gradually made our room under the eaves a
place not only for school work but for the entertainment of
our friends. We built bookcases; we put up pennants and
pinned photographs to the walls with thumbtacks; we sat at a
double desk, facing each other, as we read assignments or
wrote compositions; and on Friday nights we took boys up
there to laugh over the bad stories—the good ones, too—that
all boys tell. In time we even smoked and played cards: this in
terror lest my mother learn of it, for she would never have
approved. But my keenest recollection of this room concerns a
fight I had in it one day with Frank. For we did occasionally

fight, and this time I thought I wanted to kill him. I had been downstairs when some old friends of my mother came from Hope—women in their late forties whom to my amusement she called "girls." I was helping to entertain them, probably without enthusiasm, when my mother told me to go for Frank so that they could see him too. I ascended with the message, and could hardly believe he meant it when he said he would not go down. "But," I said, "they heard her tell me to come and get you." "That makes no difference," said Frank; "I'm not going." It seemed to me that I was trapped. If I did not return to the living room I would be called and told to do so. If I did return, how could I explain my being alone? "You've got to come." "Well, I won't." And in another second we were making such animal noises on the floor that my mother had to run upstairs and stop us. We never did go down, and I have no idea what excuse she improvised. Nor do I remember that our rage outlasted the sound of her step on the bottom stair. Mine, though, must have nursed itself longer than Frank's. A full hour, anyway.

With such rare exceptions we were close partners in every act; as when for example we combined one afternoon to deceive Paul, who at the time could hardly have been more than two. My mother, having to go somewhere, left us in charge of our youngest brother with directions as to what we should do in this or that emergency. An emergency she had not mentioned arose, however, as soon as she was out of sight. Paul, whom we always considered old for his age because he was large-eyed and solemn, began crying for Mama to come back. We supposed at first this would not last long; we brought him things and explained that she had not gone for good. But the cries increased to howls, and in what seemed no time at all his face was so red that we wondered if he might not end by destroying himself. We did not really believe this; but we decided to pretend we did; and pretty soon we were talking to each other, quietly, as if for his good he ought not to overhear, about a baby we knew once who had cried himself to death—

33

he burst blood vessels in his brain, we said, and things like that. The crying abruptly ceased, and we had a story to tell my mother when she came home; except that we did not tell it. We thought we might have been too drastic.

Frank was not my partner in a trick I played on Paul when he was old enough to know he had been abused. It was October, and the leaves had fallen. We had spent the afternoon raking them into an enormous pile, which we were about to set afire when my mother called us in to supper. Paul, because he thought he might not be allowed to come out again, was the loudest of us in his lamentations; indeed he could be got indoors only by the promise that when supper was finished he would be the one to light the match and drop it on the pile. At the table he could scarcely eat a bite. But neither could I, for I had wanted to be the one. And now I did a strange thing. I slipped off when nobody was looking and started the fire. Soon there was the smell of smoke and my brothers rushed out. There was no way of course in which I could justify myself, nor did I try. Once the thing was done, I could no longer comprehend my passion to do it. It was the passion of a child, Carl said, a baby younger than Paul. I was nine or ten, and such a remark—lenient in the circumstances—was punishment enough. Paul suffered less that evening than I did.

III

Guy, who kept to himself more than the rest of us did, and seldom brought his friends to the house, always when we did see him appeared to be amused by something. Mysterious chuckles betrayed a humor in him that often had no other outlet. He was not eloquent like Carl, of whom my earliest memories date from this time. At Hope Carl had been too far above me, in age and preoccupation, for any clear impression of him to form in my mind. And even now, being nine years older than I, he satisfied in many ways my idea of an adult.

Naturally he had concerns which he never divulged to his small brothers; he could be moody, he was driven by ambitions and anxieties, and he had a temper—as for that matter we all did. But on plenty of occasions he relaxed in our company and ravished us with a mock sermon, or a pompous political oration, which could go on just as long as we showed we enjoyed it, for his command of language was superb. Both of our big brothers seemed to us humorists, following the example of my father; but here was something special, something complicated, something artful, and I was unable to conceive where the sentences came from.

Nor was I ever prepared for Carl's practical jokes, which had a quality quite their own and of course never hurt anybody. One Saturday morning, for instance, when he and I were both helping my mother with the wash, he went up the outside cellar stairs but soon came down again, saying: "Mark, you're little and shouldn't work too hard; go out and play now till the mailman comes; I'll do everything down here." I went at once, and at the top of the stairs saw the mailman entering the yard. Carl had seen him too, and had chosen this way to pull my leg. Then he told me he had meant tomorrow; I was through for the day. This was something like his jest with Paul and me years later when the three of us were driving from New York to Illinois in Paul's car. Carl had insisted when we started that all expenses be Dutched; none of us was to spend one penny more than his share of the gasoline, the meals, and the lodgings. But as we approached the Susquehanna he proclaimed that he alone would bear the expense of the toll across a particularly long bridge he told us lay ahead; he did none of the driving, so it was only fair that he should pay our way this time. We protested; then consented; and when we got to the booth saw a sign saying: "Toll, 5 cents." He had been there before, and we had not.

I might in those days have said to myself that Carl's magic sentences came from the books he incessantly read. Even then I could recognize in him an extraordinary student; though I

Mark Van Doren

missed the full import of his example because I did not yet
know that study is best done when one enjoys it. His relish in
books was so natural that I could have thought it was not
serious. One evening he brought home his best friend, Glen
Mullin, and the two of them let me stay in Carl's room while
they read Rabelais to each other. This was study too, but I
took it for a lark—which among other things indeed it was.
Carl's suggestions as to books I myself might read—the works
of Dickens, for example—were always made in the same
natural way; and this meant that I was free to ignore them,
though I seldom did, and certainly not in the case of Dickens,
whom I went through month by month in the bay window of
our southwest room downstairs, often without turning the
light on when I needed it, so that my mother worried about
my eyes. I can remember Carl's telling me before this that it
was time to stop reading the Horatio Alger and Oliver Optic
books I brought home daily from the public library. I can
remember too, when he spoke of a certain book (but I forget
what book) which discussed an important subject (I forget
what subject), that I asked him if it did so in story form, and
he said rather sharply that I was old enough to dispense with
such a consideration. He never hesitated to correct me, just as
he never refused to advise me. He had chastened me when I
burned Paul's leaves; but I remember just as well, when I had
manifested as usual my desire that everybody like me, his
remark that such an ambition was "complacent"—his word—
and hence unworthy of anyone who wanted to be distinguished. As for books, he made little effort to direct my
wanderings among them, good or bad; he believed in great
latitude on this point, as in general he was tolerant beyond
the wildest understanding. His generosity has had no parallel
in the world I know, and four lines that I wrote about him
after his death were true from the beginning:

Like a great tree
Spread over me,

36

Urbana: 1900–1915

With love in every limb:
I worshipped him.

Carl's eyes—he was nearsighted—would not have permitted him to play baseball with Frank and me had he wanted to do so. But he played with us in a hundred informal ways of his own devising. He was large and strong, with high spirits that could invent on the instant some fantastic wrestling or running game, or some antic with chairs, rugs, and tables. Being the oldest of us all, he took seriously his duty to entertain us, whether with muscle or with mind; and this had more to do than we imagined with the fact that our lives seemed happy and full. They were suddenly less so when in 1908 he went to live the rest of his own life in New York. The drama of this he has himself described in *Three Worlds*. I did not see that drama then. I merely missed him as a wall would be missed if it fell out of a house.

IV

But this is getting ahead of the story, if Urbana is a story, as I started by suggesting it was not. Meanwhile, with our family still intact, all manner of things went on. My mother—let me not forget—cooked marvelous meals, beginning with bread that we ate like a confection, though it was plain bread, baked twice a week in lots of a dozen loaves. We liked it best when it was fresh and hot, and butter melted into it like a last ingredient added by ourselves; but it was always good, as were the potatoes she prepared in any form, though we preferred them fried. Her fried chicken, her fried mush, her fried anything was manna to our tongues; even her fried bread, for sometimes she merely broke slices of that into a hot pan where butter or bacon grease, and her own mysterious touch, did whatever else there was to do. Any of her gravies, poured liberally on her bread (I keep coming back to the bread),

37

would make a meal by itself. But it was rarely called upon to do so, for she excelled in her meats and her major dishes too; and in her whole hominy, served in salty, peppery hot milk; and in her pies—apple, cherry, pumpkin, mince, and above all, gooseberry—which were indeed confections of the highest order, though her pancakes in the morning, which she let us cover with as much butter as we liked, compete with them now in my opinion.

Is my opinion prejudiced? But it agrees with that of all who came to visit us, and—this may sound odd—with that of the tramps my mother fed on the steps of our back porch. She loved to feed people, and never turned away a tramp. The profession must have known this, judging by the numbers that came. But the point is that they got more than food: they got wonderful food, and I have heard many a man moan as he tasted it. Perhaps she had given him nothing more than half a dozen thick slices of bread and butter and a bowl of hot coffee (she herself loved coffee more than any woman I have known; I do not speak of men, myself for instance) with cream and sugar in it. I have seen such a man, however, sit there after such a feast unwilling to get up and go about his dreary business of begging for the means to live. This was life itself, as some of the tribe, hats in hand, attempted to say as they shuffled off.

My father not only kept on with medicine; he gave a good deal of his time to the farm at Hope, and in a few years had bought another farm of the same size near Villa Grove, eighteen miles south of Urbana; and after that he bought a third, so that for a while he owned—but there were mortgages —roughly a thousand acres of the best land in the world. He went back and forth between these places, first with a horse and then in a car, in the intervals of his practice; or it may be more realistic to say that he saw patients when he was not seeing crops. In addition he purchased a few acres to the south of us in Urbana and created a subdivision, with a park in the center of it which he gave to the town; Frank and I, graduating from neighbors' lawns, mowed this park with two Pennsylvanias and made more money than we had before. My father, it need not be said, was now a busy man. Yet he always had been busy, and I am not sure how clearly I noticed the difference. He was the same man at home: indulgent, playful, serious when he chose, sometimes absent-minded, and old-fashioned in his speech (he said "deaf" to rhyme with "leaf," and "wound" to rhyme with "sound"). It was years before I realized that he had crushing problems with his farms and the other enterprises he took on. I saw him chiefly on the side he presented to us. I remember such things as the fire I started in the living room one Christmas Eve when the head flew off a match I had struck to light the candles (real candles in those days) and ignited the cotton (real cotton) spread under the tree; he tramped the flames out, but in doing so broke many presents piled about. And one morning when I was putting on my shoes to go to school I broke one of the laces, which were brown; there was only a black lace available, and my father said to wear that; I refused, claiming to know that the other children would tease me; he sent me off as I was; the children, far from teasing me, never noticed the anomaly; but I told him at supper that they had—a fib too trivial to confess to him next day or any day, yet I have remembered it for more than fifty years.

Coming home tired from a case or from a trip to one of the farms, for now he could be tired and we could see that he was, he would lie down on a leather couch we had and sleep soundly for fifteen minutes, on his left side with his knees drawn up and his right hand flat between his thighs. He called this "taking a little pan"—he still fooled with words—and it was a marvel to us that so little rest refreshed him, for then he was up again as if a new day were beginning. As often as I could I drove with him to see his patients. I sat outside, holding Marguerite's reins, while he went in and stayed—he would promise this—as short a time as possible. But on those occasions I did not care; it was fun to be in charge of Marguerite, and I could ask myself once more whether I wanted to be a doctor. He usually came out before I answered the question, and on the way home he might tell me a little about the sick man he had left.

As I grew older, and lost myself in studies I was still young enough to doubt he could understand, I am sure he would have liked to hear me talk about them. I was sure of it even then, but I did not respond to his desire. And I have always regretted this, in the helpless way of those who wish too late that they had been perfect toward their parents. Parents live with similar regrets about their children: they were too harsh on one occasion, too lenient on another. There is no way to live a perfect life except this rather sorry way of patching up the past with imagined alternatives to what one did at moments that may not be relived. In a poem called "The Monument" I have sought an image for the guilt a father feels about his children. But in another poem, "Sin of Omission," I go directly to a moment in Urbana when I failed my father. It was not that I did the wrong thing; I did nothing at all; which was of course the wrong thing multiplied. I was alone on the third floor, reading or writing, or perhaps it was both, when I heard him coming slowly up the stairs. He did not stop on the second floor, as would have been the case had he been going to bed, but kept on, though with a certain hesitation, until he stood beside my chair and table. I must have looked up, and we must have exchanged a few words; I do not remember what did happen; I only remember that I let him stand there, clearly desirous of communication, and gave him none. I was thinking of the work I must go back to; he was thinking heaven knows what—probably that he should not have interrupted me. At any rate he turned after a while and went down again. And all at once I felt toward him what I would have given the rest of my life to express. Yet I was tongue-tied even then. And there is where the poem starts.

> He will remember this; the cunning Fates,
> Seeing all seventy years laid flat ahead—

Urbana: 1900–1915

The spring-tight coil of days unrolls for them,
Their little and deep long eyes forewatch the dead—
The mouse-eyed Fates can number the known times
He will remember this, the thing unsaid.

Only to say it now would soothe that man,
His father, come to sound him in his room;
Most friendly, but the stairs are still acreak,
And the boy, deafened to another doom,
Says nothing; he is guilty of desire
For the mind's silence, waiting to resume.

What it was filled with, he the least of all
In a far day will know; remembering then—
So the Fates reckon—how he ran and called,
Hoping to bring the shoulders up again;
But only called half-loudly in his pride,
And in the pride of him the best of men.

He will remember this, and loathe the hour
When his fair tongue, malingering, stood still.
He will rehearse the sentences not said;
Pretending that he climbed the lonely hill;
Pretending that he met him at the top,
Articulate, and cured him of his ill:

His need to know, so innocent, how sons
Read in their rooms the dark, the dear-bought books;
How in his own good flesh the strange thing grew,
Thought's inward river, nourishing deep nooks,
Dyeing them different-green. The boy will feign,
Concealing his long sighs, his backward looks—

Will fabricate warm deeds and laughing words,
His hand upon a chair, his cheeks alive;
Instead of this cool waiting, and this gloom
Wherein no starting syllable can thrive.
He will remember even as he runs.
The Fates run too, and rapider arrive.

My father at that time was deeply troubled. The last of his
enterprises, an electric railroad that would run north and
south through Urbana, was still in its earliest stage; yet even
then he may have had more qualms about it than he was ever
to confess. The line would compete not only with the Illinois

41

Central railroad, which it paralleled, but with automobiles and trucks—more numerous every year, and destined in the end to bankrupt this little Kankakee and Urbana Traction Company of which he was president. People put money into it because he asked them to; they believed in him as he believed in it, for his initial faith in it was very strong; and thoughts of these people were to rob him of much sleep before he died. The railroad never did prosper, though it ran for years: not so far as Kankakee whose name it bore but at least as far as Paxton, which scarcely qualified as a terminal point. We all witnessed the dismal, slow disaster without any power to stop it on our part. It was eventually, in combination with the agricultural depression of the 1920's, to take away from him whatever wealth he had; my mother, by buying a few houses and renting them, and by renting rooms in her own house to university people, saved them both in so far as they could be saved. All of this was a heart-rending spectacle, and I am ahead of my story once more through mentioning it now. I do so because it suggests one further thing that may have moved my father to ascend the stairs in search of comfort from his son.

V

We had many relatives, most of them on my mother's side, whom we visited with a regularity of which I have never ceased to be glad; and glad not merely for the general reason that relatives are good things to possess, since a great deal is learned from them that cannot be learned from strangers, but for the particular reason that these in question, considered merely as persons, were a joy to know as now they are a joy to remember. First among them were Grandma and Grandpa Butz, whose house in Potomac was for Frank and me our favorite place to go to out of Urbana. We took a train from Champaign to Rantoul, a matter of fourteen miles, then changed to a branch line that took us nineteen miles east, through Gifford, Penfield, and Armstrong, to the small town in Vermilion County on the edge of which my mother's mother and father lived. And how they lived! Or so we said to ourselves then. Everything up there was somehow more charming than what we had at home. The house was not large, and certainly it was not rich; but for one thing it was on two levels— the front door led into the second story, from which narrow stairs descended to the living room and kitchen, which were not wholly subterranean because the ground at that point sloped down to the barn and the river, and if we followed a cement walk to the rear we could enter the kitchen directly from outdoors. However reached, the kitchen was the heart of the house. It was wide and low, with a cement floor covered in places by linoleum; and the chief object in it, at any rate for us, was the big covered box at one end through which water constantly ran. This was artesian water, a thing for which Potomac was famous; and it was all Grandma needed to keep her butter, milk, meat, cream, eggs, and vegetables cool. We loved to lift the wooden lid and see the crocks in which cream was rising, or a dish of cold chicken (we could always take a piece), or at the far end, where a pipe brought the water in, wonderful accumulations of bright red rust that signified its mineral content.

Yet the living room was delightful too. It was long, with a double bed in it where Grandma and Grandpa slept; and at the end where the high windows were, for this room was partly underground, huge ferns that decorated the window sills hung in some cases clear to the floor. Grandpa's chair, in which he sat a great deal with a newspaper in his lap, had one wide arm on which he did his correspondence; he was remarkable for the number of words he could get on a postal card, in a fine, firm hand that he kept in perpetual practice, for he liked words, written or spoken, and filled with them half the world he knew. He was an excellent storyteller, and entertained us every evening after supper with tales of his youth. He had

43

come to Illinois, with many others of his generation, from farther east; his family started in New Jersey, but migrated by stages through Ohio and Indiana, just as Grandma's family, the Tillotsons, had done. One story he particularly liked to tell was about some hogs he drove as a boy from Upper Sandusky, in Ohio, south across that state. He pronounced the name so that it sounded like Uppersondusky, and it was years before I knew how it should be spelled. Grandma rocked in another chair while he talked, and frequently went sound asleep. She had heard his stories, and she herself was not given to talk. She was a large, bony woman, as speechless as she was good. She was never comfortable when he praised her, as he incessantly did—for her cooking, for her looks, and for her goodness. I am sure she thought she was not good-looking, though in her powerful way she was, and sometimes she took the trouble to call him foolish for saying so. He would only groan at this, and complain of the way she ruled him. He had a neat white beard which he was always smoothing with his hands.

He was censorious of sinners. Drunkards were the worst; he claimed he was one of the original Prohibitionists, and so knew all about the evil; in 1919, when Prohibition became national, he went out on the street and yelled so loud that he dislocated his jaw, and for days could not utter a word. He was against smoking, too. Once in Urbana, seeing me on a bench in the park alongside a man with a cigar, he took me for the smoker and knocked me off so that I fell to the ground; and never apologized, for *had* I been smoking, this would have been what I deserved. He was an old man privileged in his own opinion to say anything he thought at any time. The people of Potomac, to whom he was a character, indulged him in this with little complaint; for he entertained them too. He was a bright ancient, more interesting than most of those he entertained. And for all his foolishness—he did have plenty—Frank and I found him as fascinating as we found Grandma kind. He took us fishing in the Fork below the house, arguing as he went with Izaak Walton, whose book he knew by heart but did not accept as gospel. He preferred Seneca's *Morals;* he said that nobody could read it without being a better man.

We found him fascinating for his works no less than his words. He who had planted trees at Hope was forever improving his place here. He built a greenhouse and grew things he would never have seen otherwise: begonias with superlarge leaves, and sensitive plants. On one of its walls I saw my first gourd; he had it there, with a small hole in it, for wrens. And down the hill, past the root cellar where he stored potatoes and turnips, was a grove of plum trees planted so thick that the sun never got through to the ground; or if it did, and grass started, Grandma's chickens plucked it out. He still planted trees, at least one new kind every year; there were persimmons in the yard, and he knew the names of more apples than I supposed existed. The big barn below the plum grove was also on two levels, for the land kept falling away; the animals in it he overfed and underworked, so that some of them were laughably fat. One mare, I remember, he suitably called Chunk.

But the artesian water was the thing we never failed to marvel at. It rose to the surface, once a drill had found it, with such force that any pipe had to be partially plugged lest a geyser form and a new stream be created on the ground. And these wells were everywhere. Potomac was a paradise of water. Grandpa even had a ram—a mechanism whose click and gush we never tired of looking at and listening to—with which to elevate into the kitchen the stream we worshiped there. In another place he had impounded enough water for a fishpond: a source of misery to him, he sometimes said, because boys tampered with the outlet and once drained the whole thing dry. He maintained a feud with the boys of Potomac, who if they were as pesky as he said they were probably enjoyed the spectacle of his rages, and even strove to see what new names they could make him call them. The horse tank by the barn, however, was the place where we got most pleasure out of

Potomac water. The stream that fed it was so strong, the bubbles were so active, and the water itself so cold, that we never wearied of hanging over the metal edge and plunging our arms to the bottom, then holding them there as long as we could stand it.

No wonder we liked to visit Potomac, as Paul in his time did too. I have never forgotten a day when the rest of us took Paul to the train at Champaign for his first trip there alone. I cannot be sure how old he was, but I know we were distressed, as we stood on the platform and watched him at the window while the train prepared to move away, because he cried. We thought this meant that he was too young after all. But when he came home he explained to me that he had merely felt sorry for us because we were not going. Seeing us down there, doomed to be stationary while he rode the cars, filled him with such pity for us that he wept. It must also be true that he pitied us for missing Potomac. He loved it as we all did—as Frank and I had loved it one summer when we were there for weeks, and under our pillows in the bedroom upstairs kept secret cakes of Baker's sweet chocolate which we nibbled at each night before we went to sleep. I have no notion why this had to be kept a secret; Grandma would not have minded; but there was enough squirrel in us, I have no doubt, to account for a desire to climb and hide our food. Surely it was not for lack of food downstairs. Grandma was of the generation that believed in six jellies or preserves at every meal, and pickles of every shape, and meats of many kinds.

We ate in a dining room between the kitchen and the room where the ferns were. An oil painting, from I know not what source, hung on the wall. It bore the title "Sunrise at Lake Chautauqua"; a deer was drinking at the water's edge, and there were woods and mountains in the background. It was an old picture, smoky with age, so that details were difficult to make out. And it may not have been a good picture. But for me it represented all painting, and I lived a life of my own among its dusky particulars.

My mother, one of Grandma Butz's six children four of whom by this time were grown men, kept in touch with all of her family. Her older sister, my Aunt Laura Collison, was the mother of Inez who had heard Frank and me practicing our profanity at Hope. But my uncles, whom I saw less often because they had gone to distant parts, whenever they did return to Illinois brought with them breezes of a bigger world which I almost literally felt on my face. Uncle Clint (DeWitt Clinton) returned least often, and finally disappeared, not without mystery, into Idaho. Uncle Mark, however, for whom I had been named, lived as a bachelor in the Indian Territory (after 1907, Oklahoma) and came up frequently enough for me to develop a great pride because I bore his name. He had taken a homestead near the southern border of the Territory, and farmed there alone in a log house; he was tall and bony like my grandmother, with a lean weathered face which I fancied to be Indian, though his eyes were burning blue and he laughed more than Indians were supposed to do. In May of 1915 I had a letter from him saying that after being Rip Van Winkle for twenty years he had married, and he invited me down to inspect my new aunt Cora. I did so twenty-four years later, as shall be seen.

The other two uncles, Warren and Wallace, were twins, and they too lived in Oklahoma, but not in the wilderness. They had elected to grow up with the city of Muskogee, which in fact did not develop at the rate they expected. They were polished and knowledgeable, as Uncle Mark was not, though in their own ways they had a largeness too, and I never wearied of listening to them as they spoke of Choctaws, Chickasaws, Creeks, and the new oil fields that were opening up. Uncle Wallace brought his bride, Aunt Helen, to the house on Oregon Street; I remember this because of a circumstance that meant much to me at the time. They had the front bedroom upstairs, at the right of a broad hall, and I happened to be in that hall one afternoon when they ascended together and walked to their door. Only, they did not walk; Uncle Wallace suddenly put his arm around Aunt Helen's waist and they waltzed, humming as they did so and filling me with wonder at a demonstration of delight in each other such as I never before had seen married couples make.

And yet the Knights at Muncie, only a few miles east of Urbana, did not suffer by comparison with these uncles from afar. Frank and I, going out there on the interurban, first to the farm north of town which Uncle Lon (Alonzo) managed for its owner in Danville, and later to a house, the westernmost in Muncie, to which he had retired, found ourselves in an atmosphere so natural, so easy, and so warm with cousinly talk that we always felt at home and happy, and wanted to go back whenever we could. By cousins I mean chiefly the four daughters of Aunt Frant. Ora and Ed, their older brothers, we scarcely knew; but Dorothy (Dot), Mary (Mayme), Laura, and Julia were marvelous talkers, as their mother and father were—Uncle Lon was a droll humorist with a long face proper to the type—and it was this talk we loved. It never stopped, and it was always exciting, even though much of it concerned other Tillotsons—uncles, aunts, cousins and second cousins—whom we knew nothing about. But no matter whom it concerned, it could keep us at the table for hours after supper, with the dishes still unwashed, just as in the parlor, about the upright piano whose top was a forest of photographs, it might go on to any hour at all. Once it went on so late that nobody remembered to open our bed for us in the spare room where we were to sleep. We found our way there ourselves, but then knew so little about how to open the elaborate counterpane and bolster, which looked as if intended for royalty, that we gave up and slept on the floor, and the next morning were laughed at for our scruple.

I say there were many Tillotsons I did not know. But there was annual opportunity to know them all, at a reunion, usually somewhere in Vermilion County, to which hundreds of them came, though naturally many of those who came had other names. They all, however, were descendants of Ephraim Buell

Tillotson, who married Mary Ann Cronkhite in 1834 and had by her twelve children—these included Grandma Butz, Aunt Frant, and Aunt Mary Henry, mother of Gladys, my playmate at Hope—who in turn had more offspring than I can count. They would come for the day, often from considerable distances, and renew their memories not only of Illinois but of Indiana, where Ephraim and Mary Ann had lived when they were first married. I went some years with my mother to this fabulous gathering, and was identified to innumerable relatives at the same moment that I labored to identify them. I was seldom successful at this, and yet the entire experience is one I cannot forget. Nor can I forget what I saw one summer through a door inadvertently left open off the downstairs hall of a farmhouse where the reunion was being held. I was on my way to the kitchen; I glanced in, and there on the edge of a bed, pulling up her stockings, was a strange woman whom I knew at once, by the wild way she stared at me, to be—I remember saying it to myself—crazy. In those days and in that place the insane, if it was possible at all, were kept at home instead of being sent to institutions. The thing that most impressed me then was not the condition of the woman (a cousin? an aunt? I never knew) but the assumption that I should not learn of her existence, or if I did, that I should not let on to others. My mother, when I told her what I had seen, was horrified; I must never mention it, she said. Yet even this one indelible detail is rivaled in my memory by the whole air that hung about any Tillotson reunion to which I was lucky enough to be taken. The crowds of people and horses (later of cars), the hot sun, the flies, the long tables, the Homeric food, the children, the young couples, the ancient ones who sat in chairs under the trees and had infants brought to them for a sort of blessing—never of course called that—the whole air still hangs about me as I write, and I know it will never go away.

By the standard these occasions set, my father seemed to have next to no relatives. He had a great many, but with one

exception we seldom saw them. They were not the visiting
kind. We heard him speak of them, and once he went all the
way to Roswell, New Mexico, because he was concerned about
the health of his brother Frank, for whom my brother Frank
was named; he came back with a good report, and talked for
days about the irrigation systems he had seen there for the first
time in his life. He had, I think, more brothers and sisters
than my mother had, but most of them we knew by name only,
and then in connection with the illnesses they had, or the even
worse misfortunes of which there was a grim abundance. His
father died in 1903, in Saunemin, a town to the north which I
never saw but with which I associate numerous members of
the family. His mother, who did not die until 1911, spent
many days of her widowhood with us in Urbana. She had been
Hannah Chapman, an English girl who when she was still
young crossed the Atlantic—it took six weeks—in the steerage
of a ship she still shuddered to remember. Now in her old age
she was small and sad, and sometimes I thought more humble
than she should be. Silent a great deal, sitting always in black
dresses that were strangely made, for they had folds and
pockets the like of which I had never seen before, she maintained as her one topic the importance of her not being any
trouble to us; at meals she never took a second helping, saying
simply, "No, thank you, I have plenty." She did not try in
other words to entertain us; and so in our thoughtlessness we
gave her little attention. At least I gave her less than I have
since wished I had. For she was my grandmother, and in spite
of the fact that she cried, quietly to herself, when I saw no
reason for her doing so, or indeed because of this, I know I
should have let her tell me things that of course were on her
mind. As it was, detecting in her no share of the energy and
spirit my father had, I mistakenly supposed her to be in no
more than some academic sense the person who had brought
him into the world.

With his brother in Champaign it was entirely different.
Uncle Walter, several years younger than my father, we all

considered to be a genius, and in fact he was. He was tall, stooped, and unbelievably thin, with a high-pitched, rather weak voice that said shrewd and witty things. He was one of our humorists, and indeed the best, though he also attended seriously to the business of farming, which after running for some years a successful drugstore in Saunemin he had retired to Champaign to practice. He was the owner of several fine farms which he was always driving to inspect, dressed in the least possible number of old clothes because he cared nothing about his appearance; once, I remember, when we saw him off on a train to Mississippi, where he had bought some black cotton land, we remarked that he had no collar or tie, and for that matter no luggage; he said he had a toothbrush. The energy of my father was in him too, in spite of many suggestions to the contrary: his languor, his air of being tired, and his love of sitting and talking without end. He once remarked of his children, Esther, Earl, and David, that they were more timid than children used to be; till they were six, he said, they were "afraid to step over a cob." I have no idea why he said this, for they were like any other children; he probably did not think it, but only amused himself with the figure. We were late one Sunday for dinner at his house—it was something like our house, high, square, and brick—and we apologized. "Sit down," he said, for they had started eating; "but everything is cold, except the water." Aunt Lena, his wife, a hearty, laughing woman who I am sure had kept everything hot, did not bother to correct him; she considered him as crazy as we did, and knew better than we could how brilliant he was. For instance, at games. The university champions came to play chess with him, and he always won. But checkers was just as good a game in his opinion, or any kind of cards. Not that he ever seemed to work at it. Play was play, a thing you might suppose he had invented.

VI

Urbana during all this time, famous for its elms whose shade in the hot summers blackened every street, was doubtless an uneventful prairie town, but it was never without its charms for me. In the business district Sol Reimund's confectionery store was assumed, perhaps rightly, to have no peer in the world when it came to chocolate nut caramels and pineapple nut sundaes. I patronized its fat proprietor whenever I could; yet there was equal pleasure in carrying home from one of the groceries a paper pail of oysters—not fresh, of course, but opened near the sea and sent here, a thousand miles inland, in cold containers where they soaked in their own juice—which my mother would make into a stew.

There were the annual excitements, too, of Chautauqua and the Champaign County Fair. My clearest memory of the fair I have preserved in the story "Dollar Bill," where a boy who accurately corresponds to me teases his mother for money with which to go to the grounds on a day when the rest of the family have not planned to go. She gives him a dollar, the smallest amount she can find in her purse, and presses upon him the importance of his bringing half of it back; admission for him as a child will be a quarter, and with the other quarter he can buy good things to eat and drink. He goes at last, a little ashamed of having teased her into consenting, but comforted by the prospect of the lemonade and hamburgers he can buy with that second quarter. But a scoundrel at the window, pretending not to notice he is under age, gives him an adult ticket with only half a dollar in change, so that he enters the grounds not merely in shame but in despair. He tries to get interested in the free exhibits; smells hamburgers cooking; decides that one such indulgence will be forgiven by his mother; goes up to the counter; is given the sandwich; and before he can eat it hears the man telling him his half-dollar is counterfeit. I do not tell in the story how my father, when we all went the next day, passed the bad coin in at the same window and heard nothing further from it. I looked at the implements and animals again, and in the grandstand saw pacing and trotting races. There was no horse like Dan Patch, the world's champion pacer whom we had read about and admired; but the sulkies, the drivers with their silk caps, the starters and the judges, not to speak of the horses themselves, so gaily harnessed and at the finish line so dark with sweat, were a spectacle of which I could never get enough.

Chautauqua was of a different order—some said, a higher one. It was the place where we heard lectures and music, and if we were young watched magicians; also, the first movies ever to reach Urbana. The headquarters of all the Chautauquas in the country were at Lake Chautauqua, New York, where one summer our family went by train and spent a week. But the Twin City Chautauqua, so named in honor of Urbana and Champaign, was good enough in ordinary years. People rented small tents and lived on the grounds, close to the big tent where the programs went on; and of course there were concessions for food and drink. Automobiles, movies, radio, and television have long since done away with the institution, which in its day deserved more praise than it always got. We saw and heard William Jennings Bryan, Senator LaFollette of Wisconsin, Senator Beveridge of Indiana, and Captain Cook who said he had discovered the North Pole. We also listened to bell ringers and cheap evangelists, and to professional lecturers who had nothing to say. Yet the average was not bad, and I considered myself well employed during two summers when I acted as assistant secretary of the local show. I rented tents, corresponded with lyceum managers, got notices into the newspapers, and sometimes took trips on the interurban to places as far away as Danville and Decatur where business had to be transacted. The cars bounced merrily between the cornfields, and I always opened the window by my seat so that I could smell the hot country flying past.

Crystal Lake, on whose shore the Chautauqua had its site, was suitable for canoeing in summer and skating in winter. I never became as proficient as Frank in either of these arts; I was not especially good at any sport; I never learned how to play tennis or golf, or to swim more than a few strokes. But I did like our canoe; and when we went with other young people to Homer Park, changing interurban cars at Ogden on the way, I threw myself with enthusiasm into the none too elaborate amusements there. The town of Homer was and is on the Wabash Railroad; it is east of Sidney, where a branch line used to run up to Urbana, and west of Sidney is Philo—three great names for three small towns which a stranger on a Wabash express train would scarcely notice. Coming out on such a train decades later than the time now in view, and whizzing through those towns in a matter of minutes, I reflected on their former importance to me and the reflection resulted in a poem that for a title has their names:

> Homer, Sidney, Philo,
> Strung along the Wabash:
> Beads in the black land.
> Corn grows, but no change
> In these little towns.
>
> After forty springtimes
> Nothing to look out at.
> Seven miles, eight miles—
> Strangers in the blue express
> Yawn and despise them.
>
> So would I, certainly,
> Except that I remember
> Homer Park on hot days.
> We took the interurban.
> We kissed in the shade.
>
> Sidney was our junction;
> Six trains a week there.
> We rode the dusty local—
> Opening all windows—
> Then to Detroit.

Urbana: 1900–1915

Philo we drove through,
Cold nights, with horses.
Once there was a dim lamp
Showing, and my father
Stopped for oyster stew.

After forty autumns,
Only I am different.
Here they are as always;
They cannot remember
Themselves as I do.

Philo in those days had the peculiar distinction of being halfway between Urbana and Villa Grove, so that when we drove down to my father's second farm—the first one was always Hope—we cherished it as a landmark, visible a long way across flat country and welcome evidence that we were getting on. It took three hours for Marguerite to trot or walk the whole eighteen miles to Villa Grove; she had to walk, or even to stand and blow, whenever we ascended one of the "hills." For the country was not as flat as a table, though neither was it as wrinkled as the Rockies.

. . . the slow buggy, appearing and disappearing,
Slipped in and out of moon and maple shadows, down
Those least of earth's depressions, up those low,
Those prairie rises. Eighteen miles
From town to sleepy town, and not a lamp
In any passing window—oh, so slowly
Passing, as the mare's feet
Shuffled, and the delicate wheels
Answered, invisible in windless
Dust.

So I wrote in "No Word, No Wind," a poem that owes its existence to these trips. We took them in all kinds of weather: sometimes cold weather, and it was on such a night that my father, reaching Philo with Frank and me, and aware that the laprobe was inadequate to keep us warm, stopped there at a little restaurant—I recall its dim lights—for oyster stew.

Mark Van Doren

VII

The farm at Villa Grove I remember best out of this time, for we spent our summers there. Hope remained a mythical place seldom visited by anyone except my father; although our pony Dick, transported to Villa Grove where he would die at the extraordinary age of thirty-five, could have reminded us of many things had he been more talkative than he was. He grew as a matter of fact more self-sufficient and stubborn every year. He seemed to enjoy being sat on when there was no place to go; but I remember thinking one day I would ride him into town, and discovering that he had different ideas. He was willing to cross a bridge over the nearby Embarrass River (pronounced Ambraw, and so spelled in *The Mayfield Deer*), but beyond that he would not budge, no matter what I did and I did frantic things. Perhaps he did not want to step over the tracks of the Frisco railroad, newly built for fast freight traffic between Chicago and St. Louis, and the cause in recent years for the growth of Villa Grove; west of the "old town" had sprung up a "new town" where the Frisco shops were and the locomotives changed. I came back on Dick, having failed to complete my errand, and was told I might have known he was not my slave.

Dick was more tractable, indeed he recovered his old ambition, when Frank and I, with other boys who were visiting us, included him, small as he was, among the mounts we called our "calvary" until Carl corrected us. Four or five of us would gallop about on Sundays—it was only then that we had access to the other mounts, farm horses or even mules who should have been left to their day of rest, and even if they had been fresh were far from dashing—we would lumber up and down the barnlot and sometimes out on the road that led to the Ambraw bridge and the Frisco crossing. The Ambraw, a muddy stream which lower down in Illinois became a sizable

56

river and joined the Wabash, wound at this point through oak woods which were the only wild place on the farm. Otherwise, north and west from here, the level land was divided into rectangular fields of forty acres or more where corn, oats, wheat, and hay were grown. At first Frank and I were too young to help with the main business of the farm, though Carl and Guy did; but eventually we took our turn at plowing corn, shocking oats or wheat, and on the days when we thrashed, driving wagons of grain in to the elevator at Villa Grove.

My central memory of the place, however, has to do with a warm, lazy world where for the most part we played and watched grown men work. The house, set well back from the road, was high, with tall narrow windows, and on its right a lane brought buggies to the back door. This lane was lined with soft maples which in a wind would show their silver undersides so that I could think of the whole row as turning pale. There was a front porch where we sat in the evening—the inside of the house did not cool off till midnight, and sometimes never did—and listened to the maple leaves or, farther away to the south and east, the Frisco freight trains rumbling on their way to St. Louis. We had the house to ourselves, for another house across the road accommodated the hired man and his family. In June my mother transferred her duties and her worries here; my father, detained in Urbana by his practice or at Hope by the older farm, would come down only when he could; in September we moved back to begin another year of school.

Frank and I slept in the same room. There was a legend that on steaming, quiet nights you could hear the corn grow. I never did, but once when Frank had been up to Urbana and back he told me something that kept me wide awake long after he thought I was asleep. Beth Knowlton, he said, had been seen riding on a white horse behind another boy. He had not seen this himself, he had only heard about it. Beth was not to be my girl forever, but now at twelve I wept for jealousy and wondered if there was anything I could do. There was nothing, and the agony passed; but in "Only For Me," though it reverses the situation and speaks of one called Linda Jane who did the weeping, I reconstruct the distress, half terrible, half sweet, I felt that night:

> When I was twelve in that far land,
> And was in love with summer nights,
> And was in love with Linda Jane,
> Whose very name was dancing lights
> About my dark, my country bed,
> Once I dreamed that she was dead.
>
> And woke; and not one window star,
> As I looked out, but wept for me.
> I looked again, and my own tears,
> Like magic lanterns, made me see
> The very eyes of Linda Jane
> Weeping everywhere like rain.
>
> Then the sunrise, cool and red,
> And the new day, white and hot,
> And after that the growing up
> And the forgetting—oh, but not
> The selfless woe of one that died.
> Only for me, for me she cried.

It was sweeter at least than another distress I felt on several nights when I walked in my sleep—a habit I kept for years. In the present case I was without qualification miserable. I would partially wake up and find myself feeling the walls of the house, over and over, upstairs and down, in a hopeless attempt to find my room again. In the total dark I could see nothing, and anyhow I suppose I was still substantially asleep; but I can hear my hand sliding over the wallpaper as I moved from room to room, entering to touch the sleepers there who were not myself, then out again and on until I was fully awake and of course could locate my bed at once. So far as I know I never woke anybody up, and I never told about it in the morning. Possibly I dreamed the whole thing: merely dreamed that

I was lost—or, weird though this may sound, that I was dreaming.

An even worse experience that I connect with Villa Grove, or rather with the drive between Philo and there, has nothing to do with dreams. West of the road at one point, in a thicket of trees, was the shallow grave where Harold Shaw, an older boy we knew in Urbana, was buried by another boy who had killed him for his racing car, a contraption which Harold liked to drive around the streets with its muffler cut out. The car and its owner disappeared, and it was several days before they were found here. This was my first near view of murder, and for that matter my last. The road to Villa Grove was never the same again.

VIII

Yet nothing ever dimmed or altered the joy I then took in my existence or in that of the world with which I thought I was identical. Some days my happiness seemed a mad thing, or if not that an imbecilic thing, that inspired me to walk spasmodically, my arms jerking as if they had no better way to express their pleasure in being my own arms. I have tried since, for the state persists though it is soberer now, to find words for that nameless joy in poems such as "The Ecstasy":

> For he so loved the world today
> That he fell down like dead, and lay,
> His left arm dangled at the sofa's side,
> Smiling inanely.
>
> You would have said he searched the rug
> For signature of pin, of bug,
> Of sunbeam. But the silence of his eyesight:
> That explained him.
>
> That was the symptom: nothing seen,
> Yet the whole world washed dark and clean

By his acceptance—oh, a mile away
Horses were grateful;

Curveted, and clipped the ground
While here, relaxing from all sound,
He let the mohair heft him: light as wheatstraw,
Harvested lately.

In those days, however, it must have had something to do with
the fact that at home I still stuttered, sometimes absurdly so,
and that I was always breaking or spilling things. Hardly a
week passed but I knocked over a glass of water; once I turned
a wrong faucet in the cellar and the tank in the attic over-
flowed, ruining three ceilings; and I broke twelve dozen eggs
by tampering with the leaf of a table on which my mother had
placed the box that contained them. My fits of abstraction, like
my jerks in walking, I know were not unique with me, since
all boys are afflicted with them when they feel good. But their
degree in my case may have been something truly special, for
one of Carl's favorite questions, put to me with the mock
solemnity of which he had long been master, was: "Mark, what
poem of Wordsworth do you remind me of?" I always answered: " 'The Idiot Boy.' "

Carl might have said I was doubly right had he been inside
my mind during the long, lonely walks I took, preferably in
mist or rain, after I became an adolescent. Of course he had no
need to be there, since he must have taken those very walks in
his own time; all children do. But I assumed, again as all children do, that I was unique in wanting to wander through dead
streets, thinking to myself—sometimes saying to myself—the
strangest things; and feeling, if the truth be known, alternately
proud and sorry that nobody would ever understand the remarkable person I was. One evening, when I had come home
from such a walk and was asked where I had been, I answered
as I went upstairs: "The Lord is abroad tonight." I had read
this somewhere, but it was now my own; and I thought it quite
natural that everybody should laugh.

IX

High school and university, for all of their importance to any future I might have, were then but incidents in what seemed a present that would never end. They occupied nine years of the fifteen I lived in Urbana, and during the last of those years I wrote my first book: proof, if any was required, that I had ceased to be a stammering child. Yet even so my memories of school, of home, of town, of farm run all together in one timeless, even placeless pattern, so that to separate any one set of them from the others is more than difficult; it is unreal. As student then, as teacher since, I have never found that books and studies, however much I loved them, filled the world. I have loved as many things outside as in.

I do remember, though, the first day I went with Frank to the Thornburn High School, on the north side of Urbana near the Boneyard and the interurban tracks. I was twelve, I still wore short pants, and doubtless I seemed an infant to the sophomore who sat on a wooden fence and said to me: "Mark, do you think you can do the work?" I was at once convinced that I could not, so that I went on in as one doomed to humiliation. I did go in, however, as I had not done at Hope; and soon enough had lost my fears. For one thing, I began to study Latin, and through this to understand grammar and syntax better than I had before, or rather to understand them for the first time, and to think of them, as I have ever since, as beautiful things so basic to the mind that if they are not known, nothing is known. German did this for me too, though Latin was the more attractive language, with something elegant in it like the mathematical idiom I learned from Mr. Bowditch, a soft-voiced old man—at least I thought him old— who taught plane and solid geometry, and then for a climax trigonometry. Mr. Bowditch, as strict as he was gentle, conveyed to me a lively sense that mathematics is grammar and rhetoric no less than logic: is language too, and a way of reporting upon the mind's adventure through the world.

These things prepared me as nothing else could have done to move among the mysteries of my own language. And here it was my good fortune to have for a teacher Arthur Tietje, a hawk-faced, not very robust man whom it was a discipline to hear talk, and who when he criticized my compositions went so directly and swiftly to every weakness in them that I could wince at the prospect of his reading me at all, though I could rejoice too when he commended a paragraph. For some reason I have never forgotten his writing on the blackboard a sentence of mine in which I had tried the trick of alliteration: "He joyously jumped across the stream." Tietje explained to the class that alliteration could be done both well and badly; in this case it had been done badly, for the result was a silly phrase; "jumped joyously" would have been a little better, but another pair of words might have been better still.

Then there was the day when Miletus Flaningam, an old friend of the family whom my father, then a member of the school board, had brought down from Potomac to be principal of the high school (his first name had been given to Paul for a middle name, now never used), came into our English class where *Macbeth* was being read. He electrified us by talking about the whole play as if it were a single thing instead of a series of things—of scenes—which under another teacher, a well-intentioned woman who this day was ill, we had been studying for weeks as if there were little connection between them. Lete, as we privately called the principal, was of course not prepared to do what the teacher would have done; so he drew upon his knowledge of Shakespeare generally. He said that *Macbeth* was a tragedy; told us what a tragedy was; spoke of Shakespeare's other great tragedies, *Hamlet, Othello,* and *King Lear;* distinguished each one of them from *Macbeth* by describing the passion that obsessed its hero; and ended by scarcely having to talk about *Macbeth* at all, at any rate to me, because now I understood and felt the play, and somehow knew that I would never in my life encounter a greater poet than this one who understood everything about grief, jealousy, pride, and ambition. Before that day I had wondered if my father was right in bringing Lete to Urbana. Now I could have no further doubts. In forty minutes he created a world— perhaps *the* world—and I was never to forget it. This was powerful teaching; it assumed maturity in us who listened; it spoke to that maturity; and in so far as such a thing can be done to a boy of thirteen, it made me a reading man.

Soon after that the Ben Greet Players came to the university, and since Carl was still at home he saw to it that I went to all of their performances. For the first time I heard Shakespeare on the stage, in this case an outdoor stage with cut boughs for scenery: the players came and went through openings in maple leaves which their costumes brushed, releasing I thought a delicious woodland fragrance. I still associate that fragrance with Shakespearean comedy, or at any rate with the three examples of it I witnessed then: *A Midsummer Night's Dream, As You Like It,* and *The Tempest.* The company included, in addition to Ben Greet, a family of Vyvyans, all young and charming to my eyes, and a still more charming girl named Sybil Thorndike, with whom as Rosalind and Miranda I fell in love. I once told her this in New York, when she was Dame Sybil; I said with some hesitation, because I did not know her views on the passage of time, that it was thirty years ago. "Oh, no," she said, "it was thirty-five." She remembered the tour, her first in America, as happily as I did. But the plays were the thing. If I did not hear or understand every line, and if I had no Miletus Flaningam at my side to tell me what comedy was, I seemed nevertheless to know why the players were always smiling as they spoke, as if the felicity of Shakespeare were their own inward secret, communicable at last in this way and no other.

I was still in high school then, going to dances on Friday nights with the Saintz, a club of boys to which Frank and I belonged together with Chancy Finfrock and a dozen others, or else with the Barbs, a club of girls organized by Miriam, Beth, Laura, Betty Baines, Fran Nichol, and several more of our good friends. Lucile Needham, a brilliant girl whom I admired, was not a Barbarian. I knew her chiefly as a contributor to the *Thornburn Thistle*, the school magazine of which I was editor in my senior year—I can scarcely see why, for in the bound volume of its numbers that I have kept I can find no contributions by myself, except I suppose for some polysyllabic editorials now quite impossible to read through. There is a story by Frank, and he figures in the athletic pages, for he was on the football and track teams; but I remained anonymous, perhaps because I knew I could not compete with Lucile, who should have been editor in my place. Then it was time for Commencement; my mother gave Frank and me gold watches with inscriptions inside their hunting cases; and we were ready to be students at the University of Illinois.

X

There it was, in the fall of 1910, after years of being together in school, that Frank and I parted company. He studied agriculture, and I elected the liberal arts. He had always said he was going to be a farmer; I knew why, for some of my sentiments leaned that way too; but I was already following Carl, and if I was not as sure as he was that I wanted to become a writer, at least I felt most at home in literature, and could imagine no other study to pursue. Guy had elected architecture, and Paul was to elect business. As I recall those college years, with a few exceptions my English courses are the only ones that stand out. The exceptions were Latin, French, German, meteorology, astronomy, and logic. In Latin I read Horace and Catullus, in German I read I do not remember what; the instructor himself, a subtle, shy, dedicated young man in whom I recognized a strange intensity, was more important. He was Leonard Bloomfield, and his dedication was not so much to German as to Language, for his scientific study of which he was later to become famous. I remember a day in his class when we were wondering how to translate *sollte;* I suggested "was to," and he seemed pleased. Years later he was to tell me, perhaps with this in mind, that I was the only student he was sure he had ever been able to teach any German to; I could scarcely tell him how much of what I learned (it was much less than he thought) I had by that time forgotten. In mathematics and science I made sorry progress. College algebra, which I completely failed to understand, was the last attempt I ever made in that direction; and since I was free under the elective system to ignore physics and chemistry—I have never ceased to regret that this was true, and that I took advantage of the freedom—I chose two "easy" sciences to dabble in. Not that the descriptive course in astronomy was without its great power over me; I learned the constellations, and got some idea of the universes beyond them; but I did none of the hard work which sooner or later this lonely science demands. Logic was made exciting, not to say terrifying, by B. H. Bode, a swarthy, eagle-eyed professor whose class in the subject was very popular; and in another philosophy class I discovered Spinoza. But outside of English my intellectual adventures were for the most part desultory, and certainly too amateur for me to remember with pride.

As for English, I began now to read by myself: Robert Louis Stevenson in prose, for example, and Wordsworth in verse. These were my first enthusiasms. I thought Stevenson a master; and as for Wordsworth, whenever I could I shut myself in a room to intone "Tintern Abbey" aloud—very much aloud, for sometimes the family heard me, though nobody complained. Meanwhile, however, I had come under the spell of the finest teacher I was ever to know, and his subject was Shakespeare. Stuart Sherman, with whom Carl had struck up a close friendship during his last year in Urbana, now became my idol. He had a gift which I have since realized is rare among teachers: he thought while he talked. And since his mind was rich, he was always discovering new depths in his own understanding. This happened before our very eyes; we could see it in his face, which was remarkably revealing and mobile, just as we could hear it in his voice, an excellent reading voice, too, so that many of Shakespeare's dramatic effects were delivered to us without loss. But the main thing was Sherman's mind, at once a critical and a creative instrument; he gave it all to Shakespeare, and Shakespeare responded as he ever will to those who bring him their whole selves. Nor did the talk have reference to art in a precious or finical sense. Its final reference was to human life as Shakespeare had explored it: a bottomless subject, nor did Sherman seem to think he could exhaust it in the few things there was time to say. To the extent that he was aware of my presence in the class he may have thought of me merely as a neighbor boy who had stayed one night with his infant son while he and his wife went with Carl to see *Antony and Cleopatra* in a local theater. As he walked out of the door he pointed to a plate of bananas on the hall table and said to me: "Young man, when we come home I don't want to see a single one of those." Nor did he. I had an adolescent's appetite. And it was long a family joke that when Carl spoke next morning at home of my having eaten a dozen bananas in three hours, I protested angrily: "There were only eleven!" But now as many as five years had passed; and Sherman, less aware of that than I was, may not have realized how much of him I was understanding.

I was editor of the *Illinois Magazine* in my senior year, as Carl and Allan Nevins had been before me, but I still did not print anything under my own name. I was N.N.K. (the initials of that name spelled backward), or I.B. (Idiot Boy), or Adulescentulus Fatuus (the same thing)—this last pseudonym appearing over a long essay about Youth and Age, a topic to which youth is queerly addicted. I also wrote essays on contemporary poets, chief among them John Masefield, whom Carl in one of his many letters to me from New York had recommended that I read. And I even published a story and a few terrible poems; I had no ear yet, and no common sense. It was probably my editorship of the *Illinois Magazine* that got me elected to Mawanda, the honorary senior society, and afterwards to the presidency of the senior class; though for that there had to be a campaign, which those who "ran" me based upon two inconsequential circumstances: I was only nineteen, and I belonged to no fraternity. Frank and I, living at home as students and being still such excellent friends of each other, had refused to join the fraternity of which Carl and Guy were in fact no longer zealous members. I am afraid that I had no better claim to office. Anyhow I was elected, and with Fran Nichol led the grand march at the senior ball. When I graduated in June, 1914, my mother gave me the works of Nathaniel Hawthorne in twenty-two volumes.

There was no doubt in my mind, or in Carl's who had watched me closely, that I should go to the university for at least another year. Frank went to Villa Grove to manage the farm there for my father; but I returned to Stuart Sherman, and found that a course of lectures he gave in the prose writers of the nineteenth century was as fine as his Shakespeare class had been. I took other courses; I read innumerable books in Lincoln Hall, a new building which contained a special library for English students; I even wrote a semisatirical sonnet about one of those students, a girl, and it was accepted by Mr. Mencken for the *Smart Set*—my first published poem, and the last for seven years. Sherman, however, was the center of this present year. I can still see him as he talked about Carlyle, Arnold, and Newman, with side glances across the Atlantic at Emerson and Thoreau.

I had to write a master's thesis, and Thoreau became my subject. I read him for months, then wrote for three days and nights until the essay was done. Its view of Thoreau was determined not only by Sherman but by Paul Elmer More, whose *Shelburne Essays* I devoured that year with the result that I considered myself a "humanist." The label seems irrelevant now, and I soon ceased to deserve it if I ever had; yet the essays of More, since they trained me to look at literature with a single and altogether serious question in my mind—is the author before me powerful, or is he simply wild?—were an education in themselves, and I am glad I had it. Sherman, who was More's star contributor on *The Nation* and who of course knew where my ideas came from (they came from him too), read the essay and asked me to come to his office in Lincoln Hall so that he could discuss it with me. The discussion was painful at first; I had misused certain words, and others had run away with me. He pointed to every such case, advised a change, and in the end, since there were so many cases, had me in despair. But then he raised me up again; he said that the essay might be good enough to publish; he had thought of sending it to Houghton Mifflin, Thoreau's publishers in Boston. They accepted it—the condition was a subsidy of two hundred dollars which my father was proud to underwrite—and the next year it appeared. But as I was about to send the manuscript off I heard from Sherman that it had still further defects: there were in it some "excesses of erudition." Of course there were, and there still are, though I removed as many as I could see. What I could not see at the time was that I had never concealed my reading, but rather had paraded it; I cited or quoted too many authors, some of whom had no place in the book at all.

Frank, whom I visited in his solitude at Villa Grove as often as I could, was as proud as my parents were that I could soon refer to myself as the writer of a book. He would be alone only until spring, when he was to marry Grace Gay of Quincy, Illinois, whom he had met in college. The world had been at war since the August after our graduation, but I do not remember that we talked much about that. The only conversations on the subject that I recall were those I had at the university with Jerome Head, a candidate with me for the master's degree. Jerome was eventually to study medicine, and to become an eminent surgeon in Chicago, but his interest that year was in poetry (we wrote verses to each other on the flyleaves of *Beowulf*, in our Anglo-Saxon class)—and in war, which he tried to convince me would always be with us: it was a permanent condition of existence. I resisted him with instinct, not argument, and continued to like him although the things he said, surprising in a man so gentle, disturbed and shocked me.

But even this war seemed far away there on the farm, which for Frank had become a serious business: how serious he did not yet know, for in a few years he was to suffer with my father from the depression that drove prices down and made mortgages look impossibly large, as indeed most of them were. I am sure we talked of Carl and Guy, now years away from home. In 1910 Guy had married Verla McCray; I played the march at their wedding in Danville, for at that time I took piano lessons; and a few months later Frank and I went on the train to see them in Muskogee, where Guy was setting up as an architect, though he came back soon enough and now, after several years in Urbana, was in Detroit. This had been when we were freshmen in college. The next year we went to visit Carl in New York, and met Irita Bradford whom he would marry at Tallahassee in 1912. We may have spoken of the hour we awoke on the train that took us east and heard the locomotive whistling in a way to end all whistling: we had often recalled this together, and I was to put it into a poem, "Uncle Roger":

> He can remember a wet dawn,
> He can remember a stopped train
> In Pennsylvania, and the hoarse,
> High notes—again, again—
>
> That tore the mountain walls apart,
> That split the cold, the dripping oaks;
> And still he hears the lean yell,
> And still the dewy engine smokes.

I think we must have talked of that, and of the nervous night we spent in a New York hotel because Carl had been unable to meet us. The next day he did, and then he more than made it up by taking us to theaters, ball games, and amusement parks until we thought we had seen all of New York there was. Frank did not go to the wedding, though, the August after this; I went with my mother—it was a long trip by train—and at eighteen served as knowingly as I could in the capacity of best man. It was my first experience of the South: of its heat, of its elaborate and pretty manners, and at least in Tallahassee of its tall pecan trees which I forever wondered at. Irita's sister, now Margaret Boni, was maid of honor, and there were dances and receptions. My mother and I rode back through New Orleans, then up along the Mississippi to Illinois.

In 1915 even these things seemed far away in time, which was taking on a new reality. By fall I would be gone from home too, leaving Paul at sixteen as my parents' only son in residence. I was going to New York where Carl was, to study at Columbia where he had studied and was now a teacher of English. I might be such a teacher in my time. But I suspect that Frank and I thought constantly, however seldom we mentioned it, of the fact that our twenty-one years of intimacy were over.

I See the World

SINCE I was the fourth son to leave home, no special drama attended my departure for New York in September; there were only the feelings proper in any set of lives to such a moment, and indeed these were strong enough. But they were modified by the fact that my parents were moving out of the big house. Guy had designed another one for them next door, and the weeks before I left I spent with Paul carrying furniture across the space between. If there was any drama at all, it was a muted one connected with money. I needed six hundred dollars for the year at Columbia, and my father took me to a bank in Champaign so that I could see him borrow them from Mr. Mattis, the president. There was no difficulty about this, for Mr. Mattis said he considered it a privilege to lend Dr. Van Doren money; he approved, too, of the use to which it would be put; I can hear him saying this as he swung in his chair and looked at me; but eventually I was to be aware that my father had so proceeded in order that I might know it was not so easy as it would once have been for him to pay my way; it was he, not I, who met the note when it was due. As for what lay ahead of me at Columbia, I had the comfort of knowing that Carl was there and had made all the arrangements it was possible for him to make. He had gone first, as being the oldest of us he had done everything first; many problems never presented themselves to me as problems, for he had solved them.

His counsels when I arrived were characteristically large and free: I was to enjoy myself as a student, to let the experience of Columbia be as it were a natural part of my whole experience then and still to come, and to keep always in mind the possibility that I might write books as well as study them. These counsels were implied rather than expressed, but I understood them, as I was always to understand that Carl's faith in me had no perceptible limit. At the moment his chief expressed hope was that I should find some good friends among the other students.

I did, almost at once. I lived in one of the dormitories, in a cell from which I went daily to lectures or the library; and pretty soon there were a dozen young men with whom, either on the steps of Philosophy Hall or in the reading room of the library, I found myself chattering. We were all engaged in the same enterprise: we were reading English literature, ideally from the earliest word of it to the latest, though of course that program must remain ideal; we were listening to lectures about certain portions or periods of it; and we were discussing it with one another. We continued thus for two years, until the war scattered us across two continents. Meanwhile, or at least this is how I remember those two years, we talked remarkably little about the outstanding event of our time. We had our own concerns, and I think we assumed that we could keep them. We were Neff, Dibble, Glen Mullin (Carl's old friend from Urbana), Mead, Beaty, and Krutch, to name no others now. And before long my closest friend was Joseph Wood Krutch, hereinafter to be known as Joe.

Many times since then I have tried to date the moment when I knew this to be true. I think it was one evening when the two of us stood in the vestibule of a subway train bound for Times Square, to a restaurant, a theater, or both. The train was noisy so that we had to shout, but the circumstance seemed unimportant. The important thing was that we had a great deal to say to each other, and that each was really interested in what the other said; also, that each was eager to speak when it came his turn, and was confident that what he said would be worth hearing. We like those who inspire us to talk well, to talk indeed our best, which in their presence becomes something better than it ever was before, so that it surprises and delights us too. We like least those persons in whose presence we are dull. For we can be either, and company brings it out; that is what company is for. Joe Krutch from this moment was famous company for me, and the conversation begun then has never stopped. It has ranged without apology from the grandest to the meanest subjects; it has a natural facility in rising or in sinking; but the point is, we have never run out of things to say. In those days we often discussed the people we despised or admired. We always agreed about them, and that was good. Friends do not need to agree about everything, but they must have the same heroes and think the same men fools. Friends do not judge each other; they judge the world, and by identical standards. If this is arrogance, then be it so.

We did not say such things as this, nor talk about the fact that he had come from Knoxville, Tennessee, as I had come from Urbana—he thought Urbana a funny name, and for the first time I thought so too. He had a few stories to tell about Knoxville—from the start he was a perfect storyteller, natural and brief; his power of abstraction permitted him to abridge whatever subject might be tedious—but for the most part we exchanged ideas about literature and about what we thought was life. It seemed to me that he knew more about life than I did; he was more sophisticated, and at times he could be more positive. He had an intellectual grasp I all but envied; on certain days I did envy it, and sought to put it in its place by dismissing some discovery of his as commonplace. "Everybody knows that," I would say. But this was not the case, and even then I knew it. What he had discovered was of course true for him; and then, because he felt it with such force and stated it with such clarity, it was true for others as it had not been true before. He always overlooked my rudeness, of which there was less as time went on.

But we did not always discourse upon large topics. We had a

73

game we played in our dormitory rooms; one of us would read a paragraph from a book whose title he concealed and challenge the other to say who wrote it, in which half of what century. This was to make us at home in the history of English literature, yet it was also a pastime of which we never tired. Or we would simply walk the streets and talk of what we saw. Late one night on Amsterdam Avenue Joe saw something I did not see until he stopped in distress and pointed it out. A big gray cat, prowling in a butcher's window, had slipped from a metal rail and been caught on his way down by a hook that passed through his underparts and left him hanging so that he could not get up again. He was writhing and crying, though we could barely hear through the glass the sounds he made. I too was distressed; but Joe was in visible agony until we found a policeman who could unlock the door and release the cat. As we walked on—the cat was not seriously hurt, nor did it want any further attention than that which it gave itself by licking the torn skin—Joe revealed to me how devoted he was to animals, and particularly to cats. There was no metaphysical basis for this, at least so far as he then knew; or if there was, it connected itself with the sympathy he felt for any creature who depended on men and was ill-treated by them.

The sympathy extended to men themselves. I remember his growing white with rage when he read in the paper of how a judge had lectured a man he was sentencing. The sentence was enough, said Joe; the lecture not only was gratuitous, it was a form of bullying, it was something a judge had no right to abuse his power by inflicting upon a man defenseless before him. Years afterward, when Joe was a professor at Columbia, he spent hours in a magistrate's court explaining that an old Negro whom he had seen a university policeman rebuke for washing parked cars was inoffensive and should not be bullied —that word again, for it was central to his conception of human evil. Not that he generalized about such matters, or claimed to be virtuous because this was the way he felt. But

I have always known his feeling to be as powerful as his thought.

Much of our time we spent of course with the other students. Half a dozen of us might go down Broadway several blocks in search of a better dinner than we usually had; then coming back we would be likely to assemble again in one of our rooms to talk until we had to go and work. This might be Roy Dibble's room. He had brought with him from western New York a manuscript book full of resounding Shakespearean sonnets; he was willing to read these, and we were more than willing to praise them, for they had an energy we could not associate with Dibble himself, a squat, phlegmatic man who daydreamed of being back in Chautauqua County on the farm to which every third thought of his returned. Emery Neff, a more ascetic figure whom we likened to John Stuart Mill, and who next year would be off on a traveling fellowship to England and France, was the most subtle critic among us, of Dibble's sonnets or of anything else. And doubtless each one of us had his merits. But Joe would still be the center of our conversation. Tall, hollow-chested, floundering in his movements and unable to talk without walking the floor, he had the special merit of coming to literature with a lively expectation that it would be of practical significance. At the University of Tennessee he had preferred mathematics, supposing it to be both more precise and more meaningful than poems and stories. Then one day he read Shaw's *Man and Superman,* and for the first time believed that literature, as he said, could be *about* something. His conversion to the subject never diminished his demands upon it. And these demands were what made his talk so vital. We understood this, as on various grounds we understood that we would never live to know a better talker about anything, unless Carl was that talker.

We often discussed our professors, those rather remote men on whom our careers and even our lives depended. There was A. H. Thorndike, chairman of the department, a serene, slow-moving man who carried his white head on his shoulders as if it were a weight that might tumble off. There was William Witherle Lawrence, whose lectures on medieval literature, and in one term on the primitive epics of Europe, were models of organization and grace; he himself was a tall, exquisite gentleman whom we did not see much out of class. George Philip Krapp was a less formal person; he taught the history of the English language, and would one day make a singularly appealing translation of Chaucer. There was John Erskine, who also taught undergraduates in Hamilton Hall across 116th Street; a poet and a musician, he lectured on the lyrics of the seventeenth century as if their authors were his friends; his comments were penetrating because professional. And there were others whom I did not see so often.

But finally there was W. P. Trent, whom I knew Carl loved and venerated; nor was I disappointed in the august person he proved to be. He was slight, and looked much older than he was; also he talked older, for he seemed to have lived forever, both here and in the South from which he came. We called him "the Virginia gentleman," not of course to his face. He had a thin beard, blue eyes that could be both withering and kind, and a deep voice which when he read heroic couplets made them sound like Homer and Milton. Milton was his great love, though he had spent his life, or so we understood, on a biography, never to be finished, of the English author who is least Miltonic, Daniel Defoe. Because he returned Carl's affection he occasionally asked me to his house, with Carl or without him, and I could see there the grand, old-fashioned way in which he and his wife lived. He was interested in politics and history too, and said there had been no great American statesman in his time, or naturally in mine. I often wondered about the day when three friends called at his house and he was not at home. They were Henry Adams, John Hay, and Theodore Roosevelt.

When my book on Thoreau was published in the spring of 1916 the question came up whether it might do for a doctor's dissertation at Columbia. The answer was No: it had been a master's essay somewhere else, and it was not long enough. Nobody said it was not good enough, but I could think this myself, and so I began more or less cheerfully to look for another subject. It was Carl who found it for me. He said, with an insight at which I now marvel, that I should make a thorough study of some poet; and suggested Dryden, who had long been in need of critical attention. If I hesitated, the reason was that I had so often heard that Dryden was not a poet. Even Matthew Arnold had said so, and most of the English instructors at Illinois echoed Arnold, as for that matter nearly every living teacher did. But Carl was sure that Dryden would be interesting, among other reasons because he had lived in an unsettled time like ours and yet had ordered his own art amid the confusion; and he went on to show me a particular poem of Dryden's which he thought admirable by any rule. It was the elegy on John Oldham, beginning:

> Farewell, too little and too lately known,
> Whom I began to think and call my own.

This alone convinced me, and I went to work. I bought with Carl's help a set of Sir Walter Scott's edition of Dryden in eighteen volumes, and resolved to read it through as many times as were necessary to make me feel at home in Dryden's mind as he composed his poems. Professor Trent, who would be in charge of the dissertation, was pleased when I said I should like to write all of it before I showed him any part. "You take a risk," he said, his eyes twinkling in the rather wicked way I was by now familiar with, "but go ahead. I promise to read it without prejudice." He understood my reluctance to show him sections of the work before the whole of it existed; with parts, of course, but these must have such a relation to one another as would let none of them mean anything without the others. That was how I had written the *Thoreau*—rapidly, after I had seen my way through to the last word—and it is how I have written every subsequent prose book, no matter what its content.

But it would take a long time to do this—longer than I suspected then—and meanwhile summer came so that I could go home to Illinois. I went by way of Detroit, as I would do on many such trips throughout the next few years. Guy's daughter Mary Elizabeth, now almost five, was quite as much the reason as her parents. She was the first grandchild in the family, and all of her uncles adored her. I had seen her in her first years at Urbana, before Guy moved on to Michigan; and here she was again, a little older, in a strange city, and therefore needing all the more, I thought, the kind of attention I might give her. Whatever the truth about that, I enjoyed myself and then went on to the place I still considered home, and was so to consider for years to come. New York, for all of its mighty attractions, would be a second home I merely went to and returned from, on trains that I liked almost as much as I did the world at either end. I have always been at home on trains, but never so much as then; it was exciting to rush between the metropolis and the town where I grew up; it seemed to me that the young man sitting there—sometimes he leaned forward and studied himself in the strip of mirror beside his berth—was in a particularly good position to understand the whole of American existence. I do not know what I thought I understood, but I remember the superiority I felt. Also, I was a courier who brought news: to Carl of Illinois, and to Illinois of Carl and his increasing family—for he and Irita too had produced a grandchild, Anne, during my first year in New York; but I was to see more of her the second year, when I lived with them in a new apartment on Morningside Avenue, downhill from Morningside Heights.

If my father asked me about the work I had been doing at Columbia I was probably unable to tell him. I should have been, but students are tongue-tied at home, and doubtless I contented myself with the announcement that a fellowship would make me independent of his help next year. His pleasure in this was in the success it implied; I am sure he thought my studies more important, just as I am sure he would have liked to hear about them. But I preferred to talk of things there at home, and at Villa Grove where I went as soon as I could to see Frank and Grace. They told me about their cat that had ridden one day the whole distance to Urbana in the sodpan underneath the engine of the car; when they stopped on Oregon Street they heard a faint cry; they lifted the hood and there she was, terrified and streaked with oil so that her coat was never the same again. They told me too, and that evening on the front porch I heard it for myself, about the man who nightly practiced the cornet in a switchman's booth alongside the Frisco tracks. Every night he did this, mournfully, unsuccessfully (he never improved), and they wondered who he was. None of us knew, though I was to remember him long after in "The Cornetist":

> When the last freight, dusk-musical, had gone,
> Groaning along the dark rails to St. Louis,
> When the warm night, complete across the cornfields,
> Said there was nothing now, no motion left,
> No possible sound, we heard him:
> Rocked on the silent porch and heard the low notes
>
> Leave on their level errand like the last sound
> Ever to be man-blown about the earth.
> Like the last man this sentry of the switches
> Blew, and the mournful notes, transcending cinders,
> Floated above the corn leaves:
> Floated above the silks, until arriving,
>
> Arriving, they invaded our warm darkness,
> Deep in the still verandah, and we laughed:
> "Why, there he is, that pitiful lone devil;
> There is the Frisco nightingale again,
> There is our mocking-bird-man"—
> Laughed, and said these things, and went to bed.
>
> And slept; but there are nights now when I waken,
> After these years, and all these miles away,
> When I sit up and listen for the last sound
> Man will have made alive; and doubt a little
> Whether we should have laughed;
> Whether we should have pitied that poor soul.

79

You were too sure of being there forever,
And I too soon was leaving to be wise.
Not that his horn had wisdom; but at nighttime
Man has a need of man, and he was there,
Always; the horn was there
Always; and joy, I think, was why we laughed.

And slept; for there is many an hour of drearness,
Many an hour unloud with lips or brass,
When I lie still and listen for the last note
Ever some lung has blown; and am self-envious,
Thinking I once could laugh;
Thinking I once could pity that poor soul.

"You were too sure of being there forever." Frank and
Grace would eventually live in St. Louis, Springfield, and
Tuscola, and they would have their own daughter, Martha,
for a third grandchild we could take great pleasure in. But
they were to be at Villa Grove for years to come, and the
cornetist was not our only topic as we talked. We renewed our
memories of that place, and when I was back in Urbana they
drove up more than once, perhaps with Paul who sometimes
helped Frank on the farm. I think it was during this summer
that Paul took me one night in Urbana to see a movie
comedian he admired. His name was Charlie Chaplin, and
Paul thought him very funny. So did I. I had gone with Carl
to many movies in New York, for he relished the new art as
few persons did, but I had never seen anything like this. I
remember one moment perfectly. The little clown put his left
hand on his hip and stretched out the other arm to brace
himself against a slender white column of stone; except that
it was a column of water, from a fountain, and he got wet.

I returned to New York in September and found most of my
friends there, ready with me for a continuation of the grind.
I saw them as much as I had the previous winter, though I
lived with Carl, who had left Columbia to be headmaster of
the Brearley School; my understanding with Irita and him
was that I should have lunch and dinner in my former haunts,
and consider myself free to go and come like a roomer in the

house. Of course I saw a great deal of them too, and of Anne whom I liked to stay with when they went out. They had spent the last two summers in Cornwall, Connecticut, and I had been up there with them once or twice; but I could have no notion then of the importance which that beautiful place was to assume for me. It was to be my ultimate home.

Now, though, I picked up my student's routine; with this difference, that I started seriously and systematically to read Dryden. In a downtown print shop I found a portrait of him which I pinned to the wall over my table; and at the back of the table, always before me, were the eighteen volumes into which Scott had collected nearly everything I would need to examine. Not everything, of course; there were other editions of Dryden, together with biographies, particularly the one by Saintsbury, special studies of the poet and his time, histories of literature, and periodical articles which when I was free to do so I brought down from the library and propped up against Sir Walter. As I went on I found myself listening to Dryden's lines and to his groupings of them into passages of greater or less power. I tried to see what he did and did not do; I listened with care, remembered what I heard, and went back to make comparisons. I began to fear I would end up with a wholly technical study of one who seemed to me to have been a consummate master of verse, or as he put it, "numbers." I was not sure that this would be enough for Professor Trent. Yet I went on, and it remained true that nothing interested me more than those same numbers, with which my ears were now as familiar as they were with my own voice.

Not all of my time was free, however, for Dryden. There were still lectures to attend, a great deal of general reading to do, and my oral examination to prepare for. This was to be two hours of torture, we all understood, at the conclusion of which a committee of professors would tell us whether our knowledge of English literature was comprehensive enough, and in places deep enough, for us to become doctors of philosophy, provided we then wrote a dissertation and passed a second examination on that. I took my "preliminary" in December, 1916, and passed it, though in my own opinion I did not do well. Someone had told me that the best way to spend the hours before it was to ride back and forth on the Staten Island ferry. This was a thing I loved to do, among the ships of the world that plied those choppy waters, and with Manhattan towering in welcome of my return; but the headache I started with did not go away, and by the time I got up to Philosophy Hall I was literally in a sweat. Then I learned that Professor Krapp, who would have asked the hardest questions because the history of the language was my weakest subject, was unable to attend; and the other examiners were benevolent enough to ask me easy questions. Or so I thought. Perhaps I should have remembered Mr. Bowditch's saying to me, when he met me with my father on a street in Urbana, that he had given me 100 on that day's geometry test; I explained that the questions had been easy, but he smiled and said: "That was because you knew the answers." I always expected impossible questions, and in this examination the prospect of them brought back my old habit of stuttering, to the astonishment I suppose of my inquisitors.

Nevertheless I was told I had done well enough; and I could laugh a little later at Joe Krutch's tale of how he had been so nervous that he picked to pieces the cane seat of his chair, and only when he got up noticed a heap of litter on the floor. He was more desperate than I when it came to expecting the worst. He did so in all things; and correspondingly rejoiced even more than I did in any happy outcome. He answered his questions particularly well, and was thunderstruck to hear that he had. In those days we called him The Pessimist. He accepted the name, insisting only that when some good thing did occur he was happier than anybody. We could see this for ourselves. His exultations equaled his despairs, and both were wonderful to witness.

II

The ensuing spring of 1917 was of course the time when President Wilson and Congress declared war against Germany. We saw this coming, and in the dormitories talked more and more about it. We considered the matter in its larger context, and then we wondered how it would affect us. We already knew, in fact, because national conscription had been from the first a subject of which the papers were full, and we had no reason to doubt that those of us who did not enlist would find ourselves in the army sooner or later. Most of us decided to watch and wait. Joe Krutch and I, separating in June, had no idea when we would meet again. It would be in January, 1919. I was to see Carl before that, when he came to visit me in camp. He saw me off for Urbana now, and did not conceal the depth of his anxiety, which had its counterpart at home in the anxiety of my parents.

Anxiety. It was not merely that the American people had been in no sizable war since 1865, and had long since begun to suppose they would never be in one again. It was also that by 1917 this Great War had become a spectacle of continual, senseless death which sickened all who saw it. So many Frenchmen had died that already it was said, correctly as things turned out: France will never be the same. England, too, and Russia, which had quit from exhaustion and repudiated its Czar—the changes were catastrophic, and nobody knew what lay ahead either for any country or for any individual in that country. In my own family, to name an inconspicuous case, I was the individual whom at the moment there must be anxiety about. My three older brothers, being married, were assumed not to be subject to the draft; and my younger brother was not yet of sufficient age. So what would happen to me? Nothing ever did of the sort my mother and father certainly imagined; but they did not know that nothing would, and neither did anybody else.

A less war-minded family can scarcely be conceived, nor one less given to heroics. It was not that any of us opposed the war; it was simply that we did not know how to think of it in terms personal to us. Yet that had to be done now, and the result of my father's thought was a conviction that I should raise food instead of fight. There was much public emphasis upon the world's need of food and upon the obligation of the American farmer to produce it. Well, we had farms and I was familiar with their ways. So I should start at once and thus be in a position to apply for agricultural deferment. I had my own doubts about this, but when I registered in June I was willing to put down my occupation as "teacher and farmer." I was not yet a teacher, and strictly speaking I had never been a farmer, yet so at my father's suggestion I described myself. And then we had to decide where I should farm.

At first it was Villa Grove; but then, since Hope was more in need of help, I went there and remained until my number was called in late July and my father's request for deferment (I made none myself) was summarily rejected—to my own secret relief, for I had not been comfortable in the role, and for all I know my father was not either; I am sure my mother was not, nor many others, though none of those confessed the doubt in words. Perhaps in the beginning they would really have preferred that I enlist and have it over. But I did not, and so two months of the summer passed, happily in so far as I was at Hope, unhappily in so far as I questioned my own status.

Hope itself was a revelation, a myth made actual after what seemed many years of absence from its charm. Doubtless I was in need of exercise, sunshine, and a total separation from books. And I enjoyed the work, which it was a pleasure to do faithfully. But my deepest pleasure was my rediscovery of this wonderful place where I had been a child. I was all but a child again. I liked the dust, I liked the rainy days. I liked the hired man and his wife, I liked the other help. The ash and walnut groves again were perfect in my eyes. And in the barn, or before sunup when I went out to call them to their stalls, the horses and mules became, at least so far as my own feeling went, twelve excellent companions to whom I could never say enough of what was on my mind. To me a work horse in a stable is still the symbol of friendship that cannot talk back. Doubtless he has no thoughts at all; but he stands there, benevolent and patient, while you rub his nose and open the most subtle, the most tremendous subjects for him to consider. I have endeavored to state the relationship in many poems: in "The Gentlest Beast," for example, and in portions of *Jonathan Gentry* and *The Mayfield Deer*. But such huge creatures as Charlie and Baldy, who occupied the first stall at Hope that summer, must always resist rhetoric. They are ineffable, and may be left at that.

My father found frequent pretexts to drive out and see how the work was going on, and every Saturday afternoon he came to take me home for a good Sunday dinner. My cousin Charlotte Beardsley, his niece whom I had not known before, was in Urbana with us then, and so was Nell Littler, whose family came from Potomac and who herself was a schoolteacher in Oak Park, west of Chicago; she was gentle, and the nearest thing I ever had to a sister. Frank and Grace would come up on some of these days, with Paul who was working at Villa Grove. Then my father would take me off again, laden with advices from my mother as to how I should eat well and keep cool. She seemed to think I was already in the army, as to be sure in a few more weeks I was. My number as I have said was called in July; I was examined in August; and I left in September, before daybreak on the sixth of that month.

In the next war, or in the years that followed it, my own sons went off alone; that had become the code. But I was seen off at the Big Four station by my father and mother and by Frank, Paul, Charlotte, and Nell. Luckily there was little time for talk at a time when there was nothing to say. As the train pulled out for Peoria, I settled back in pleasurable excitement because everything was now decided; I had nothing to think about except the new things I would see. Eight of us were going from Urbana in the first contingent of its drafted men. Three of these, including Bill Lee and Harry (Piffie) Smith, I had known in high school. And one other, Roy Somers, I had known too. He carried his violin, for he was studying music. The next summer I heard that he had been blown to pieces in the Argonne. Five of the eight were to see France, but I was not. I would stay in this country till the war was over, and furthermore my principal duty would be paper work.

But I did not know this that morning as the train went on to Peoria and was exchanged for another that took us, smoking and playing cards, to Des Moines, Iowa, where still another conveyance bore us north to Camp Dodge, a sprawling cantonment still in process of being built. We arrived after dark and were assigned to the 349th Regiment of the 88th Infantry Division; and I was taken with Bill and Piffie to the barracks of Company L. As we were being assigned to that company at battalion headquarters we were asked among other things about our education. When I admitted that I had been seven years in two universities I was given a second glance by Captain Child of Company L, but I thought no more of this until five days later I was called to regimental headquarters to make out morning reports.

Meanwhile I did what the other recruits did, supposing I was never to be separated from them. The first night was remarkable for one thing that happened to us all. It was cold, and there were not enough blankets to keep us really warm. I remember lying for a while after the lights went out and smiling to myself because I could see Piffie's wrist watch, which had a radium dial, shining outside of his covers on the cot next to mine. Soon I was asleep, only to be awakened after an hour by the sound of someone tiptoeing up the stairs. It was Captain Child, with new blankets which he had found and now proceeded to spread quietly over us. Nobody moved in his bed, but the next morning we all testified to having been awake when this was done. I wrote my mother at once and said she was not to worry about the physical welfare of her soldier. Incidentally, my first few letters home were so interesting to my father that he took them to the editor of the Urbana *Courier,* who printed them without deleting any intimate detail. When I heard of this I stopped it, to my father's surprise and disappointment.

From the day I was set to work at the morning reports I was no longer a true member of Company L. Soon I was transferred to Headquarters Company; I slept in the headquarters building; and the next four months passed among documents which Captain Anan Raymond, a lawyer from Omaha, administered as adjutant. I rose in the noncommissioned ranks until I was a regimental sergeant major, but I never drilled or touched a gun. I am told I should have been bored, yet I was not. When I learned in January that Joe Krutch, after returning to Columbia, had enlisted in the Psychological Service and would soon be giving intelligence tests to illiterate recruits, I wondered if that might not be more interesting than what I did; but the truth is that I enjoyed my whole time in the army, and particularly this time.

One reason was Sergeant Major Jacob Jacobsen, an older man from the regular army who appeared one day at headquarters to take charge of us "civilians." This was not supposed to mean Captain Raymond, since he was an officer. But for all of his conspicuous and rather fastidious intelligence he had been only six months before this a lawyer in Nebraska, as Captain Child had been a lawyer in Minnesota. These were men who had gone to officer's training schools in the spring, when I might have gone; had I done so, I would now be a lieutenant at least. I am glad that I was not, for then I should not have known Sergeant Major Jacobsen, or heard the tales he and other old-line sergeants told us of the Philippines and other such faraway places. Jacobsen himself became my special friend. He was a blond, stocky veteran whom I amused by my innocence of army traditions; but he tolerated me as one with whom he could talk about other things. Within a week he had headquarters running perfectly, so that all of us, including Captain Raymond, could relax into the routine we followed until January. One item of this routine I remember with real joy. The first sergeants of the various companies had to appear daily with their little morning reports which we consolidated into the big one we sent on to Division Headquarters. Sergeant Barnes of Company B had his own way of making an entrance. A fat, black-headed fellow, he burst in every morning and began shouting in a high voice, usually to Jake: "Major, I craveth a conversation with thee." Even Jake, who was born in Schleswig-Holstein and had his sober side, could not help laughing at this absurdity, nor of course could I.

My family did not forget me for one instant. Carl wrote me a postal card every day I was in the army. He never failed to do this; and when I protested, saying it took too much of his time, he explained that he kept a pile of cards on his desk which it was no trouble to cover with words—the least thing he could do. The others wrote regularly too; and sooner or later all of them came to visit me. Because I could not get leave to go home Christmas, my father came then. My mother had come before, and was reassured by what she saw. She said the nights at headquarters would soon be colder, though, and when she went back to Urbana she sent me warm clothes to sleep in; she was right, and they were welcome. Frank came at another time. Carl's visit in the spring—but then I was no longer at headquarters—was unannounced; he liked surprises, as I always have.

In January I started a new life: I entered an officer's training school at Camp Dodge, renouncing as I thought for good the career of protocol, reports, and correspondence. Not that I had found it dull; one of the clerks, Corporal Harry Noel, often sat up late with me by the headquarters stove, which it was my duty to keep going but which on subzero nights burned out before reveille, and entertained me with tales of the little town he had come from in Illinois. We were likely to have Jake with us too; I was always glad when we did, for there was something tremendous about him which his speech did not express, and I tried to state this to myself, without succeeding. But it was a discipline, merely trying. Jake, against all of his enlisted man's instincts, entered the school for officers with me, and was not too sorry on his own account when after a few weeks he had to drop out because of his German birth. Unhappily for me, I seldom saw him after that.

For one thing, the school kept us busy. In three months we were expected not only to learn what every soldier learns but to develop the arts and habits of command. Exhausting drills alternated with periods of study; we dug trenches and floundered through them, then after dark in the mess hall spread maps on the tables and worked at problems of scouting and deployment. It was labor that left us little time for anything else; though we had a school library where I managed to do some reading of the sort I did, in that place or elsewhere, whenever I could. General Grant's *Personal Memoir* and John Muir's *My First Summer in the Sierra* are two of the autobiographies I encountered in the army. For some reason I found autobiography especially interesting then; perhaps the reason was that I myself lived a new life every day—not merely at this moment the life of the officer's school, but at all moments the life which contact with a variety of men makes perpetually fresh and different. A large army has literally every sort of man in it, and if sooner or later one ceases to be surprised, at least the novelty cannot wear out. By coincidence one of the books Carl sent me was *The Autobiography of a Super-Tramp,* by the English poet W. H. Davies. It was different from the others, but all the better because of that.

In April, 1918, having become a second lieutenant and bought my first officer's uniform, I got leave to go home for ten days. Paul, approving of the uniform, did not tell me of his own plans, if he had made them then, to enlist in the

Marines; he was about to finish his freshman year at the university, and I assumed he would return there in the fall. But by that time he had completed his training on Parris Island and been shipped to France—on a transport, as I learned from him later, many of whose passengers died of the influenza epidemic then active on both sides of the Atlantic, so that when he reached Brest the first thing he saw was tiers of coffins waiting to take the dead boys back. But I left for Camp Dodge without even dreaming that such things could happen; and by June I was on my way to Camp Pike, Arkansas, near Little Rock, presumably to train recruits in that replacement center. My father, who soon would have a second son to worry about, and with much more reason than in my own case, still thought of things to warn me against. When I wrote from Arkansas that the heat was like nothing I had ever felt before, he sent me word that it might be wise not to eat too much, since food itself was heating, and the two things together might be serious. They never were for me, as in good time I told him.

The 87th Division had been stationary at Camp Pike as the 88th had been at Camp Dodge, but by the time of my arrival —or our arrivals, for lieutenants were pouring in from everywhere, so that it looked now, somebody said, as if the draft had got down low enough at last to bring in even officers—it was moving off to France, where the 88th had gone too while I was in the training school. Nothing but confusion seemed to be taking its place, nor was order ever conspicuous at Camp Pike during the six months I spent there. Depot Brigades and Casual Detachments—the very names suggested improvisation and temporary status. And so I found myself weekly, if not daily, in new circumstances and surroundings and among new men, and sometimes with odd duties to perform. By and large my duty was the processing of recruits. This meant meeting trainloads of them at the station, forming them into columns of fours, marching them to barracks that had been assigned, and keeping them there for brief periods while they were uniformed, examined for disease and illiteracy, inoculated against further disease, indoctrinated with respect to the Articles of War pertaining to desertion, taught how to stand at attention and salute, drilled a little, and then sent on either to companies where they would receive full training, or perhaps to France without further training on this side.

My first company consisted of 133 men from Mississippi County, Arkansas. I had four enlisted men from one of the Casual companies to help me with these strangers—the four had no noncommissioned rank, but I called them sergeants— so that I was not utterly alone when I reached the station. Nevertheless I was in a fever of excitement. I was not sure I would know how to behave. "The habit of command" was suddenly a phrase out of which all meaning had drained. I had never commanded one person, let along 133. Luckily, my "sergeants" had no corresponding fear of the unknown. They lined up the recruits, marched them off with little attention from me, and when I arrived at the barracks reported that they were mine to do with as I would.

A thing happened then that reassured and saved me. The recruits crowded around me with questions. Where could they get a drink, for they were mighty thirsty? What address should they send the folks at home? How soon would supper be ready? When would they get their uniforms? Was it all right to shoot a little crap? What was my name, and where was I from? They were like so many children; none was my enemy, none was there to see if I did right or wrong, none of them was judging me. They thought I knew everything, as I remembered having thought Captain Child knew everything. So my three weeks with them passed without any of the pain I had anticipated. More than a third of them turned out to be illiterate; most of them had never been away from home before; and they listened like lambs to everything I told them, whether in the barracks or out on the sun-brown field where I lectured and drilled them. They were of all sizes, from the little wiry ones who came from the banks of the Mississippi to the hulking farmhands from bottoms farther inland. They all chewed tobacco, and some of them it was difficult to discourage from spitting in formation. But they could learn; they did learn; and I myself learned how to teach—something I would be glad of two years hence, though now I was aware of no resemblance between recruits and freshmen. I was sorry when I had to send them on. My next company of 150 men, not sunburned like these because they came from the cities of Iowa, seemed by comparison, or because my initiation was now over, no problem at all.

My third and last company, though, was not what I had reason to expect. Orders were sent me one day in August to prepare three barracks for the reception of 500 Negro recruits about to arrive. I was given as usual four enlisted men to trust with the details, and the assumption appeared to be that this was simply another assignment like those I had completed. But 500! And black! I was staggered; though not as staggered at that moment as I was a few days later when I discovered that instead of 500 there were 707. Yet by then, though I can scarcely believe it any more, my panic was past. I was in fact enjoying the nightmare. For one thing, I created out of the ranks as many as a dozen "corporals"—I picked those who wore glasses, on the theory that they would at least have spent some time in a town, and this turned out to be right—so that I could delegate duties and free myself for important things such as listening to Zack Washington when he came into the company office to complain about his clothes. There were nine Washingtons, of whom five had George for a first name. But Zack was the one who came to me. He was a black giant, perpetually and hugely amused, who called me "Boss"—most of the company did, though some said "Sergeant," that being the highest rank of which they had heard—and told me this first day that he was disappointed because the shoes he had been issued were not "classy." He had expected something better than he got; oh, sure, they were big enough, but they had no class. He came other days and talked of other things: his mother, his brothers and sisters, and his own women of whom I gathered there were more than he could count. And finally he confessed himself delighted with his uniform; even with his shoes, which he kept clean and even tried to polish, though they were not made for that.

So were they all delighted with their uniforms; and with everything that happened during the two weeks I was with them. Such laughter—seas and whirlwinds of it when they played between the barracks, lashing one another with their belts—I had never heard before and have not heard since. To express the fact that they were in quarantine until preliminaries were over I had borrowed somewhere a machine that painted a white line around the three barracks, and had told them they could not step over this. They never did, but they would walk up to it and lean over it as if they were about to lose their balance, and roar with pleasure at the imagined disobedience. They even laughed and applauded when I stood on the outside stairs and read them the Articles of War about desertion. Realizing that they had not understood one word, I translated the passage. I said it meant that if they went away without permission they might be put to death. It still seemed funny, though some of them sang out: "Don't worry, Boss, we'll stay right here!"

They did stay, of course, and some days I thought they did nothing but eat the creamed salmon of which, perhaps through the cook's laziness, their diet too long consisted. The kitchen fed them in shifts, so that the mess hall, odorous beyond description with the "simons" they freely told me they found tiresome, was never empty. When on the last day it suddenly was, because trucks had come and taken them to Fort Roots, on the other side of Little Rock, where they were to be organized into labor battalions, I missed them fantastically. They even said they would miss me—Zack Washington was positive he would—and a few weeks later there was evidence that they did. Having occasion to run over to Fort Roots on a motor truck, I asked the driver to take me past the 78th Casual

Company where I knew they were. As I flew by I recognized hundreds of them, and they in turn, big Zack among them, recognized me. Hats were thrown into the air and I was shouted at till I was out of hearing. I think I was prouder of this than I would have been of a salute from General Pershing —or as they would have said, from Sergeant Perkins. I have not forgotten the day at the barracks when one of them informed me that "a couple of sergeants" wanted to see me outside. I started to say: "Sergeants? Then bring them in to me." But when I was told they were on horses I hastened out, and sure enough they were a colonel and a lieutenant colonel, come to inspect the garbage cans.

My army career, such as it was, had now achieved its climax. The rest of the way was downhill to the Armistice in November. For I returned to paper work. Lieutenant Alfred Cooper, to whom I had gone every afternoon to report upon the welfare of whatever company I was struggling with, asked me on one of those occasions whether I wanted to be relieved of recruits so that I could go with him as assistant personnel officer to Casual Detachment Headquarters. I begged him not to do this to me; I had had enough paper work in Camp Dodge; I preferred to be with soldiers. And he seemed to consent, merely adding that he would see. In the middle of August he did see: an order was issued assigning me to headquarters as assistant personnel adjutant.

In the end I was not sorry, for Lieutenant Cooper, later Captain Cooper—all of his personnel work then fell to me, and when we moved to Headquarters of the Development Battalions I became his assistant adjutant, with the lofty rank of first lieutenant—was one of the most interesting men I met in the army. He was very intelligent; he was high-strung and sensitive, with nervous dark eyes from which I was never able to look away; and he was eloquent as only some men who do not write books can be eloquent. He was eventually to tell me about the death of his wife in childbirth, just after he entered the army, and I was to remember this in my novel *Tilda*. But now I merely knew him as one whose conversation was singularly arresting and acute, and who in the final office where we worked together permitted me to write all of Colonel Smith's letters, both those that went down to his subordinates and those that went up to the War Department in Washington.

Captain Cooper, in other words, was a diversion; worth knowing in himself, he transcended our routine. And there were other diversions. Three of my uncles visited me: Warren and Wallace Butz from Muskogee, and Walter Van Doren from his farm in Mississippi which he had come down from Champaign to see. Uncle Walter appeared one morning at the door of headquarters, collarless of course and unshaven, and looking very tired, and stayed with me there till noon, when we went to the officers' mess for dinner. I left him then in my quarters, recommending as long a nap as he desired. When I saw him again at the end of the day he was refreshed and shaved, and we talked on the verandah of the Hostess House, which overlooked the valley of the Arkansas River and commanded a view of Fort Roots, until suppertime; after which I took him to his train. He enjoyed the officers at the mess, as certainly I did, for Lieutenant Muse of North Carolina and Lieutenant Koch of Arizona were among my best friends in camp. They too were diversions, as was the coming of Fran Nichol to serve as dietician in the base hospital—war work for her, but pure delight for me, since I saw her many evenings when both of us were free. Sometimes she came bearing pie or cake from the hospital kitchen; sometimes we merely sat under the trees and gossiped about Urbana; but once or twice I was able to borrow horses from the Remount Depot so that we could ride—I suppose this was on Saturdays or Sundays—far enough out of camp to see the Ozarks, queer misty shapes in a West that I remember as always distant-looking and strangely blue. Then there were days when I disappeared into the camp library and read Bernard Shaw; some citizen had donated all of his works written by that date, and I caught up with the ones of which I was ignorant. And in the fall there were weekend trips to Conway, where Captain Cooper had made the acquaintance of some girls he wanted me to know. One of these I wrote to for months after I left Arkansas; another one, a visitor from Louisiana, nearly fainted when I told her I had published a book.

But this was after the Armistice, when there was an abundance of leisure and most of us merely waited to go home. We had learned of the Armistice when cars raced one afternoon through the camp with young people in them waving flags at us and singing. There was no radio then; the newspapers for the day had not appeared, and even if they had we might not have read them, since we had ceased to be interested in what we called current events; but soon enough this event sank into our minds and we knew our life at that place was over. The only question for any of us now was: When would it be over for him? For me the date was December 24th. I caught a train for Memphis, and managed things so that I walked into my mother's kitchen while she was cracking black walnuts for a Christmas cake. She almost dropped the bowl. Then my father came downstairs—tears were in his eyes—and we telephoned to Frank.

III

During the five weeks that passed in Urbana and at Villa Grove before I returned to New York by way of Detroit I fancied I was forgetting the war. Once any war is over it becomes incredible, and this one was no exception; at least it is no exception for me now. But the act of forgetting it then was dramatically delayed. Back in New York in February, 1919, I found myself alone as I had never before understood "alone." My student friends had not returned. Joe Krutch was soon to show up, but he would be as busy with his dissertation (published in time as *Comedy and Conscience after the Restoration* —I suggested the title) as I would be with mine. Carl and Irita were as kind as ever, but they had now a second daughter, Margaret (Barbara would be born next year), and I insisted on living in one of the dormitories. I installed myself among the notes on Dryden which I had left in Urbana while I was away, and with Scott's edition facing me again across a table. But something was wrong. I could not concentrate my attention on Dryden or on anything. At dinner with Carl and Irita I would be absent-minded; at lunch in one of the Amsterdam Avenue restaurants I sat some days unable to swallow a single bite. I met Raymond Weaver, who had come back to teach at Columbia after three years in Japan, and he was so astonishing a person, with what seemed to me so mannered and yet so charming a style of speech—he was surrounded, too, in a room which had the air of a private museum, with fascinating prints and books, and with objects of curious, unfamiliar beauty—that I wondered why I could not at least concentrate upon him.

But nothing filled my void. For that was it: the life I had been living for more than a year, withdrawn so suddenly from me now, refused to let any other life replace it. I was homesick for the very army I had thought I was glad to leave. So many men simply would not be forgotten. I tried hard, but with every effort I failed worse, until there was a moment when I thought I might die of a loneliness I still could not understand. Then I cured it by buying a bound notebook of nearly three hundred pages and sitting down to fill it with facts about the exciting, noisy, ever-varying society of which until Christmas I had been a member. First I made a title-page: *A Plain Account of All that I Can Remember about the Nineteen Months from June, 1917, to December, 1918.* Then I wrote down everything: every name of every man who had been of even the slightest interest to me, every chance, every change, every thought I could recall having, every look of the ground or sky between Hope and Little Rock. I actually drew maps: of the fields at Hope and of the stalls where the horses stood, of the various headquarters where I had worked, of the

97

squad room at the officer's training school, and of Camp Pike entire. I did this without stopping, night or day, until in a week I was well of my unease. I had forgotten the army by remembering it all, and by putting it in a place where it would keep—where it has kept, too, though most of its details are unintelligible to me now. I was free at last to go on listening to Dryden's verses written more than two hundred years before.

As winter and spring went quietly on I paused now and then to wonder whether there was any point in my applying for a fellowship that would take me abroad next year. Carl, who had gone one summer to Europe with Stuart Sherman, urged me to make the application; and the more I thought of it the better I liked the idea of seeing still more of the world before I settled down—to teaching, I supposed, though I was not perfectly sure of that. I did apply; and learned a little later that Joe Krutch had applied too. There was a William Bayard Cutting fellowship that annually subsidized some student's work abroad, and whichever one of us got it, if either of us did, would be a lucky man. But each of us was uncomfortable; each wanted the fellowship, yet to get it would be to triumph over the other, and neither he nor I could bear to think of such a thing. When we left for Knoxville and Urbana in late May we made speeches wishing each other success in the lottery. Both of us meant these speeches, so that I for one, when I was notified at home that I had been chosen, wondered how I could write Joe and tell him. But the problem did not exist. The letter I wrote was crossed by one from him saying *he* had been chosen. There were two fellowships that year— the war had held one of them up—and they were ours. The coincidence still seems to me nothing less than miraculous. Then it certainly seemed that, as in our excitement we corresponded about the boat we would take to England in August.

Almost at once it occurred to me that if I could write the Dryden book before I sailed I would have all of my time in Europe free for simply living there and seeing the Old World I had not seen as a soldier. A letter from Carl encouraged me

in this; and before long I was back in New York, this time in
his apartment, for his family had gone to Cornwall for the summer and he was alone most of each week; he had left the Brearley School, was now literary editor of *The Nation,* and had of
course to be at that office during the day. I started the work
with fear and trembling—not a bad way to start any work—
but found it easier to go on with each morning, so that when
Carl came home I would have a surprising number of pages
for him to read. He always insisted on seeing them before he
did anything else. He would lie on the floor, a pillow doubled
under his handsome head, and read every word I had written
since yesterday; and most of the time he would approve,
though one night when he found that I had said "values" when
the word meant nothing, as usually it does in literary criticism,
he leaped to his feet and said with a kind of moan: " 'Values!'
Good God, you can't say 'values'! Decide what you mean and
then say that!" I have never used the word again. But this was
Carl's only outburst. Every other evening he was complimentary
to a fault, so that I went on happily, if strenuously, until in
six weeks I was done—except for a few passages I would revise
in England, and for quotations I would check there in books
which some of my authorities had cited. I would take the
manuscript with me (it was in longhand, in ink); I would
type it when every correction had been made; then I would
send it back to the professors.

Meanwhile it represented my best understanding of Dryden's career as an artist in verse. It was a complete study of
one poet from that point of view. And since I had come to
admire his music, that music was to be the chief determining
influence upon the poems I myself would write. The time for
this was by no means near, but when it came I would never
forget the feeling Dryden had given me for melodic structure.
Somebody's phrase (I cannot remember whose) for his effect
as a poet would continue to haunt me: "Like a great bronze
ring thrown down on marble." Whenever I have revised a
poem I have done so with sound in mind and the movement

99

of sound. I have made statements, as Dryden did, but also I have endeavored to make music. Neither one of these is potent by itself, any more than the third thing is—symbol—which criticism sometimes treats as if it were. All three should finally be one. But music must be there, and must be heard. I have never forgotten that, though I have remembered too that music in words should never try to resemble the music of pure sound, and have said so in "Another Music":

> In them another music, half of sound
> And half of something taciturn between;
> In them another ringing, not for ears,
> Not loud; but in the chambers of a brain
> Are bells that clap an answer when the words
> Move orderly, with truth among the train.

Joe and I were soon to sail on the *Haverford* from Philadelphia, where it was understood we would meet on the morning of August 9th. Only one thing troubled me. Paul was returning on a transport from France at about the same time, and I was afraid I would miss him. The exact date of his arrival was still unknown. Then at the last minute another miracle occurred. Carl and I got a radiogram from him saying that he was on the *Siboney,* due at Newport News, Virginia, on the 8th. So I could meet him, providing the *Siboney* was not delayed. I got everything in readiness and went by train to Newport News on the 7th. The next morning, after agonizing hours of rumor that she would not come until tomorrow, the *Siboney* appeared. The pier, dressed for her with streamers and already rustling with confetti, now became loud with bands and the cries of people each one of whom hoped some boy on deck would hear and be happy. As ropes pulled the hull in, packs of cigarettes and bags of candy went up and either landed or fell back into dirty salt water. The rails were crowded with waving Marines. When I failed to see Paul I was not surprised, for I knew that not every passenger would be visible. But as the gangplanks were lowered and the companies came off, and at last his company was there, I still could not see Paul. The next company was coming; there were only a few stragglers along the deck. One of them limped, and dragged his duffle bag behind him. There! That was Paul, already aware of me and waving. I have never been gladder to see anybody. But why the limp? A few more minutes, and he told me. On the road near Brest he had been hit by an army vehicle and his back had been hurt. It was not much, he said, but he could carry no weights. I followed him to his bunk in some building and talked with him and his friends until I had to go. There was a ferry I thought I must take in order to make my train for Philadelphia. I was wrong about that ferry, I found out; I could have waited two more hours. Yet as it was I had had four hours for the thing I wanted so much to do, and as the train took me north in the night I said that nothing stood in the way of my starting with a clear mind for England and Europe.

IV

Joe was waiting for me at ten the next morning, and at noon we slipped off down Delaware Bay. We had thirteen days of the ocean ahead of us, for the *Haverford* was small and slow. Most of these days were the fairest one man of the ship's crew said he could remember; the sea was a looking glass without patch or wrinkle, as if its own mind had become clear and intended to stay so. I took this for a good omen: a reflection of the high probability that there would be no more wars. The Great War being over, surely there could be no other. Doubtless Joe had no such illusion; I credited him then, as I still do, with having none at all; and if I did not put mine into words the reason may have been that I suspected it of *being* an illusion.

But there were other things the smooth sea and the empty sky reflected: my own freedom, for example, to relax from every effort I had ever made, and so to float toward England like a piece of it that once had been cast off but now was coming back. My expectations had no limit I can now recall. Nor can I recall, during the eight months that were to follow, any moment of disappointment, sharp or mild. If the other passengers could take our common destination for granted, that was because they had been there in this life: they were British, and were going home at the first opportunity peace presented. One of them was a pretty girl who had worked in the United States as a telephone operator since 1915, and who was returning to visit her father in Liverpool. Joe and I became rivals for the privilege of walking or sitting with her on such deck space as the *Haverford* had. She saw to it that our opportunities were equal, more or less. When mine were less, the circumstance seemed—well, comparatively unimportant. The important thing was that England lay ahead.

Our plan was to go north from Liverpool and spend perhaps two weeks exploring the country before we settled down in London. We went first to the lakes and mountains that Wordsworth had made famous; we walked among them, we climbed Helvellyn, we bought a volume of Wordsworth and read it aloud to each other in appropriate places—for example, "up the tumultuous brook of Greenhead Ghyll," the scene of "Michael"—and we sat among the stones of at least one Druid circle. All this, like Liverpool itself and every town or city we had seen, was wonderful in our eyes. But then at Keswick the question had to be answered whether we should go still farther north into Scotland, which had been visible from one of the peaks we climbed. I wanted to see Scotland, and Joe did not. It was almost as if he knew he would one day become famous himself for a life of Dr. Johnson, whom no one except Boswell ever persuaded to penetrate those wilds. I was no Boswell; so in the hotel at Keswick, after two hours of argument on a rainy day, there was nothing to do but toss a coin. I lost, and did not see Scotland for thirty-six years.

I have wondered since whether Joe ever really wanted to see anything besides London; in those days he was a passionate lover of cities, and this one then, even for me, was the city of all cities to be seen. Of course if he had lost he would have gone loyally to Edinburgh; but as it was we turned south through Chester, Lichfield (Dr. Johnson's home town), Coventry, Stratford, and Oxford to London, which we reached on September 4th and found to be precisely what we had dreamed. We took lodgings at 62 Guilford Street, near Russell Square, next door to the house where Carl had lived nine years before. And that very evening, unable to wait longer, we walked through Fleet Street and the Strand, then on to Piccadilly, Pall Mall, and Hyde Park. At Oxford the day before Joe had bought a copy of John Gay's *Trivia, or The Art of Walking the Streets of London,* and only last night we had read portions of it aloud; so we could laugh with a knowing joy when the street signs at one intersection told us we had come to the place "Where Catherine Street descends into the Strand."

One reason, in addition to Carl's advice, that we had looked for lodgings in Guilford Street was a desire to be near the British Museum, in the reading room of which we would work at our dissertations, I less regularly than Joe but still there were those quotations to check. Our manuscripts, forwarded in trunks, did not arrive until September 20th—a delay that worried us, but meanwhile we tramped more streets and at the Museum itself made ourselves familiar with the routine we eventually would follow through weeks and months of cold, foggy weather. It took us no time to learn that any place in London was warmer than our room in Guilford Street. In this second winter after the war there was still a shortage of coal for private dwellings; theaters and restaurants were favored, and so was the Museum.

In the reading room I studied old and new maps of London which located for me all the places where Dryden had lived, published his poems, been assaulted by his enemies, or otherwise made literary history. I resolved to see these places with my own eyes, and soon enough I did, though I knew it would make no difference so far as my essay was concerned. I was as sure now as I had been at Stratford, even at Greenhead Ghyll, that such associations have no depth. Perhaps in this case they were only an excuse, if any excuse was needed, to lose myself deeper in London. And as for the Museum, there were other things there than the reading room to entertain Joe and me. I shall never forget the Etruscan sarcophagus on whose stone lid the figures of two lean, laughing men still sat after twenty-five centuries and conversed. They were so modern that one could think one had known them before they died yesterday. They could even be Krutch and Van Doren.

When our trunks came we got down to work, though we never slackened in spare hours or even days our effort to investigate every last corner of London. I particularly loved the Temple (the Inns of Court), into whose grounds I would duck through a low passage from Fleet Street. I bought books at the second-hand shops in Charing Cross Road—more books than I could afford—and when I took them home at night would read them to Joe at his request. He liked to lie on his bed and listen, and stop me so that he could remark upon a sentence or a page. Voltaire's *Letters Concerning the English Nation,* a first London edition of which I picked up one afternoon, delighted both of us, I distinctly remember. Or we would go through the reviews in the *Athenaeum,* to which George Saintsbury, the ancient tory critic with whose works we both were intimate as students, and whom I knew best in connection with Dryden, was a frequent contributor. On such a night, reading a review by Saintsbury of some book on wine, we grew thirsty and ran down to a pub for several glasses of port; and coming back, were just elevated enough to believe he would like a letter from us; we wrote him about what we had done, and went to bed well pleased with ourselves.

Not that we always stayed in and read. More often than not we went to a theater, or to dinner at the Strand Corner House, merely to keep warm; but also, of course, to see what we could see. And then next morning we would be in the Museum again, where I for one would check quotations and improve my prose of last July—or, when this grew wearisome, call for first editions of great English books and stare at their title pages: *Robinson Crusoe, Gulliver's Travels, Lycidas,* and the Shakespeare folio of 1623. I often sat as I did this next to a hideous, half-starved man with a yellow raincoat buttoned to his neck, who watched me from his chair and once confided to me that he was an astrologist. He was a reader of horoscopes, ancient and modern, and he wanted to read mine. He never did, though he scribbled notes on scraps of paper and seemed to be preparing some prodigious revelation.

But there were several days when I was off at Cambridge, having left Joe ill with tonsillitis in our lodgings. He was convalescent the morning I went, yet I felt some guilt over the desertion, and could only hope the doctor I had found would take as good care of the patient as he promised. He did, while in Cambridge I interviewed a scholar who had written about Dryden's *Mac Flecknoe*—he was more interested now in his cats than he was in his article on that poem—and went out to see Ely Cathedral, my favorite English church ever since that day. Then before going back to London I wandered over into Northamptonshire where Dryden had been born and where certain villages were associated with his family's name. At Canons Ashby I called on Sir Arthur Dryden, a collateral descendant whose house, which he completely opened to me, had its own intrinsic merit. I remember the rooks that flew over the garden in great numbers just before sunset. The next day in Guilford Street Joe was himself again.

In the Lake Country we had met a Mr. Langton Cole and one of his daughters. They were kind to us there, and now we looked up the address we had been given for them in London. He was architect to the City of London, with offices near St. Paul's where we visited him and learned things we would never otherwise have known about buried Roman walls and remnants of the medieval town. But the daughter who was with him in the North had rooms by chance in Guilford Street; and the rest of the family lived only as far out as Surbiton, in Surrey. We spent a number of weekends there, exposing to Mrs. Langton Cole and three more of her daughters the full quaintness of our accents, which they never ceased to find amusing at the same time that they were willing to hear us on the odd subject of English character. We all got on pleasantly because of the differences between us. One of the daughters was an unreconstructed partisan of Charles I; I found a copy of the *Eikon Basilike* and took it out to her one time, and she was pleased. Mr. Langton Cole's study, which we had the impression no woman ever entered, was cluttered with papers, architectural designs, and models of ships. He was writing something, I could not discover what, but I decided then and there that I knew how amateur English authors produce their often very remarkable books—they work at them between tea and dinner, a matter of three or four hours daily, which is quite enough for the purpose. Mrs. Langton Cole was a vigorous old lady who because of her weight preferred to go about in a wheel chair. Her questions, always frank and surprising, came at us broadside and had to be answered. Once, though, we could not tell her why something she said made us laugh. We had been asked to read some American poetry, and one of us had just finished Vachel Lindsay's "General William Booth Enters Into Heaven," so impressive for the way it renders the soul and even the sound of the Salvation Army. Mrs. Langton Cole, however, was not impressed. "Humph!" she said. "That isn't poetry. It sounds to me like the Salvation Army."

The Langton Coles were very kind. They fed us well, too; I remember how happily Joe and I grinned at each other one evening at dinner when the house was cold—at least we thought it cold—and a hot, steaming tart was brought in for desert. Nevertheless as the weeks went on Joe pined for further company; he said we were not meeting enough strangers. So in November we tried something else. After obtaining credentials from the American consul to the effect that we were

not vicious or predatory, we persuaded the *Times* to let us
insert the following notice in its "agony column":

> Two young Americans, literary,
> but interested in everything,
> desire London friends.

And after six days, thirty letters came. Those that assumed we
were lonely we ignored, for we were not lonely; we also ignored the Americans who answered, for there were plenty of
those where we came from. We sifted the remainder ruthlessly,
and replied to perhaps a dozen that seemed promising. The
total result of the experiment was neither great nor lasting, yet
we did have agreeable encounters: with a journalist in the
City who showed us the Law Courts, with several pairs of girls
with whom we went for tea and dancing, and with a young
woman, half English and half French, whom we would see
again across the Channel. We were never sorry that we had
sent our raven forth.

By December 3rd my manuscript was typed and ready to
send home. The typing had been done on some days with my
overcoat and hat on: anything to keep me warm except, of
course, gloves. I took three bundles to the post office, one for
Carl, one for Professor Trent, and one for Professor Thorndike. And by another of the benign coincidences which pur-
sued me that year, on the same day a letter came from Carl saying that he had described the *Dryden* to Will D. Howe, who
was about to start a new publishing house with Alfred Harcourt and Donald Brace, and that Howe would almost certainly accept it as one of their first books, though a subsidy
might be called for. This was good news, but now I had to
wait and see how real it would turn out to be. And having for
a while no work to keep me occupied, I fell to wondering
what I would do next year in the United States.

Would I teach or would I write? Or both? And in any case,
where? I found myself trying to decide between Urbana and
New York: the only places I knew, and there were universities

in both. But it was a genuine question for me: where? I wrote to Carl, elaborating the dilemma, and heard from him that although he voted for New York he must leave the decision to me. Then on December 22nd he cabled: "Dryden accepted unconditionally. Merry Christmas." He meant, accepted by Harcourt, Brace, and Howe without a subsidy. I would not know what the professors thought until May, when my final examination was scheduled. Joe, who had not finished his own book, rejoiced with me over the cablegram; yet for both of us, since it made us think of the future, it was sobering too. And I for one continued to be torn between two places, not to say two careers, which I fancied I was free to think about. As to a career of writing I was of course quite vague. What would I write, and could I make a living by it? Carl was soon to send me books to review for *The Nation,* and these I handled as expertly as I knew how—I remember being harder than need be on some volumes of new verse. I was beginning, at this comparatively advanced age, to consider whether I myself might not become a poet. I had written few poems, and they were bad, but this did not have to mean—and there for a moment I stopped. When a letter came from Professor Thorndike offering me an instructorship in Columbia College I hesitated longer than now seems possible to answer and say Yes. That was a decision, to be sure, but I still did not feel it to be final. It took care, I told myself, merely of next year.

But the decision was made in Paris. The time had come for Joe and me to inspect the Continent. I left London on January 27th, by myself because I wanted to see Holland on the way and because Joe, whose name was not Dutch, had no desire, he said, to see windmills; he would meet me in France a week later. Leaving London was not easy. I have continued to love it as I love no other city except New York. But then I did not know I would ever love New York, so London was my city. It was beautiful, it was powerful, yet in some mysterious fashion it was intimately mine. It even smelled good—of fog, tea, tobacco, and I knew not what other essences. Fleet Street and the Strand still have no equivalent for me even in New York. A bus ride from the Houses of Parliament to St. Paul's is like nothing in the world. Yet Paris was necessary too, and I could not pass it up. There was no coin to toss, for Joe had no doubts about Paris. The only difference between us was as to how we should go there. After farewells to the Langton Coles and our other friends I took a boat from Harwich to the Hook of Holland, and spent a week in the little country I took pleasure in knowing my ancestors had come from.

They had come as long ago as 1699, and when I am honest I admit that I recognize nothing in me that is Dutch; but now it was fun, when I signed my name in a hotel register, to have the clerk look up at me again. The name had originally been van Doorn; so I went to Doorn, where the Kaiser lived in exile, and fancied I was on home ground. Most of the week, however, I spent in the famous cities that are so close together: Rotterdam, The Hague, Delft, Haarlem, Amsterdam, and Utrecht. In galleries I sought out the pictures not only of Rembrandt but of Vermeer, for I had not forgotten an article on Vermeer, years ago in *The Nation,* by Frank Jewett Mather. On the streets I admired the houses, all so much alike yet each with its character too, as in the paintings of Vermeer. In the country, traveling perhaps by a steam tram to Edam or some other city famous for its cheese, I marveled as everybody does at ships with sails that seemed to be moving over level land but of course were in canals. And whenever I had breakfast I luxuriated first in the odor and then in the taste of consummate coffee.

I stopped in Antwerp and Brussels, but France was next and I was eager to be there. The express train that took me, slowing down over frequent stretches of new track where not so long ago there had been no track at all, started me looking out of the window for signs of the war. And soon there were plenty: towns wholly or partially in ruins, and here and there and everywhere, between zigzag trenches that had not been filled, single graves, with helmets on them, of men who had died and been buried on the spot. Colonial troops were still busy digging and decorating these solitary graves, the number of which, additional I knew to vast military cemeteries already in the making, appalled me even more than the rubble and the trenches did. I was prepared then for the marks of mourning, innumerable and inescapable, I was soon to see on the body of Paris. When I arrived there I found the city as beautiful as I had known I would, but it was nowhere without its sadness: its wounded men, and its women whose men were gone forever.

The city I began next day to enjoy with Joe was nevertheless the city that cannot, no matter what waves of misery wash over it, lose altogether the brightness for which it has been loved in every generation. I loved it too—a little less than London, but I rarely made the comparison. I tend to approve of any place I am in, simply because I am there. And because Paris was doing its best to forget the war at the same time that it signified its inability to do so, I fell in with the first mood and explored the city for itself. We took rooms in the Hotel Corneille, across a narrow street from the Odéon, and within a minute's walk from the gardens of the Luxembourg where I was often to sit alone and say to myself that I was in paradise. We had elected, that is to say, to live on the Left Bank; for were we not students, and did we not want to feel the utmost freedom, if this meant merely the freedom to do nothing? There were the Boulevards close by; and there was the rue de Seine, remarkable for its old print and book shops, that wound down to the great river with its many bridges, one of which I often crossed as I went on foot to the Bibliothèque Nationale, where I made out that I had further authorities on Dryden to consult, and which I would reach only after a walk through the gardens of the Tuileries, so charming for their gravel paths between the winter flowerbeds and for their stone figures of queens and goddesses, a little less than life size, disposed cunningly in recesses of the shrubbery. Back at the hotel I would sometimes sit cutting the pages of French books

I had bought—again, more of them than I could afford, so that soon I would have to write my father for more money, and of course get it—or else I would start out with Joe, and eventually with friends we made, on a tour of some new section of the city.

We did not miss, of course, Versailles and Fontainebleau, and once we made a dismal journey to Rheims and the battlefields beyond it. I ran into Sol Cohen, whom I had known as a boy in Urbana and admired for his skill with the violin—he was now studying music in Paris—and took a special trip with him one day to a forest where as an observer during the war he had sat in the top of a tree and almost been blasted out of it by German shells. Joe and I were invited once to Vernon, in Normandy, where the children of our hosts followed us about in a garden and let us overhear them practicing their English: "Yes-s-s!" "Thank you very much!" "Look out!" "Good-by!" They would say these things and giggle; but especially our sibilant affirmative amused them: "Yes-s-s!" A neighboring place, an ancient farmhouse in open country, I remember for the grizzled old man who inhabited it alone, and who came out of the fields to sit with us in an exquisite drawing room while we drank champagne which a late sun pouring through the windows turned into amber fire.

Then in Paris again we would lounge among the cafés, or on certain evenings listen to the actors of the Comédie Française as they delivered, like messengers straight from Parnassus, the lines of Corneille, Racine, and Molière. I myself spent other evenings with Marguerite Favre, whom Emery Neff had known when he was in Paris with the army. He sent me her address, and she became an excellent friend to both Joe and me, though I saw her oftener than he did as March and April passed. She was in mourning for her father, who had not died in the war but whom she could not forget. She lived in Montmartre with her mother, supporting them both by the sale of embroidered bags. Formerly she had thought to carry on her father's jewelry trade in the provinces, but she was unable to bear the customers' constant talk of him when he had been alive. In spite of her grief she was a merry guide to places in Paris I would never have found alone. She laughed at the French in my notes to her concerning our engagements to meet. And she was particularly gay over a tale I told her about the walk I decided to take one night all the way across Paris from her apartment to the Hotel Corneille. I lost my bearings and followed a side street which I thought would lead me to the proper avenue. It did, but not before I became alarmed by footsteps that followed me. I thought of Apaches, the tough men of Paris, and looking quickly behind me in a dark place I believed I did see signs that the man there, who always kept the same distance from me but at the same time always came on, was too much interested in my back. At last I made up my mind to stop suddenly and see what he would do. What he did was turn and run. He too had been afraid; which was why he never overtook me.

But all this time I was deceiving Joe. I had started to write my first serious poem—or I should say, had become serious for the first time about writing one. It was in octosyllabic couplets, and was a narrative. It took off in part from Dryden's tale of Cymon and Iphigenia in the *Fables* and in part from the story I have already told of the girls in school who terrified me with their laughter and their kisses. It dealt, in short, with the green-sickness of the very young: probably a hopeless subject, for me at any rate. But a journal I kept all the time I was abroad tells me that I "versified" (my word then) to the tune of as many as forty lines a day, and that I did this whenever I was alone: by a fountain in the Luxembourg gardens, on a bench in the Tuileries, or at a desk in the Bibliothèque Nationale. This last was the regular place, for in February and March it was usually too cold to compose outdoors, though sometimes I did that, complaining proudly to myself because my fingers had difficulty with a pencil. The journal says that on the night of March 30th, Joe and I being then in the hotel with nothing to do, he proposed that we read something aloud, this time in English—on other nights, I take it, we had been trying to make our French intelligible to each other.

"What about my poem?" I said, endeavoring to sound casual.

"Yours!"

"What do you think I've been doing in the Bibliothèque?"

"Well, I wondered."

So I read it all, out of a durable notebook into which I had copied it after making many corrections, and the record states that Joe generously approved. So did Sol Cohen, who heard it a few days later on a bench in the Tuileries. Then I should have been well pleased. But the journal makes it clear that I still waited for a critic whom I could count on not to be kind. Strangely enough this was Carl, who could indeed be frank with me but who at all times wanted more than anything else to believe the best of whatever I did. It was for Carl that I continued to revise *Simple Cymon* all the way across the Atlantic in the lounges of *La Touraine,* which left Le Havre on April 10th and arrived in New York on the morning of the 20th.

How could I know that from the moment of landing, caught up as I was in so many new concerns, the poem would diminish in importance even for its author, and that when Carl, as eventually he did, convinced me it was not good I would be more than willing to believe him? Neither could I know that at noon on this day I would meet the young woman who was going to be my wife.

I Start to Work

1920–1928

FIVE years of being a student in New York, a soldier in Iowa and Arkansas, and a traveler in Europe came to an end for me the instant our ship docked. I do not remember what happened to Joe, but I know I was met by Carl and Irita and taken straight to the offices of *The Nation* where both of them worked. And soon it was time for lunch. I had met the editor, Oswald Garrison Villard, who I think did not go with us. But Freda Kirchwey did, and Lewis Gannett, and Arthur Warner, and several others of whose identities, with one exception, I can no longer be sure.

The exception was Dorothy Graffe, who had been in Barnard College with Freda and now read newspapers for *The Nation* and filed clippings that might prove useful to the editors. She has told me since that I paid no attention to her and even did not know she was there; she doubts in fact that I remember her being in the party. She is wrong, but I must accept her story that so far as she was concerned she expected the newcomer to fall far below the figure Carl and Irita had described. They had overpraised me, she thought. And of course they had. Since Carl's death, which came thirty years later, people have told me of the things he never wearied of saying about me. I can believe them, for if he could tell me plainly enough that something of mine—for example, *Simple Cymon*—was not well done, he never admitted my defects to others. So I am certain that Carl had been extravagant in his advance notices of the younger brother who was about to appear. If he did not spoil me, then or later, it was because his expectations were themselves a challenge.

He had plans for me even now. He needed his summer free so that he might complete the manuscript of his *Contemporary American Novelists,* due to be published next year, and he hoped I would take his place on *The Nation* between June and September. I was to act as literary editor, assigning books for review and corresponding with the reviewers; but I would spend my weekends in Cornwall where I would be given whatever advice or instruction was in order. I accepted gladly; it was a kind of post, and I felt I had been untethered long enough.

But first I must take my final doctor's examination at Columbia, and then I must visit my family in Illinois. The examination in May, in a stately room of what I still call the old library, though that is not its official name, was one of the surprises of my life. The professors—not merely those I had studied with but eminent ones from other departments—rose when I entered the room and did not sit down until I had. This is an age-old custom, and a beautiful one; since then I have seen many candidates so staggered by it that they scarcely believe their eyes. For some reason no candidate is ever told that it will happen; or, when the questions begin, that they will be asked with respect and even with deference, as from old authorities to a new one they are adding to their number. Nobody had told me either, so that I fairly floated through the experience, and heard myself informed of certain errors I had made, and of generalizations I had overstated, with no sense of being other than an equal of the courteous gentlemen who addressed me.

In Urbana, whither I went as usual by way of Detroit, I found my father and mother eager to hear about whatever things I had failed to mention in my letters from London and Paris. I had written many letters, some of them long, but there can never be enough detail to satisfy the appetites of those who stay at home. Paul told me more than he had had time for at

Newport News. His regiment of Marines arrived in France too late in the war to see action, so that most of its work was guarding warehouses of supplies near Bordeaux. I knew this from his own letters, but now he added such items as that when a warehouse contained food they passed their nights on duty with greater gaiety because of the cans of peaches they opened with their bayonets and consumed; or of the black, rainy moment when his gun went off by accident and made a racket on the corrugated-iron wall of the depot before him. I also learned that he was not content any longer with the University of Illinois. He did not like the dean of men. At Villa Grove Frank and Grace were starting another such summer as I myself remembered there, though my own memories were of play rather than of work, whereas the farm had become for them a wholly serious occupation. Yet we sat on the porch at night and talked as we always had. And one of their cats— she reappears in my poem "Midwife Cat"—impressed me by the responsible way she walked along a rafter and watched beneath her a white sow giving birth to perhaps a dozen little pigs.

Back in New York I established myself in the Old Chelsea, a rooming house on 16th Street, from which I went every morning to the building on Vesey Street, opposite St. Paul's, where *The Nation* was edited. My own operation there, with Carl's help, ran so smoothly that I recall no crisis of any sort. But from an allied operation I was to learn something important. One day as Arthur Warner was leaving for lunch he suggested that I look at the proofs of an editorial by Mr. Villard—or O.G.V., as he was normally referred to—and see if corrections were needed. Arthur of course meant typographical corrections. When he came back, however, he found the article rewritten on his desk; I had changed every sentence. I watched him as he read, and the only sign of his disapproval, even of his anger, was that the back of his neck became slowly red. At last he turned and told me that what I had done could not be done: we had not been engaged to put the boss out of business. Now this had not been my intention. I merely supposed the boss should write as I did. The pugnacious liberal who had replaced the *Nation* of More and Sherman with another one to his liking should sound, I thought, like those exquisitely cultivated sons of Matthew Arnold and Sainte-Beuve, or at least like me as their imitator. No supposition could have been more absurd. I had still to learn how O.G.V. in his own style could strike the stoutest blows then being struck at public liars and thieves.

My weekends in Cornwall, happily as they passed, still gave me no hint of the years I was to live there later on. Dorothy Graffe and her mother, having heard so much about the utterly peaceful beauties of the place, had taken rooms this summer in the farmhouse of Noah Rogers, a neighbor whom Carl was to write about in *Other Provinces* under the name of Matthew Bradford. They spent only weekends there, as I did in Carl's house nearby; but I saw them and their friends who visited them—one of these friends, Hedwig Koenig, who would later study medicine and become our doctor, I clumsily tipped out of a canoe into Cream Hill Lake—and often on Sunday nights I rode down with Dorothy on the train. The noteworthy feature of our conversation was that we found the same things funny; very funny, so that we were always laughing; but again I got no hint that this was the person with whom I would live in Cornwall through decades to come. I was too busy thinking that marriage was a thing for older men than I was, men who had solved all other problems first.

As summer aged and September came on I said not merely to myself but to anyone standing by that although I was soon to begin teaching at Columbia I had no expectation of doing so for long. I still held out for the writer's life, though I remained ignorant of how it could be a living, and I had few enough ideas as to what in fact I might ever be author of. At worst, I said, it could be a double life: half teaching, half writing. And I felt so strongly about this that when Joe Krutch came up from Knoxville to teach at Brooklyn Polytechnic we

had no difficulty in agreeing as to where we should live, supposing we lived together, as without further question we decided to do. The place would be Greenwich Village, five miles
downtown from Columbia and perhaps as many miles across
the East River from where Joe was to meet his classes. Our life
would be double at least to the extent that we worked and
slept in different sections of New York. We found an apartment in a small house on Barrow Street and signed a lease with
Mrs. Brady committing us to stay there for a year. Joe stayed
two years, and I stayed seven; and always I have lived within
a five-minute walk of that house.

The Village has the reputation of being Bohemian, but I
have never been interested in that. I still do not know whether
it deserves the name; I like it for its low brick houses and
its narrow streets where the coming of a flower-wagon in May
can be an event. Here at 43 Barrow Street even the ceilings of
the rooms were low: a fortunate circumstance, since we had to
heat the place ourselves, in the back room where Joe lived by
a gas radiator and in my front room by a pot-bellied stove
that burned hard coal. We built bookcases and hung the walls
with prints and with pieces of colored cloth. Across the street
lived Donald and Lyle Clark; he had been a student at Columbia and now was one of its teachers; his special subject was the
history of rhetoric. And next door in 45 we found Dorothy and
her mother, who had moved downtown a month before we
thought of doing so. In time I was to spend as many evenings
there as I did at 43; Mrs. Graffe, a fine cook, had for me the
additional virtue of not caring at what hour I came or went.
Dorothy and I had a signal that preceded my coming over. I
would whistle the low, rather mournful notes I had used to
bring the horses in at Hope—she laughed at the association,
and so did I; then if she was home she put her head out of the
window and discussed with me the question of what should
happen next: a late call, or a night walk through the empty
streets. Paul, who had solved his problem by coming to study
for two years in the Columbia School of Business, sensibly

took a room near the university; we visited each other by subway, as was the case with Carl until he and Irita moved still farther down Seventh Avenue to Charlton Street.

I am sure I had no illusion that the Dryden book would prove anything about my chances to live as a writer. The summer's contact with professionals had proved nothing either, for I was but Carl's deputy at *The Nation*. Nevertheless I had great curiosity as to how the book would be received when it was published in the fall. It was praised but not bought; after two hundred and twenty copies had sold very slowly the rest were remaindered in drugstores. My only satisfaction could be in the sources of the praise. Stuart Sherman's review in *The Nation* gave me pleasure almost too deep for thanks; and after some months the London *Times Literary Supplement* devoted a leader to the book, or rather to its subject, Dryden as a poet. This was so accomplished a piece, and so understanding of the points I had done my best to make about this poet and all poets past or future, that I marveled at my luck in finding such a reader. I did not know his name for four years; then T. S. Eliot published a pamphlet, *Homage to John Dryden*, and the article was in it. This had everything to do, I assume, with a demand for the book which continued until Gordon Fraser wrote me from Cambridge, Dryden's own university town, proposing an English edition. It appeared there in 1931, and in 1946 a third edition was published in New York.

Yet in that fall of 1920 nothing could have pleased and amused me more than the correspondence I had with George Saintsbury, to whom I sent one of the first copies of the *Dryden*. For I admired his own book on the subject; I had used his reprint of Scott's edition as well as my copy of the original; and as I have said, I esteemed him anyway. Back came at once a most agreeable letter, courtly and full of compliment, which I acknowledged not only with thanks but with the revelation that I was one of the two American students who had written him after he inspired them to drink port. I took it for granted that he had paid little attention to the names at the bottom of our letter, and certainly that he did not remember mine. He replied with alacrity again, saying on a card, in handwriting which had long been legendary for its difficulty, but which his failing eyesight now made worse:

> 1 Royal Crescent
> Bath
>
> Then I owe you *two* pleasant experiences instead of one: in fact with your letter I may say *three*. I am not clear whether you have seen my reference to your and Mr. Krutch's action in a little book which must be terribly heterodox and almost contraband in your country now. But I shall hope to reciprocate his and your courtesy again this very day.
>
> Saintsbury
> 12.12.20

The reference, of course, was to Prohibition, now more than a year old. Saintsbury had a different view of it from that of Grandpa Butz. But what little book of his could be contraband in this country? Joe and I found a copy of it as soon as we could. It was *Notes on a Cellar-Book,* published in July, 1920, and on page 40, in the chapter on port, we found this footnote:

One of the most agreeable incidents of my life in connection with Port is quite recent. Soon after I had published something about wine in the *Athenaeum,* and since America "went dry," two students of that misguided country wrote to me saying that they had found it impossible to refrain, after reading the article, from sallying forth, purchasing some so-called port wine (I hope it was not very bad), and drinking my health in it. It would be difficult for a teacher to have a more gratifying testimonial to the efficacy of his teaching; especially when he remembers the boasts of Prohibitionists as to bringing on prohibition by sowing pseudo-scientific Taradiddles in U. S. school-books.

A sequel to that correspondence gives me, now that I return to it, a still heartier satisfaction, or maybe I should say, a subtler one. In 1925 I reviewed for *The Nation* a volume of Saintsbury's collected critical essays on French writers together with his *Last Scrap Book,* and in course of praising their author took occasion to speak not only of his tory opinions but of the lumbering style he had developed with age—lumbering, yet with its own seasoned charm, so that I praised it too and even paid it the tribute of affectionate parody. I saw that a copy of this review was addressed to him, then waited—with some doubt that I should have sent it, for I thought he might find it impertinent—to see if there would be any acknowledgment. There was, in the last communication I would have from him. He died in 1933 at the age of eighty-eight. I give all of his letter that I have been able to decipher:

1 Royal Crescent
Bath

March 11.1925
Dear Mr. Van Doren

I have no doubt that the American, like the English, stock or store of "chestnut" stories contains that of the wicked man who having transgressed against Prohibitionism, found the world rather *rotatory* afterwards; sat down, however, and expressed his intention of continuing to sit "till his house came round to him."

You have made my house or apartment in the *Nation* come round to me . . . swept of some derelict French writers . . . and inhabited by a most undoubted crank in the sense of—well—a spirit not exactly elliptic. As you know the *Last Scrap Book* I needn't give more details.

But please accept my hearty thanks.

Yours sincerely,
George Saintsbury.

II

But I must go back to September, 1920, when I started to teach —with the notion, as I have said, that I would not do it long, although the fact is that I have done it without interruption for almost forty years. I have done other things too, but Hamilton Hall, where Columbia College has its being, is my one professional home that has never changed. I found myself at once in hospitable company. The older professors in the College were not too different, it seemed to me, from the colonels in whose headquarters I had worked as sergeant major and lieutenant. I respected them without being afraid of them. Nor do I remember feeling any panic when I faced my first classes. I must have been nervous, as annually I continue to be; but I was not afraid of freshmen either, for I had learned in the army that they were bound to be at least as apprehensive about the demands I made on them as I was about their opinion of me.

And three of my younger colleagues were old acquaintances: Raymond Weaver, now busy with Herman Melville, his biography of whom (suggested by Carl) would determine that author's vogue for a generation; Emery Neff, who proceeded deliberately, wisely, with his dissertation, *Carlyle and Mill;* and Roy Dibble, whom recent events had curiously transformed. Rejected by the army for physical reasons, Dibble taught the war through in Hamilton Hall; and since he was required, in addition to teaching his chosen subject, to indoctrinate his students in something called "War Aims," something he had to feed them, as he put it, from a syllabus which left him no discretion in matters either of judgment or of emphasis, his normally vegetative nature had rebelled, so that he now considered himself a literary radical, and fired by the example of Lytton Strachey's *Eminent Victorians* set out to write a series of essays on *Strenuous Americans:* themselves, as essays, strenuous and surprising, and successful enough to call for other work of their kind before he died in 1929 of the weakness that had exempted him from military service. There was Irwin Edman, too, in another department. Carl had known him as an undergraduate in the College, when he amazed his instructors by writing final examinations in rhyme. Now he taught philosophy; and continued to write verses; and for many years was my warm, bright, playful friend.

My elders were benevolent men. George Clinton Dinsmore Odell, who had been a student in Columbia College before it moved uptown, and who did not mind giving us the impression that he had lived much longer than even that, was a massive, genial, smoothly civil and considerate New Yorker whose one passion was the local stage. He was only then beginning to plan the *Annals* of that stage which in many tall volumes would make him famous; but his talk, when it did not have to be about the sections in freshman English which he so leniently administered, was likely to turn back in time to Edwin Booth or Adelina Patti—there had been no soprano worth the name, he said, since Patti. John Erskine, a New Yorker of the next generation, I had known before: as a lecturer in the graduate school, and as a friend of Carl. His energy manifested itself in rougher and directer ways. He was a poet and a musician; as a man he held strong opinions and expressed them without reserve; as a teacher he was powerful; as a colleague he was kind. He was to leave the university after the success of his novel *The Private Life of Helen of Troy,* as Carl had already left it except for the graduate lectures in American literature which for years he came back from *The Nation,* the *Century Magazine,* the Literary Guild, or wherever else he was, to give in Philosophy Hall. Harrison Ross Steeves, no less a New Yorker than Odell or Erskine, impressed me that year, as he would do through all the later time when he administered our College department, by his utter quiet and his impregnable reserve. Speaking always in perfect sentences, and maintaining a decorum which nevertheless could not conceal a dedication to the best that there can be in books, he was not to tell me until I knew him better than I could then that he might just as well have studied law. Precision would have been his strength in any case: precision, and a sense of honor which nobody ever doubted. Professor Trent was no longer one of my immediate superiors. He taught entirely in the graduate school, where I saw him as often as I could, but this was not often, particularly after the long illness set in from which he was to die in 1939. During this illness he wrote me, with difficulty because of his paralysis, letters of touching sweetness and good will.

If I speak of the students last it is not merely because they were the crucial persons with whom I spent my time, as must be true in any college; it is also because no way exists of describing what really goes on in a classroom once the door is closed. What goes on is a kind of secret between him who stands and those who sit. I knew this from the first; it was my secret even more than it was theirs. They had their own responses which I could hear or see them make: they raised their hands, they talked, they shook their heads, they laughed, they looked bored; and special approval or disapproval they expressed—the custom is now obsolete—by stamping or shuffling their feet on the floor. But even then I could believe that if anything of true moment was happening in their minds there was no immediate way for them to show it, any more than I could show, except by talking in the maturest way I could, and following any new idea as far as it would take me, how much our conversations interested me, and how much I learned from them.

From the beginning, I think, I assumed experience even in freshmen; and the reward for this assumption was my feeling that I had good students. I had the feeling not only in small classes but in large; for right away I had a taste of what it is like to address rows and rows of faces in rooms like amphitheaters, except that I did not do it myself; I merely assisted Brander Matthews, a fourth New Yorker among my elders who taught an ancient course in American literature which I would recast in time and teach myself. Assisting him then meant taking attendance at his lectures, reading the examinations, and answering students' complaints that they had been given the wrong marks. It also meant walking away with Brander and listening to such stories as he had not told in class. His monologues were witty, and sometimes they sounded as if they had been rehearsed. Their reference was usually to the theater, which Brander knew in his own way as well as Odell. But he was a more professional man, very knowing about authors and playwrights; and if I never thought him profound I knew that he was clever and disposed to help me if I behaved properly, as he seemed never to be positive, however, I would do.

Within two years I had a large class of my own. It was called Six English Authors; it was entirely my invention; and I remember being surprised when upon suggesting it I was permitted to give it and see what happened. It was conceived in reaction against a survey course that skipped too rapidly, I thought, over too many writers. Why not reduce the number to six and read each of them as thoroughly as possible? What happened was that the course succeeded beyond anyone's expectation: certainly beyond mine, for I had not dreamed that as many as 250 students would want to take it. The authors varied from year to year, though Chaucer, Shakespeare, and Fielding were always there; the others might be Milton, Pope, Swift, Byron, Browning, or Hardy (as a poet). I do not know how many of the students listened carefully, but at the moment this did not seem to matter; the readings were copious, and I found that I had a great deal to say, nor did I mind if what I said had been said by others before me. I read aloud, I called attention to good things, I generalized about literature and life to the limit of my capacity. Perhaps the chief novelty consisted in my assumption that nothing was too difficult for the students. I told them not to worry about Chaucer's Middle English but to read him fast for what they could get out of him; they missed a good deal, but I think they got the heart of that master comedian. So with Shakespeare's plays, *Paradise Lost,* and the *Prelude:* I considered each work as a human whole, and ignored many literary problems. I was to teach this course for something like ten years, and was never to grow tired of hearing either myself or the students talk; for I insisted that they continue to talk, in spite of their overwhelming numbers, as if the room were small.

The small room, that is to say, was standard in my mind. And no wonder, for my experience had been chiefly there, with twenty or thirty students considering in seats before me the principles of reading and writing. Professor Odell properly supposed that the two arts went together; so in every section of freshman and sophomore English we read and wrote, which meant among other things my reading aloud what the students wrote, or copying it on the blackboard and discussing its every fault or merit. The small room, indeed, must forever be the model of what teaching is when it is personal and patient and alive. I soon discovered, of course, that my students were persons—in class, that is, where for me it mattered most what they were. I never encouraged intimacy with them outside, and I have not done so since; I have no illusion that students and teachers can be friends in the fullest sense, since there is by statute an inequality in their positions; Aristotle is right about that as he is about most things. Yet this has at no time prevented certain ones of them, if they persisted in the effort, from breaking through whatever barrier there was and becoming, if only in after years, some of my finest friends. In college as such I have always taken for granted that what we had to give each other was to be given in the small room we inhabited together for fifty minutes daily; that was where I discovered what I knew, and the same thing would have to be true for them.

Not that the very first class I met was without its young man who engaged me beyond the call of duty. This was Whittaker Chambers, whose eyes were always upon me as if he thought he had found in this strange place a person who would understand him. I cannot claim that I did, for he was continually astounding me. Early in the term he was delinquent with a paper; and when I asked him why, he told me he was busy with politics: he was distributing handbills in favor of Calvin Coolidge, the Republican candidate for Vice President in November. "Why Coolidge?" I asked; and Whittaker asked me in turn whether I had not heard about that great man's action in settling the Boston police strike. I had a different view of this action, for I was a reader of *The Nation* and already a contributor to it of frequent reviews. But the argument did not go on; his politics were not my business, and anyway he was so passionate a Republican that he would not have listened to anybody. Within a year he had ceased to be interested in politics. He was passionate about poetry, philosophy, and all manner of abstract things; and his poems were good. Toward the end of his junior year he published in *Morningside*, the college literary magazine, a little play about Jesus in the tomb, the point of it being that Jesus, called upon to come forth, preferred to sleep forever. During the rumpus that followed I defended in the *Spectator*, the college newspaper, Whittaker's right to publish such a piece; and was rewarded by a word from Brander Matthews that he disapproved of both Whittaker and me. Whittaker himself was expelled from Columbia; and though he was reinstated the next year, he never again felt that he belonged. Shortly after his graduation he wrote me that he had joined the Communist Party. This also had for me an abstract sound, and I could not take it seriously. Dorothy, on the rare occasions when he came to see us after his Columbia days were over, noticed that two or three of his front teeth were broken, and asked him whether he intended to have them fixed. He told her he preferred to leave them as they were: they made him look, he grinned and said, like one of the people. He disappeared from view in time, though cards and letters would come from various places, here or abroad, and not too seldom a poem, able and warmhearted, which I printed in *The Nation*. Then ten years passed during which I never saw or heard from him at all.

An altogether different student must remain anonymous. His writing was so poor that I could not possibly pass it. Not only was it clumsy and incorrect; there seemed to be no mind behind it. He came into my office one day, closed the door, and proceeded to explain. He said he was a physical training instructor in a gymnasium downtown. I looked at him again and realized that he was strong; he was not tall, but by the very way he held out his hands, which were trembling with anxiety and excitement, he expressed muscles I was unable to see. He informed me that with those hands he could bend iron bars; he could even tear a piece two inches square out of the upper left corner of the New York telephone book. I glanced toward the door, wondering what next. But I had misconstrued the man. He had come for no other reason than to tell me what I *could* admire him for. At least he was strong. He was older than the other students; he had thought he could be a student too; but he supposed now there was no use in trying further. Gentle, like most giants, he touched me so deeply that I did my best to spare his feelings. He did not want them spared. He wanted my honest opinion, which I ended by giving him. Before long he left college.

There was no resemblance between him and another student, an able writer, who when he failed to hand in a term paper was furious because I would not overlook the failure. The time was May, and he told me he had been in love all spring. I said: "You don't love her very much." He stared at me with greater fury. "How can you say that?" "You won't sacrifice a mark for her." He could think of no answer to this, and for the time being I am sure he hated me—as still another student must have, for he wrote anonymous letters to all of the New York newspapers saying I had insulted them. He was a journalism student; and it was true that one day, irked by the fact that the composition class of which he was a member seemed incapable of finding subjects other than those suggested to them by the daily press, I had stated Thoreau's opinion of newspapers as if it were my own, and at the moment it more or less was. I even announced that I never read the sheets myself; I preferred books, or even better, my own thoughts. The result of his action was a rush of reporters and photographers to interview me in Hamilton Hall. They left me in peace when I reminded them that his letters had been anonymous, and the incident, which I confess shook me, was closed; except that the *Times* lectured me in an editorial for my addiction to darkness.

It was not long before I found I had the reputation of being partial to Jewish students. I doubt that I was, yet it is true that among the Jewish students in my classes there were many who fascinated me by their brilliance and by the saliency of their several characters. I accent "several"; for it was the variety among these students that impressed me most. Perhaps I had entertained the vulgar notion that as Jews they would be all alike. Of course they were all different, and somehow they did become my friends—so much so that when one of them happened to tell the editor of the *Menorah Journal* about it he invited me to describe them in an article. I did so in 1927, under the title "Jewish Students I Have Known," and those of them I still see tell me I was fairly prophetic as to their futures. The students described—as individuals, for I refused to generalize—were Henry Rosenthal, Clifton Fadiman, Meyer Schapiro, John Gassner, Louis Zukofsky, Herbert Solow, Lionel Trilling, and Charles Prager. I shall not repaint them here; yet to read the article again is to be reminded how early character is formed, and how little it ever changes. In the case of Henry Rosenthal I emphasized the sardonic, satirical genius which his friends still fear in him, though with time he has mellowed. In Clifton Fadiman I noted the gift of mimicry and the fund of knowledge which everybody continues to associate with him. I spoke of Schapiro's "passion to know and make known," particularly in the field of fine art and its history. John Gassner I represented as "drunk with literature"; if I had added, dramatic literature, I would have left nothing out. Louis Zukofsky remains "a subtle poet" with an "inarticulate soul." Herbert Solow, I said, had "brown bored eyes" and was ironic without bitterness. I reported of Lionel Trilling that he was "sensitive" and "fastidious" and that he "spoke diffidently, with a hushed and harmless voice"; I found in him "dignity and grace," and foretold that whatever he eventually did "will be lovely, for it will be the fruit of a pure intelligence slowly ripened in not too fierce a sun." Of Charles Prager, whom I greatly liked, I predicted that he would do nothing so arduous as to become "the man of letters we thought he wanted to be." He never did, nor in fact do I know what he did.

John Erskine, who in France after the war, waiting to come home, had helped organize a program of reading for himself and his friends, decided when he did come home that the same program would be good for the students of Columbia College. It was a revolutionary decision, made at about the same time I came along, and it was not accepted by the faculty without a fight. The revolutionary thing was Erskine's faith, inspired in part by his old Columbia teacher George Edward Wood-berry, that the best books are not too good for undergraduates. The opposition said they would never understand them; they would only pretend they did, and the result would be a butchery of the classics, or at the best a travesty upon them. Students should read about them rather than in them; text-books were still the teacher's most dependable tool. Erskine did not agree. The books he and his colleagues in the French enterprise had read and discussed were the greatest books, from Homer and Plato on, that they could find; he wished he had read them, however imperfectly, when he was young; and he proposed that the education of American youth be no longer neglected. The sooner they made contact with noble minds the better for their own. There is always the first time that any book is read; then in these cases, why not now?

The outcome was a course in the College called General Honors: the ancestor of innumerable courses and even cur-riculums in Great Books which the colleges of America have created since that day. General Honors was not prescribed, nor could freshmen elect it. Only upperclassmen were invited to the feast. They came, not in great numbers, to sessions con-ducted weekly for two hours on Wednesday evening; seminar rooms were used so that the students could sit informally around a long table and smoke; and at the end of this table were two teachers, not one, so that benefit might be derived from differences between their views of Aristotle, Euripides,

St. Augustine, Dante, Rabelais, Montaigne, Shakespeare, Molière, Voltaire, Goethe, or whoever else was being encountered through one of his masterpieces.

It was at such a table that I learned how powerful Erskine himself was as a teacher, for I sat in with him during my first evenings as a member of the staff. One night the book was Dante's *New Life,* and a student had begun the discussion by saying that so far as he was concerned it was nothing but a story of a man who stood in the gutter and made remarks about some girls who passed. The rest of us, sensible of the outrage, gasped; but Erskine only smiled and said: "Mr. ——, will you open the book and read?" "On what page, sir?" "Any page." It was a perfect solution, so quietly arrived at that even the student knew he was refuting himself as he read aloud—I do not remember what, but as I now open the book at random I find this sentence: "And these words said, all this my fantasy vanished suddenly by reason of the great portion of himself that methought Love gave me; and as though transformed in my appearance, I rode that day very pensive and accompanied by many sighs." Nor can I forget another time when some student undertook to explain all literature as economically determined. "Can you give me an example," said Erskine, "of a book or an author so determined?" "Why, yes. Sir Walter Scott. He wrote his last novels to pay his debts." "I would have thought," said Erskine softly—and this was all the more remarkable because he was not soft by nature—"that the sense of honor had something to do with it." There was an answer to that, perhaps. The sense of honor may be a badge of class. But the student did not think of it, and neither have I until this moment.

Before long I was teaching my own section of General Honors with a man younger than I. This was Mortimer Adler, whom I had barely known as a student in the College but who had reappeared from the department of psychology to engage in Erskine's experiment. Mortimer was soon to consider himself a philosopher rather than a psychologist, and as such he has taught me, throughout thirty years of a lasting friendship, more than I am able to add up. But then he seemed to think he was being taught by me, in the intervals at any rate of his own inimitable discourse, which was rapid and fiery, and illuminated at every turn by formal logic—itself, as he manipulated it, a shower of sparks. I had not known before, and I have not known since, such high spirits in any man occupied with wholly intellectual concerns. He had other concerns too: trains, girls, movies, food, and indeed all the things that natural people love, for he was entirely natural; but when it came to ideas he blazed with excitement; he would bounce in his chair as he fought to defend a distinction; he would talk so fast that his tongue, as I once told him, fell over itself; he would be deadly serious, and then he would laugh like a happy madman—not that he was ever mad, but he could be happy to the skies over a philosophical discovery. I began to see him away from the university as well as there; he told me of his triumphs and his troubles—mostly his troubles; and I witnessed in him the conversion of a teacher to the cause John Erskine had espoused. Once Mortimer had begun to talk with students about great books there was no need to convince him of their beauty and might.

He professed to believe that I was the only one of us who knew anything about poetry; then when I protested, he talked about poetry in such a way as to fill it with meanings—utmost meanings—I myself had forgotten or never known. To him it was a form of knowledge, and its chief function was to tell stories. He was Aristotelian about the art, as he was in process of becoming about everything. At this point my education under him can be said to have had its beginning. Nor was the end of it in sight three decades later when I wrote "Philosopher at Large" with Mortimer in mind:

> The ancient garden where most men
> Step daintily, in specimen dust,
> He bulldozes; plows deep;
> Moves earth; says someone must,

If truth is ever to be found
That so long since went underground.

What truth? Why down? He shakes his head.
He does not know. But roots and rocks
Go tumbling, tearing, as his blade,
Shivering from its own shocks,
Bites farther, and upturns pure clay
He does not pause to smooth away.

And horrifies those men, by hedge
And dust plot, whom the top sufficed.
They thought the garden theirs. And still
It is; but the dear air is spiced
With damp new things dug up. Or old,
He says; like God, like buried gold.

III

I must go back again—the story now is not a thread but a
woven cord—to the summer of 1921 when after a single year
of teaching I went west a thousand miles to what I still called
my home. This was the last summer save one when I would
think of it that way. I went again in 1922, but then the center
of life shifted for me to where I worked and where Dorothy
was. Both summers I wrote poetry. *Simple Cymon* having been
put away for good, I recovered heart and composed a poem
of some length, in heroic couplets, about Grandma and
Grandpa Butz, whom I called Agatha and Larry; the title of
the poem was simply *Agatha*, for Grandma was its heroine.
I sent it to Dorothy, who wrote me that she thought it good,
though there were "a few little things"—the phrase has since
become familiar between us—she supposed might be changed
or made clearer. She was the only reader the poem ever had;
I wanted her opinion, for I had become dependent upon her
opinion by and large; but in the end I gathered from her as
well as from myself that it was not good enough.

I was to write two more longish poems before I set that particular ambition temporarily aside. One was about Hephaestus, the Greek god in whom both Homer and Milton had got me deeply interested long ago—I liked him because he worked and limped, and I took his side because the other Olympians condescended to him and made him the butt of jokes. The other was about Jonathan Edwards, whose acquaintance I had made through Carl's volume of selections called *Edwards and Franklin,* especially in the pages occupied by the Personal Narrative, still for me a piece of writing unparalleled in its kind; its beauty and power approach infinity as a limit. For that very reason, of course, no poem needs to be written about it: it is already a poem. Anyhow, these two attempts at narrative blank verse were in their turn discarded, as were more short poems than I like to think of now.

I seemed hopelessly slow in getting started. Yet during this time I did in my own opinion succeed with some lyrics and descriptive pieces, and magazines began to accept them. They were of the least possible complexity, many of them dealt with Urbana, Potomac, and Villa Grove, and the people I loved there might have liked to read them; but for some reason I was secretive about their very existence. I remember pretending to Frank, across a table at Villa Grove, that I was busy with a letter when it was in fact a poem, though I cannot recall which one it was.

I say I was dependent on Dorothy's opinion, but the truth is that I was dependent on *her* and did not know it yet. I was holding tight to the notion that I ought to live alone, for an undetermined number of years, so that I could be free to— well, to what? I could not answer that question, so I did not really ask it. But in the summer of 1921 I could decide not to go east a month early and spend Dorothy's vacation with her in the cottage she and her mother had taken on Noah Rogers's farm in Cornwall. I wanted to do this, yet I spent the month in Urbana. Then next summer the choice was clear. They had gone to Towaco, near Boonton, New Jersey, and when they invited me there for the month of August nothing could have kept me away. Since Dorothy had this month off from *The Nation,* we were both free to do what we liked. We pulled weeds in the back yard and got poison ivy for our pains. We took in a stray dog, a little white one whose owners eventually turned up to lead her home. We bought a car with $200 that Dorothy had saved, a second-hand Ford roadster, and drove it west among the pretty mountains beyond Boonton. And then when the month was over we got married.

We had been free to do this too, but the decision waited until only one weekend was left: a long weekend, since Monday was Labor Day, yet it was not much time at that. On Friday morning, September 1st, as Mrs. Graffe waved good-by to us helplessly at the gate, we drove off in our Ford to the Municipal Building in New York and with a celerity that was possible only then became man and wife. We had $100 between us, $10 of which in my confusion I gave to the clerk who acted as witness instead of the dollar he expected. I had thought it a dollar bill myself. Then with what was left we drove across to Broadway and headed north along the Hudson, pausing only to buy ourselves flowers, to make a few telephone calls (to Carl and others), and to send one telegram. The telegram was to my mother, who told me later, laughing, that she had no trouble understanding it though it read when it reached her: "Worried today. Love." Of course I had written "married" on the blank.

So we were off in the world, together and alone, for four whole days. We could not get very far, nor did we care to. Tarrytown, our first stop, was typical of where we went. So far as I was concerned, any place was a good place to tell Dorothy, as perpetually I did, that we had done a good thing, a happy thing, of which I had not expected so completely to approve. This may sound absurd, but it is exactly what I said, and she pretended to agree that the idea of getting married had never been tested out by any man and girl before 1922. What I would have found it harder to say, because I was still unfamiliar with it as a fact, was that my days henceforth would be ordered as I had never dared dream days could be ordered.

My job, once we were back in New York, was to send word to Joe Krutch in Knoxville that we hoped to have the apartment at 43 Barrow Street, beginning very soon, all to ourselves. He consented, which is to say he let us put him out, and was married himself within five months to Marcelle Leguia, a Basque girl who had come to America to be a nurse. We already knew her as an earthly paragon of affection and devotion, and nothing could have made us feel less guilty over having evicted Joe. Meanwhile, in the hours and days we had free from work, we were busy with our first apartment, which Dorothy, by magic it seemed to me, transformed from the bachelor quarters it had been into what was now her home and mine. We also began to hear from my relations in Illinois, who wanted to see *their* new relation. Grace, who kept chickens, sent us eggs, and later on we got from her delicious chicken meat which she had learned how to seal in cans.

We went out there, of course, as soon as we could; but this was not until next June. Then we traded our old roadster for a new one, shiny and black, and started west through Buffalo so that I might meet one of my new relations, Dorothy's Aunt Maude Lane. An hour this side of Buffalo we stopped on a bridge, got water out of the stream below, and washed our car, for we had been through rain. Then we went on in to see Mrs. Graffe's unmarried sister, the only Lane left in the city where Dorothy's grandparents had lived. Her grandfather had operated freight boats on the Great Lakes; Mrs. Graffe remembered going on one of them clear out to Duluth and back, and Dorothy cherished a barometer which had descended to her from this boat. Aunt Maude took us to Niagara Falls before we went on to Detroit, where Guy and his family introduced us to the cottage they had built on the north shore of Lake Erie, the Canadian shore to which slaves escaped before the Civil War by way of the Underground Railroad; their descendants still farmed there, in a climate, warmed by Lake Huron on the west, that permitted them to grow tobacco. We kept on then to Chicago, to see Paul. Of course he had known Dorothy in New York; but he wanted us to visit him in the room from which he went every day to work at Halsey, Stuart and Company, the bond house that had taken him in after business school. He was to marry Jessie Hess, who worked there too, and was to return to New York in 1931. Now a bachelor, he gave us his bed for a night and talked of Chase Love at the office, the man who had brought him to Chicago and who had been my overseer in Urbana the first summer I was with the Chautauqua.

After this, Urbana; and of course Villa Grove. My family, to my delight, took Dorothy in as if she were no stranger, which in a way was true because I had told her so much about them. I had even wondered whether my praise of them was over-praise; apparently it was not. Frank, for instance, was better-looking than his brother; she wished she had seen him first. At Villa Grove I helped Frank shock wheat on a stifling day in a field south of the house which was surrounded on two sides by oak woods, so that what breeze there was could not get through to relieve us. Grace and Dorothy brought us lemonade and crackers; and that night, to tease them, we pretended to have forgotten the lemonade. Crackers, we said, dry crackers— what torture for hot throats!

But then Dorothy and I had to think of starting back. We went by way of Cincinnati into Kentucky, where on another hot day we had a puncture. I thought I could fix it, but there were eleven holes in the inner tube, so that a farmer had to be asked for help. It was a time of drought, and the pond below his house had barely enough water in it to test the patches he put on. They held, so we continued through the bluegrass region I had always wanted to see—it was better than I ever thought—and from Lexington turned east again. The next night we spent at Harpers Ferry, in a hotel high above the junction of the Shenandoah and Potomac rivers. Both rivers have deep channels there, and railroads hug their banks. It seems to me that we listened all night to the combined sound of rushing water and echoing whistles: a grand, unforgettable music, worth keeping awake for. Then somehow home to Barrow Street, where Dorothy's vacation would be over although mine still had months to run. Nevertheless there were the weekends, when both of us were free.

Dorothy, an only child whose father died when she was thirteen, has always regretted that she had so few relatives to exchange for mine. But there were the Lanes. If Aunt Maude never left Buffalo, Uncle George now lived on Long Island with his wife and three tall, friendly sons. He worked in New York, at the Metropolitan Life Insurance Company, where Mrs. Graffe worked too; this had been necessary ever since her husband's death. The Lanes, I have insisted, were a fair exchange. Not only did I like their hearty voices and their abundance of good will—"God love you," Uncle George would say in a thundering voice, half humorous, half grave; in addition to that they were the first people I ever knew intimately whose entire lives had been lived in cities. I learned through them that I had been wrong if I supposed, as possibly I did, that this would dampen human nature or subdue it. Quite the contrary with Uncle George and his boys.

And certainly it was untrue of another family, not of relatives but of old friends, who lived in Jamaica, Long Island, where the father, Gurney Prytherch, owned a drugstore, and where I loved to go. Mr. Prytherch—the name is Welsh—was smaller than any Lane; he was round-faced, and his humor was more subtle and sly. He was enough in himself to make me glad of the world Dorothy brought with her as a dowry. He had a genius for conversation and for stories. In the back room of his store he regularly consorted over coffee with cronies who supplied him with even more tales than he was able to invent; or there would be a helper about the place, perhaps a colored man—one of these, he said, had called him "Mr. Pritheredge" —whom he might use to hang an anecdote upon. At home, a few blocks up from Jamaica Avenue, his wife Harriet kept two enormous male cats who I pretended to think were spoiled beyond endurance, though I endured them and admired them. Dorothy (Daudie) Prytherch had been Dorothy Graffe's best friend in her Brooklyn days, for that was where she grew up. Daudie was a humorist too, as her parents were, and as my own people were—the ones I remembered best, I mean—in Illinois.

Perhaps it is everyone's merciful lot to be born into a world of laughter, gentle or boisterous according as chance sees fit to dispose. I sometimes think, however, that I was especially fortunate in this respect. For here were these people too; and Dorothy's father, George Graffe, was said to have been always joking too in his wry, irregular fashion. His last years had been difficult, as Dorothy was to reveal in her novel, *Those First Affections,* in 1938. I learned more then than she had ever told me about the bittersweet experiences of her childhood, and about the heroic measures Mrs. Graffe had taken to maintain them both.

IV

The remainder of that summer's leisure passed in visits to my new people on Long Island, to friends in other places, and of course to Carl and Irita in Cornwall. But also there were weekend searches for a house in the country which we hoped it would be possible to buy. From the first we had taken for granted the necessity of such a house—preferably, I thought, not in Cornwall, for I was reluctant to follow Carl there and divide his solitude in two. So we drove our Ford through Westchester County and the southwestern corner of Connecticut, the corner nearest New York. We inquired in Newtown, Brookfield, and such places; the prices were too high, yet we kept on inquiring, and wasting our eyesight on houses we knew were not for sale because other people had been lucky enough to find them first. We had almost given up, for 1923 at any rate, when suddenly on September 2nd the decision was made—in Cornwall, and by Carl, who if he ever knew of my scruple disregarded it as of no moment. Dorothy's mother, being with us there for a few days, went riding one afternoon with Carl; and when they came home they were both eloquent about a house—indeed, a farm—they had seen in Cornwall Hollow. Carl, who often walked over to the Hollow, had never gone up a certain road to the Bradford place. But this afternoon he did go there, and he thought like Mrs. Graffe that it was the place for us if we could get it.

The next day Dorothy and I went up that road alone, and within ten minutes I knew Carl was right. We found a farm of 150 acres, two thirds of it pine and hemlock woods, though there was hardwood too; and at its center, surrounded by huge maples and then by open fields, was an old white house with which Dorothy says I fell in love at first sight. It was not in the best condition, nor was any of the dozen or so gray barns and sheds that grouped themselves about it. But this did not seem to matter. The farmer and his wife, sitting on a stone by the front door, said Yes, the place might be for sale. And for how much, if it was? They looked at each other before he said: "Five thousand, I guess." Which seemed a modest price, but we had no such sum. We had $200 in the bank. I wonder now what could have been in our minds when we looked at the expensive places south of there. Five thousand. Well, could we look around? We could. He would take us to see the spring.

Our walk up through the woods and across Bradford Brook to where a rotting wooden box—it is cement now—contained the spring decided me if nothing had before. Water rose out of white sand in "boils" as big as dinner plates; and an iron pipe —it is brass now—conducted it by gravity to the house. On the way back, through deeper hemlock woods where the sun never came, I did so little to conceal my delight that Dorothy, dropping back beside me, warned me against too great a show of eagerness; it was better, she said, to act as if I had some doubts. But I had none, and when we came out into the ox pasture which overlooked the orchard and the house, I knew

141

we must have this place if we ever could. Dorothy, now walking ahead with the farmer, was exactly of the same mind; and soon, indoors with the farmer's wife, she was imagining herself there on some future day as the hostess, not the guest.

We actually saw very little of the Bradford place that day. Now that I know every inch of it I can think of a thousand items we missed. Perhaps the essence of it spoke aloud, if only just above a whisper; perhaps I knew at once a certain secret I have since kept largely to myself. Here was my *old* home, my first one, long before I lived that other life in Illinois. New England has a way of doing this to people; they can be homesick for it even if they have never seen it. But the piece of it I saw was pulling me, pulling me, as if it had magnetic force; I was homesick on the spot. And it was more than the house that did this, though I have never ceased to think of its windows and its eighteenth-century roof as peculiarly right. It was the whole: a little Eden of woods and fields, surrounded at just the proper distance by hills of various shapes, some sharp, some round, some long and level at the top; patterned in the open places by stone walls that looked as if they had been there forever, but here and there as well by solitary trees; traversed its entire length by a brook which from the house was only to be heard, not seen, since it never emerged from the forest that kept its waters dark; and stamped as human after all by a cunning distribution of buildings, painted or unpainted, each one of which seemed also to have been there even before any man or beast elected to move in.

I do not exaggerate. To me it was an earthly paradise. And if it was empty of what it once contained, as Dante's was, that made it all the more attractive. The Hollow, like many such hidden places in New England, was from one point of view quite dead. History had passed it by; its population had been dwindling for more than a century; there were no large families in the neighboring houses, and some of those houses had fallen down. At the bottom, along the Hollenbeck River, there was no longer a store, a blacksmith shop, a mill, or any sign of community existence. There was only a church, no longer used; a schoolhouse which to be sure was used, but now by a handful of children instead of the dozens who once romped and shouted at recess; a graveyard; and a monument, with cannon balls about its base, to General John Sedgwick, who had lived not far from the Bradfords, up Hautboy Hill, and had built a mansion there just before the Civil War came and took his life at Spottsylvania. Even on the Bradford place there was a small graveyard, older than the one below and no longer used, where not only the Bradford who built this house was buried but many another too, along with numerous Sedgwicks, Hurlburts, and Harrisons—these had been the first families, the aristocracy of the Hollow. As for the Bradfords, no break in their line had occurred until the late war; then James, the last of them, died a bachelor, as John, also a bachelor, had died some years before, and the place was sold at auction. An insurance man in Torrington, twelve miles east, bought it so that he could cut some of its lumber off; then he sold it to the farmer we found sitting on the doorstone, disconsolate because he had not been able to make a go of it with his cows.

We knew this only later, when we learned most of the foregoing facts. But in a sense I knew all of it now. And far from caring, I was happy: I thought I had come home to a place that circumstances had conspired to keep for me until I came. For as a place it had not died. Eden can sleep, but it does not disappear. At the foot of the road there was an ancient shingled house where Will Bailey and his wife, whom I only heard about this day, had lived as tenants for many years. They belonged here too; they were remnants of a past I would doubtless have time to understand if I joined them in the drama of survival and renewal.

But could we buy the place? The farmer had guessed so, for five thousand. And we had two hundred. I asked him if there was a mortgage we could take over. He said there were two: one for $1,800, held through a bank, and another one for

$1,000, held by his father over in York State. He thought there would be no difficulty about transferring those. But this left $2,200 to be given him in cash. I proposed that I pay him $200 now, to bind the bargain, and deliver the balance a little later. He consented; I wrote the check; and a piece of paper was signed by both of us, saying that Dorothy and I were owners of the farm provided other moneys followed in due course. Then we drove back to Carl's house, in a fever of anxiety lest the transaction prove impossible; but in a fever of anticipation too, for we had already begun to chatter about the work that lay ahead if we succeeded: the painting, the papering, the cleaning up, the tearing down, the furnishing (with what?), the cutting of grass, the starting of gardens.

The first mortgage was no problem, but the second one was. The old man I went to see about it had given it to his son, but why should he transfer it to a stranger, especially a stranger from the city? He had no use for city people. I climbed onto the seat of the wagon in which he was hauling crushed stone and spent hours convincing him that I was a country fellow at heart: I had been born on a farm, and I sympathized with his fears. He accepted me at last; but now there were two thousand large dollars to be found. I wrote to Uncle Walter, proposing a loan. And sooner than I expected the money came. I was eventually to hear from my father that Uncle Walter said he was helping us "buy scenery." Anyhow the money came, and Eden was ours.

All that remained was years of labor that neither Dorothy nor I would ever give to another place; not only is there no such place, but such labor can be done only once in this life. Later that fall, when the farmer moved out, we walked over from Carl's house and slept in the big barn, in hay that failed to keep us warm; we built enormous bonfires and burned trash; we made a list of necessary repairs, including a new shingle roof; we learned from the neighbors that one of them, Sherman Bailey, a nephew of the old man at the foot of the hill, would cut the hay next summer, and that Felix Jasmin, father of the farmer's wife whom we had put out of her house, might do it the following year; we planned, and then we planned again. In the spring we drove up as early as we could with a cot, an oil stove, and four small chairs, only to discover that the road had washed out because no one was there to watch it; it was impassable by our Ford. Mrs. Bailey told us how we could drive through the fields, past the old cemetery. But the fields were wet, and we ended by carrying these objects up between us. We put them in the smallest room of the house, off the dining room that we were going to make the living room, and had our first meal of soup and beans and tea.

But that was only the beginning. Over the winter we had had a fireplace built—the old one disappeared before the Civil War, when stoves were coming in—and although there was still no hearth and no mantel we could make a token fire. Beyond this there was nothing but the future to contemplate. In that future we were to be helped many times by Carl and Paul, who whenever they came did day labor manfully in our cause; and it was Carl who as soon as the mantel was built brought an old clock he had found in Litchfield, set it over the center of the fireplace, and started it ticking. The mantel had been built by a Negro boy from Hampton Institute whose services Carl lent us for the purpose. He was helping Carl with a new place he himself had bought, the Wickwire place on Cream Hill. Another Hampton boy, James Lewis, was to spend two summers with us as a carpenter, putting hundreds of things in shape after generations of neglect or decay. But the endless story, told so many times in other places, does not need to be retold.

V

The summer of 1924 we had decided to spend abroad. This may seem strange in view of our obsession with Eden. But there were several good reasons for going now. If we should have children it would be hard to go later. And certain major repairs that I could not make myself would be finished by the time we got back. There was the new roof; the stone foundations had crumbled in several places; and just as the dining room was to become the living room, so the kitchen was to become the dining room, and back of that, in a low wing that went off at right angles, the woodshed was to become the kitchen. And there would have to be at least a modicum of plumbing: the pipe that ran with water from the spring could be moved where it belonged, into the new kitchen, and another pipe could lead to a spring box we would have built —something like Grandma Butz's in Potomac—to keep things cool in the pantry. All this we left in the hands of George Crosby, a builder in West Cornwall; and in June we sailed on the *Rochambeau* for Europe. We did have children; we did have work to do, including the writing of books; and we would not go again for thirty-one years.

Paris came first. We stayed at the Hotel Corneille, where Joe Krutch and I had stayed, and in fact Dorothy was required to relive most of my joyful experience four years ago. I made her walk so many places the first afternoon that I wore her out; but she recovered, and we went everywhere: to Versailles, to Chartres (she has never forgotten those bells), as well as to sections of the city, nearby or remote, which one or the other of us felt curiosity about. Or we simply sat in our room and looked out over a pleasant balcony at what went on below: students at the bookstalls in the Odéon across the way, or taxis as they rattled and hooted by. One rainy evening I was to remember next year in "After Dry Weather":

> If the people under that portico
> Are happy, and point at the pattering drops;
> If barehead boys are parading below
> Musical eaves of tall house-tops;
>
> If you lean out of the window here,
> Contented so with the pavement's shine,
> And laugh as the covers of cabs appear
> With passengers in them dressed to dine . . .

Or we strolled along the Seine, stopping when we were tired at cafés for coffee or wine, perhaps with good bread and pie-shaped pieces of Brie, which I thought the best cheese in the world.

Then Italy. Genoa, Florence, Padua, Assisi, Naples, Pompeii, Capri, and Rome: but the greatest of these was Rome. On the *Rochambeau* we had met Tenney Frank and his wife, bound for Rome where he was to be in charge this year of the American Academy. I knew his life of Cicero; indeed, I had reviewed it. We looked him up as he had invited us to do, and he showed us many things we would never have seen by ourselves. One evening, from a terrace that overlooked the mountains to the north, he identified Soracte. "Oh, yes," I said, "Soracte." "I suppose you know it from Byron," he said. "From Horace," I assured him; and he was gratified. One of his amusements as he went about the city was to ask little Roman boys if they could read the old inscriptions on arches and tombs. They said they could not, for they knew no Latin. But then he would ask them to read the words aloud as if they were Italian; and often, with a radiance in their eyes, they understood.

But most of the time we were alone. We had a room in a small hotel, now gone, which overlooked the Piazza di Venezia. We ate in obscure restaurants, for we had little money; we were living on my Columbia salary checks, forwarded monthly by Mrs. Graffe, and for days before one came we might subsist on nothing but anchovies, bread, and cherries, all three of which were good but cheap. On the train back to Paris we had no money at all, and did not scruple to eat the remains of a lunch, mousy at best, which had been left in our compartment by a pale woman—we decided she was a governess—who could never have brought herself to abandon so much as one crumb before.

A few days in Paris, and then we went by way of Belgium and Holland to England, retracing my route through the Low Countries but having some special adventures too. One afternoon in Edam we ran out of a sudden shower to stand in the doorway of a shop that proved when we peered through its windows to contain old furniture. Our house in Cornwall had no furniture, so we went in, if only idly, to see what was there. A small ancient man with whom Dorothy could talk German let us look at our leisure; and before long we were wondering whether certain pieces—a big china cabinet, a smaller cabinet that could be fastened to the wall, three wooden arm chairs, and one side chair to match, all ancient oak, mellowed with age—could ever be got across the Atlantic to Cornwall Hollow. Finally we took the proprietor into our confidence; and were amazed to hear him say that when we did have the money, perhaps next year in America, we could send it to him and he would dispatch these pieces by ocean freight; meanwhile he would consider them sold. And that was how it went. Next spring we sent him the money—no great amount, for the prices were absurdly low—and during the summer Sherman Bailey delivered them to us in solid crates as big as piano boxes. They were our first substantial furniture: the center about which all the rest of it was to grow.

In London there was even more for me to insist upon Dorothy's looking at right away, since I had been here longer. She says she has not forgotten our first bus ride from the Liverpool Street station. "There is the Bank of England. See the sign—Threadneedle Street? Now here is St. Paul's. As soon as we get around it we'll be in Fleet Street; beyond that will be the Strand." I was eager; I was proprietary; I suppose I was ridiculous; yet here was my own city, so to speak, that I was showing to my wife. We found lodgings in the Middle Temple, in a small house that was not to survive the next war. I was overjoyed by this good fortune, for the Temple was still for me the center of ancient London, the timeless city which I knew by sight, by hearing, and by smell. Not that we confined ourselves to the space it occupied between the Law Courts and the Thames. We went everywhere, I seem to remember. Then we struck out north to Cambridge, Ely, Lincoln, York, and

Durham; crossed over the moors by train to Keswick and the Lake Country; walked or rode through that as Joe and I had done (we even climbed Helvellyn); and returned to London through Chester and Oxford.

Back in London, we agreed that there was still one corner of England we must see. This was Cornwall, and there were two weeks left in which to see it. Reading advertisements for cottages there, we selected one at Helston, halfway along the southern coast between the Lizard and Land's End, and having made the necessary arrangements went down to occupy it. It was an old miner's cottage, not far from the sea, with walls two feet thick, small windows, and a narrow door from which a path led to the road. Inside there was a miniature iron stove that needed study before cooking could be done upon it; but the study was made, and soon we had settled into a routine that satisfied us as few things had done all summer. We took excursions daily: to the Lizard, St. Michael's Mount, Redruth, Land's End, and King Arthur's seat at Tintagel. We walked to the sea below us, winding our way along deep, eroded lanes between stone walls studded with gorse. We visited castles, and all but prehistoric tin mines to which the Phoenicians were rumored to have sailed through the Pillars of Hercules, then up past Spain and France to this lone promontory. Or we sat in the sun outside our little house and talked or read. In Helston we learned how alien our language was to the shop-keepers who spoke—not the old Cornish, of course, but a dialect of modern English which was so rapid and strange that we too were at a loss to understand.

Once, when there had been bad weather for several days, I cabled Joe Krutch for money with which to buy raincoats. "If you find that you are running short of money," he had written in June, "don't hesitate to ask me for some." It came immediately; but we did not know until we were home that Joe had got out of bed, where he was convalescing from an appendicitis operation, to go to the bank and send it. We had left our Ford for him and Marcelle to drive while we were gone, and they had enjoyed it during intervals of his work on Poe, then in progress. I knew this, for he had written to say so; but I could not have guessed about the operation. Then our two weeks were up, and we sailed from Southampton on the *Orbita*. We needed the raincoats on deck, for there were strong seas. At New York we were met by Paul, Carl, Marcelle, and Joe, the last of whom was well again and wanted to hear particularly about Paris. I did not tell him then about some poems I had written during the voyage home: these were for my second volume. The first volume was about to appear.

VI

The poems in *Spring Thunder,* published that fall, were of the utmost simplicity. People called them country poems, and doubtless this was fair even when it implied a limitation. Stuart Sherman, writing me about the book, went further and stated the limitation. "On the whole," he said, "it reminds me of Thoreau at the stage when he was perfecting his pencils. That is intended to be complimentary—with reservations. I suppose spring thunder ought to roar softly. And I suppose your poetic vein runs from a spring that you opened when you were, say, eighteen or twenty. By which I mean to suggest that the *personality* delivered by the book strikes me as a considerably earlier one than you now walk around with, except for a group of lines here and there. . . . As a matter of fact your 'tang' has a large admixture of intellectual ingredients. You are yourself for the people you live with because you cogitate and excogitate. And in order to deliver your force I think you need a different set of symbols and costumes than the quiet country yields. . . . The piece in this book that most took me was Reverie After War: 1866." Sherman was characteristically acute. He did not happen to know of the attempts I had made since 1920 to write poetry of a more ambitious order than he found in this book, or of my instinct, when those attempts failed, to fall back upon subject matter I knew perhaps only too well. Nor could he have foreseen that in time—actually, quite soon—I would make other such attempts, and "deliver" without too much loss the self that cogitated. Neither he nor I could have known that I would continue to this day to write both country poems and poems of the mind, wherever the mind may be supposed to dwell; for the country, just as it is, has never ceased to woo me into speech, and I have never condescended to it as a subject, nor did I then. Nevertheless the letter was valuable because of the distinction it drew. And I could even smile knowingly at Sherman's preference for "Reverie After War," since that had been a product of my reading, as many other poems have been since. It too was a country poem, but it had come to me by way of John Muir's account in *A Thousand-Mile Walk to the Gulf* of some long-haired men he met among the Southern hills who lived by violence even though their war was over. Years later, and by a similar process, I was to write "The Ancient Couple on Lu Mountain" because I had read one of Chiang Yee's *Silent Traveller* books; and so on—the list would be long.

The next four years were eventful in a wide variety of ways. Within that period I published two more books of poems; Dorothy published her first three novels; our two sons were born; and in addition to teaching at Columbia I worked as literary editor of *The Nation*. The books of poems were *7 P.M.* (1926) and *Now the Sky* (1928). Sherman's death in 1926—he drowned in Lake Michigan, off Manistee where he spent his summers—was and remains so grave a loss for me that it seems out of proportion to remark upon its preventing, as of course it did, his ever knowing whether these books delivered the person he had thought I was. In some measure they did, though it is not for me to apply the measure. I was growing up; I was thinking; and I was learning how to write like one who thinks—and feels, too, but my effort was to make the two activities appear as one.

A sign that they did may have been a letter from Robinson Jeffers saying that he found in 7 *P.M.* "secret and beautiful things presented with a quietness that is sometimes terrible. I . . . think of you as the only American who loves his country—articulately at least." Two years later he was to write me of *Now the Sky,* which he also reviewed: "I have a criticism, and no doubt from me it will surprise you. I think you are too (vulgar word) pessimistic. 'End of Singing' and the others in that section. Civilization is bitter in that essential way to everyone, but I think we can remember that there was a time before and will be a time after it, and can keep an important part of us timeless enough to be uncivilized. You have that timeless part, and it feels menaced and is sorrowful; as mine was gnashing its teeth in a rage a couple of years ago. But these fancies are recent and unformed and perhaps nonsense. . . . I don't know another poem like Civil War, that fills half a continent with its weirdness."

I loved my country and I felt menaced by its civilization. The pair of statements fascinates me now. I no longer feel the menace, whatever the shortcomings so easily to be seen in any civilization at any time or place; yet I have never lost sight of the subject Jeffers so delicately touched. It is the subject of any poetry that is serious; for when poetry is serious it tries to exist both in and out of time; and when it aims to express a love of the world it refuses to conceal the many reasons why the world is hard to love, though we must love it because we have no other, and to fail to love it is not to exist at all. I remember saying something like this to George Genzmer, my Columbia colleague to whom *Now the Sky* was dedicated; 7 *P.M,* incidentally, had been dedicated to Joe Krutch. I often talked with Genzmer, after lunch at the Faculty Club, about scholarly and literary things; he was to become a biographer, but then he had not specialized, so that our conversation, like our correspondence in later years, ranged over the world of books wherein this gentle and erudite and rather owlish man was forever at home.

I Start to Work: 1920–1928

When my poems did not deal with men and the habitations
of men (for instance, the houses and barns of Cornwall) they
dealt with animals and stars. "Van Doren likes animals." I
remember a paragraph in one review which began with that
categorical if somewhat childish statement. The statement remains true. As for the stars, I had learned enough about them
since college to lament the obsolescence of my beloved constellations as a sufficient guide to their number and distribution. I said so in "Now the Sky"; and twenty-five years later,
having learned still more about the utterly unimaginable size
of the universe, I said so again in "The God of Galaxies":

The god of galaxies has more to govern
Than the first men imagined, when one mountain
Trumpeted his anger, and one rainbow,
Red in the east, restored them to his love.
One earth it was, with big and lesser torches,
And stars by night for candles. And he spoke
To single persons, sitting in their tents.

Now streams of worlds, now powdery great whirlwinds
Of universes far enough away
To seem but fog-wisps in a bank of night
So measureless the mind can sicken, trying—
Now seas of darkness, shoreless, on and on
Encircled by themselves, yet washing farther
Than the last triple sun, revolving, shows.

The god of galaxies—how shall we praise him?
For so we must, or wither. Yet what word
Of words? And where to send it, on which night
Of winter stars, of summer, or by autumn
In the first evening of the Pleiades?
The god of galaxies, of burning gases,
May have forgotten Leo and the Bull.

But God remembers, and is everywhere.
He even is the void, where nothing shines.
He is the absence of his own reflection
In the deep gulf; he is the dusky cinder
Of pure fire in its prime; he is the place
Prepared for hugest planets: black idea,
Brooding between fierce poles he keeps apart.

Those altitudes and oceans, though, with islands
Drifting, blown immense as by a wind,
And yet no wind; and not one blazing coast
Where thought could live, could listen—oh, what word
Of words? Let us consider it in terror,
And say it without voice. Praise universes
Numberless. Praise all of them. Praise Him.

And Dorothy was writing novels: *Strangers* (1926), *Flowering Quince* (1927), and *Brother and Brother* (1928). Also in those years she was having children: Charles in 1926 and John in 1928. Some people said then that they could not see how she did so much, for in addition she was helping to edit *The Nation*. They were productive years for all of us. In 1926 Joe Krutch published his *Poe,* and Carl his *Other Provinces* and *The Ninth Wave*. In 1925 Carl and I had collaborated on a textbook about modern British and American literature. In 1927 I wrote at Carl's request a short volume on Edwin Arlington Robinson to be issued with his *Tristram* by the Literary Guild, of which Carl was editor. And in 1928 I compiled *An Anthology of World Poetry,* an undertaking rendered easier by the fact that Albert Boni, its publisher, had collected many of the books from which I would assemble its contents. But Dorothy wrote her novels with a celerity that made the rest of us wonder. Not that they took no effort; they took a great deal, or the people in them, notably Emily in *Flowering Quince* and Laly in *Brother and Brother,* women shut out from the fullness of life by inner difficulties which it would be inadequate to call repressions, could not have been so interesting. But Dorothy, making use of what early or late hours she had free, did write them rapidly and publish them. And she did become the mother of two sons. Charles was born on Barrow Street; but because of a dangerous illness when he was little more than a year old—Carl saved his life by giving him blood—we thought we should move into a more commodious apartment, and there the next year, on West 9th Street, John was born. Charles was named for his two grandfathers, Charles Hollister Lane and Charles Lucius Van Doren; but since he was my father's first grandson he was given a middle name beginning with L—Lincoln, not Lucius, since he was born on February 12th. John's life was saved by Carl when he was three, in the lake at Cornwall. Waterwings that had slipped to his feet were holding his head down when Carl appeared and pulled him out.

VII

Then there was *The Nation,* which for four years took three of my days each week while Columbia took two. I succeeded Irita as literary editor; Carl had left in 1922 to be co-editor of the *Century* with Glenn Frank, and when Irita left in the fall of 1924 it was to help Stuart Sherman edit the book section of the New York *Herald Tribune*—he had abandoned teaching at last. But in the same fall Joe Krutch became dramatic critic of *The Nation,* succeeding Ludwig Lewisohn; and besides there were Freda Kirchwey, Lewis Gannett, Arthur Warner, and others whom I had known since 1920. It was a busy and exciting time. In one respect I was an unsatisfactory literary editor: I did not get all the books reviewed promptly, nor was I considered to have a sense of what topics were most timely. I got on well, though, with the reviewers—not always an easy assignment, for most of them wrote more words than had been ordered, and my cuts sometimes displeased them; but this never happened to the copy of B. H. Haggin, who when he came on as music critic made it clear that he did not want so much as a comma changed, and I was happy to comply not only because he was so fine a critic but also because his English, put together with excruciating care, was nothing less than perfect. I wrote a weekly book review myself, in a column called First Glance, which gave me secret pleasure because in that column I could be as untimely as I liked, savoring reprints and salvaging unpopular titles from oblivion. And I published some new poets, or if not strictly new ones, then poets whom it was a privilege to help make better known. Mr. Villard often suffered over poems I had printed: they were difficult, they were queer, or they were "not hopeful." They were, for example, by James Rorty, Maxwell Bodenheim, Robert Graves, Laura Riding, Hart Crane, and Allen Tate.

It was Allen Tate who brought me Hart Crane's poems, just as it was he who made me sit down in his basement on Bank Street and listen to Phelps Putnam's "Hasbrouck and the Rose"; I can still hear his soft, very intelligent voice intoning two of the lines:

> In Springfield, Massachusetts I devoured
> The mystic, the improbable, the Rose.

Allen, who as one of the Fugitives of Tennessee—more specifically, as one of those wits for whom John Crowe Ransom at Vanderbilt University was the Ben Jonson of his time, counseling and comparing notes with them in a responsible, professional way—had learned to be generous with the work of others, would have been generous in any case, for that was his nature. He thought I was generous to him because I published "Mr. Pope" and other brilliant poems of his. But I found him singularly generous to me; which was gratifying, because his critical instrument had the finest razor edge, and he could decapitate with it a person or a poet he despised.

He and his wife, the novelist Caroline Gordon, were spending the winter of 1925–1926 in the same house with Hart Crane, near Patterson, New York. From there Allen came to town one day to have lunch with me, and our talk ran among so many subjects, and so easily and eagerly, that he wrote me after he went back: "I get very little 'literary conversation,' and I miss it. . . . There are few persons these days who do not mistake obsessions, missions, remedies, and purposes for ideas. . . . To hear you speak as you did of Wordsworth was worth, in itself, a trip to town; there aren't ten people in America who have that feeling for *literature*. . . . Finally, let me be self-conscious and offer excuses for a long letter in this age of 'hurry.' But, you see, I am still very young and retain my enthusiasms; 'letters' are not yet a routine, they are still a passion. But I am almost afraid to tell you that I am just twenty-five; the fact might shake some of the confidence which I very gratefully feel you have in me."

This was the first of a great many letters Allen was to write me over the next thirty years. And it was the last one that was the least self-conscious. In November, 1929, he began one from Paris, where he had gone on a Guggenheim fellowship: "Dear Mark. But who is he? Mark Van Doren? It seems to me that I knew him long ago, and even cherished much affection and esteem for him, in the days before I wrote him a letter that went months unanswered. Ah, I have him placed at last. He is the scholarly looking poet who always looks as if . . . he were going to say grace, but says instead damn. He also looks as if he had never been interrupted, but constantly expects to be. He also has a plan for every minute of the year—which rouses Tate to envy not great enough to stimulate imitation, because plan would bore him to death. He prefers to be harried, never quite caught up."

The Tates moved to New York the next year after Patterson and lived on Bank Street, where Dorothy and I made the acquaintance of their infant daughter Nancy; at that age she addressed our infant son as "Charlie Fandory." We also met their literary friends, who then, as always since, were legion; once we brewed with them a barrel of wine and called it sherry. Allen's reviews of my own poetry were on the whole the most interesting ones it had. They were generous and yet judicious, with expressed or implied reservations that seemed to come out of an age-old occupation with the art; and they were written as if I were a complete stranger to him, as when he put on his critic's robes I was. He and Caroline did not stay long in New York, and after they left we missed them. We were to see more of them in time; and for many years these warm, bright letters came from Allen. They were of course intermittent, as he had accused mine of being. In his own case the reason, I sometimes thought, was a trait which everyone had noted in him: readily enthusiastic, he could as readily be bored. He would change in an instant from a child who remembered nothing to an old man who remembered everything, and suddenly, like the soul in Emily Dickinson's poem, would close the valves of his attention. I have said of him since:

> He was the soonest friendly,
> But then the soonest tired.

Always, however, he could be the child again to whom everything and everybody was brave and new. If I tried in those days to find an explanation of all this in my own insufficiency at certain times, my thought ran on the necessary difference between South and North. Allen was more conscious of being Southern than I was of being Northern, but his conversation sharpened my sense of the difference as well as forgave me for my part in it. One thing I learned from him I should have known before. The latitude of Urbana and Villa Grove, particularly of Villa Grove, is the dividing line in Illinois between its southern and its northern halves; for if above this line the settlement was largely from New England and New York, the settlement below it was largely from Virginia and Kentucky, the most famous of those latter immigrants being Lincoln, long a man of infinite interest to me. Allen seemed to think that I had marks in me of both the cultures; my speech was not Southern, but many of my idioms were familiar to him from his boyhood in Kentucky. Nevertheless the difference remained; and I could wonder whether he alternated between remembering and forgetting it. This question of mine was to suggest itself in the dedication of *Jonathan Gentry* to Allen; the middle section of that poem is called "Civil War," and its hero becomes aware of a related question.

Another meeting I owed to *The Nation* was that with Scott Buchanan. He came to the office one day, I think in 1927, to ask me whether I would give some lectures at the People's Institute, which he administered with Everett Dean Martin;

actually, the lectures if I gave them would be not at Cooper Union, the headquarters of the Institute, but at the Muhlenberg Branch of the New York Public Library, where Scott had started a special program of adult education. I could talk about any aspect of literature, but he suggested among other things a series of talks on the great comic writers of the world. I thought I was busy, but I could not refuse him. He instantly interested me for reasons I found it difficult to define and find even more difficult now that I have known him closely for thirty years.

The central reason, I suppose, was that he seemed in some rare way to be serious. The serious man is rare at any time, but at moments I can believe that Scott is the only contemporary specimen. I mean by the word all that it usually implies and then a great deal more—so much more that the original meaning tends to disappear beneath an irony, a humorous imagination, and a lightness of soul (surely the soul weighs nothing) which are the final sign and seal of seriousness. We cannot take seriously a man who has no humor, nor a man who has nothing else. Scott's humor (as an ingredient and chief proof of his seriousness) was New England in its color and depth; its genius was understatement, inspired by respect amounting almost to fear in the presence of great things like truth and illusion. After a boyhood in Vermont, where his father like mine was a country doctor, he had lived in western Massachusetts; he had studied at Amherst, Oxford, and Harvard; at Harvard he had written a dissertation in philosophy which Alfred North Whitehead, the professor in charge, had found formidable but fine—it was to be published as *Possibility;* and now here he was administering adult education to people in New York whose minds had had no formal training comparable with his.

His own mind took delight in formal problems, but he had none of the superstition, common among professors of philosophy, that the right form had been found. To Scott the oldest questions were still new, and for all he could see an uninitiated philosopher—that is, anybody at all—might, if he were honest and if he thought as well as he could, throw valuable light upon them. He trusted even me to do that. I had never thought of myself as a speculative person; certainly I had never called myself a philosopher. But talking to Scott I became one to the best of my ability. I watched what I said with a new awareness, trying not to be superficial or absurd. Not that he appeared to be judging me. On the contrary, he seemed to think I might really say something he had never heard before. But the result was that I did my very best; which was never as good as his, for he was always ahead of me and has remained so, and yet I felt myself growing into something I had so far scarcely been. This is the experience of anyone who has known Scott: of his students, for he is a unique teacher, and of his friends. His strength lies in his faith that every living person has an intellect: the human intellect. The people who came to the Library were possibly as important, he could believe then, as Whitehead himself.

He was entirely different from Mortimer Adler, whose acquaintance he made at about this time. He seemed lazy by comparison; he never pressed an argument; his air was of one who knew nothing yet, though eventually he might have intimations. But as much as Mortimer he made me reflect upon what it means to be a poet. Poetry, it appeared, was even more important to him than philosophy. And he laughed when I said I knew nothing but technical things about it. He laughed, with the result that I myself became more serious. If I was to be a philosopher at all, it would be in the poems I wrote, which for this purpose had only to be true. Scott, like his god Plato, both trusted and distrusted poetry; it was too seldom true even to the writer's vision. Or I should say, like his god Socrates, whom more than any man I know he resembles—first of all, as I say again, for his belief that any man may be worth talking to. He came to the house, and our families became dear friends. Then like Allen Tate he was to live elsewhere over America, west and south. But we never let this matter.

The Krutches meanwhile had bought a house in Cornwall. They were not to keep it, for they thought it too far from New York. But for several years we had their company in both places. Joe at that time was not the naturalist he would become at Redding, to which they moved. But even then he experimented with sensitive plants in his garden—he would take us out in the dark to show them off by flashlight—and he luxuriated in the spectacle of his cat Minou enjoying the country as only cats know how to enjoy it. Joe was still an authority on those subtle creatures. One of the best stories he ever told was of a boy who ran away from home one afternoon, but when it grew dark and cold decided to give up and go back. All the way home he wondered how he should explain his action—his withdrawal and return. He loved these people after all, but how could he say it? He did not count on the chance that they would not have missed him. It was a large family, and none of them when he walked into the kitchen showed any surprise. He sat in a corner, still wondering how he could speak of the long time he had been away. Then Tabby strolled in. And he said: "I see you've got the same old cat." As for Marcelle, I have never forgotten the week when I was in Cornwall alone, in May, and she worried over whether I was feeding myself properly. It was a beautiful week outdoors, and I had gone up to do a dozen jobs that needed doing; but I was often so tired when I came in that I ate next to nothing, or at best fried something out of a can. Knowing this by intuition, she appeared one day with asparagus out of her garden. I prepared it as she directed, and felt that my life was saved.

I was glad in 1925 when Joe and Marcelle could meet my father. He came out from Urbana to see us, dragging one foot a little because he had had a stroke. Driving home one night with my mother from Villa Grove he stopped at a railroad crossing, and when the train was past could not feel the pedals, for his feet were numb. He had got over it well enough, and now we met him at the Lackawanna station in Hoboken—he had come all the way on passes, being a railroad man—and took him as soon as he had seen New York to the farm in Cornwall which he wanted to see even more. Like Uncle Walter he had supposed it was nothing but scenery—rocks and rills—though he had nothing against scenery as such; but what meadows there were among the mountains amazed him with their rich green grass, and he had long talks about dairy farming with our neighbor, Willis Hurlburt.

Our own place gave him the purest pleasure. He insisted upon walking over every part of it with me, in spite of the fact that walking had ceased to be easy for him. He particularly praised the brook as it descended through the hemlocks northeast of the house; and one day he created a little brook where none had been before. Across from the house, in a field with a huge boulder at its center, was an old sawmill I had begun to use for a study. Above it there had been a pond, though now it was silted full except for a trickle of water that came through. Below the building this water seeped through spongy ground until it re-entered the big brook at another place. My father took a shovel over and cut a channel between the building and the big brook. Soon a stream was running, and it runs today. I asked him then: "Is anything more fun than playing with water?" He chuckled and said No.

But water reminds me. One evening he told Marcelle, who as a onetime nurse he thought would enjoy it, his story of the patient he doused in the rain barrel at Hope. She says she has not forgotten how he laughed over it until he grew speechless. Laughter like that, she announced, was good for people. She did not know how good it was for him. The electric road and the mortgages on the farms had ceased to be laughing matters.

VIII

In 1928 the Krutches were in Europe, where *The Nation* had sent Joe to write some articles about the theater. Among other places they visited Moscow, and a letter from Vienna, the next stop, reported upon Russia. Its form of government, Joe said, might be here to stay; "nevertheless I as you know . . . prefer the present (perhaps the past too) to the future, and I am not heroic enough to care for a revolutionary society." Back in New York he found nothing more revolutionary than the spirit of the 1920's, whatever that was.

It is a famous decade, and Joe and I were in the midst of it, yet neither he nor I can define it now. There were wild parties; Dorothy and I remember being invited somewhere for Sunday breakfast, and being given even at that peaceful hour tumblers full of home-made gin, with only a dash of orange juice added to mitigate the stench. But my own memory is chiefly of hard work. It was a thriving time for literature; everything was tried out, and many things succeeded that would not have done so in a less sanguine city. Anybody could find literary employment of some sort even if he could not get his books published. Grub Street had moved uptown. The danger, Joe said in an article he called "The Curse of Opportunity," was that hack work might become too easy to find for writers who should be giving their main strength to books. Once the problem of the writer had been to keep alive. Now it was to keep free of prefaces and reviews. Yet until prosperity went over the precipice in 1929 there were few who worried about this.

It was a carefree age, of course, for those who had put their minds out to pasture. An example for me was Herbert Gorman, a free-lance writer of great personal charm whom I met through Carl. His wife, Jean Wright, was a decade later to become Carl's own wife after his divorce from Irita. But now, in intervals between novels and biographies he wrote to order for publishers who found any idea attractive, Herbert cavorted in the fields of what seemed an undying literary summer. He sent me in August, 1927, from Provincetown on Cape Cod where he was taking a rest, this Babylonian letter:

To Marcus Valerius, hail!
Your rolled missive discovered me reclining in my summer villa, Bicuspid, on Capus Codus, where, to lascivious flutes, I dream the hours away. Stretched out on beds of roses and smeared with rare unguents from Clancy's Drug Store (unguents which Aesculapius informs me will remedy the torrid macerations of the epidermis occasioned by the over-amorous osculations of the God-damned sun) I repose idly and observe the gyrations of my slave-girls brought at great expense from Bithynia. More and more I am convinced of the philosophy of Petronius: "Never give a sucker an even break." At the same time an intense ennui has settled upon me and neither rare unguents nor dancing girls nor the golden wine of Samos can move me from that lethargy that turns my days to trances. Even the wine-dark sea and the few galleys sparkling in the distance are phooey to me. In a word, Marcus, I am in that bored state where my only reply to all information is the famous crack of Socrates: "Ess dis a feck!" Send me therefore the new scrolls whereof you write and I will study them and send you some trivia about them. Also reserve for me the American Caravan. If ever the impieties and rich wines of Rome pall upon your fastidious nature pray jump into your litter—is it still drawn by the twelve white mules from Elephantis?—and journey mewards. Such a meeting would bring the flash of life back to my lacklustre eyes and we would discourse of ships and sandals and Epicurus and Epiglottis. Lay a vine-wreath at the foot of your Caia for me that she may know I am still

Herbertus Delirius,
Pro-consul of Castoria
X
Herbertus his mark

To Marcus Valerius,
Pro-consul of Cornwallia and satrap
Exzema.

But then in California there was Robinson Jeffers. I made his acquaintance, solely by letters because he never left Carmel,

after James Rorty brought me his *Tamar and Other Poems*
and insisted that I review it in *The Nation*. The book had
been privately published in New York, but Rorty, a wild
Irishman (and a good poet himself) who had met Jeffers in
California, was sure it deserved a wider audience, as of course
it did. My review in 1925 and many others that equaled it
for enthusiasm seemed to make the difference Rorty desired;
and Jeffers, a kind and courteous man who sounded in his
letters nothing like the hawk-heroes of his powerful poems,
wrote to me for several years. Once he did leave his tower to go
to Ireland, and he said he might see me in New York as he
went or came; but at the last minute he could not bear the
thought of a metropolis, so he slipped through Halifax.

One day at *The Nation* I was called into Mr. Villard's office
to meet Colonel Charles Erskine Scott Wood and Sara Bard
Field, here from The Cats, their house near San Francisco.
Her name for him was Zeus, and I could see why. He was a
massive old man with a mane of snow-white hair, and his voice
was tremendous, like the force of his gaze when he looked at
you from under impressive dark eyebrows. He had been an
Indian-fighter in the West; then he became a lawyer, and
clearly he had prospered. He loved luxury. He told me of the
wine he grew on hillsides near The Cats; he was to send
Dorothy the finest China tea he could buy in San Francisco;
and somebody whispered to me once that he kept pearls
in his coat pocket so that he could run his fingers through
them when he felt that way. He and Sara became our faithful
friends; long letters would come from both, expressing lively
interest in everything that happened to our children. When
John was born the Colonel lengthened his name to John
Donne; for poetry was his final passion, as it was Sara's. They
sent us their books in exchange for ours; we reviewed one
another by correspondence. Colonel Wood's letter about
Spring Thunder worried me when I got it, for it asked me why
I had not written about battle and sudden death instead of

alfalfa and old mares. When I answered that perhaps I should have, he demanded to know where my wits had gone. He meant, he said, that he liked the book just as it was.

The Nation introduced me, naturally, to books as well as men. I was in a position to see all the titles as they came out; and while this ceased in time to seem a privilege of great price, so that I could understand why Ecclesiastes had bemoaned the very making of books, I heartily enjoyed it for four years. There were whole classes of books that I might never have known at first hand had I not sat in their presence and considered who should review them. I owe to *The Nation,* for instance, my continuing interest in John Muir and W. H. Hudson. As naturalists they extended a tradition I had encountered in Thoreau; but Thoreau was for me a moralist first of all, and furthermore a moralist with whom I sometimes quarreled, whereas these later men had simply their rapture to report, or if that is too strong a word in the case of Hudson, their intense absorption in the life on earth that most men do not see: the life of animals and plants, and of the wooded mountains or the open fields where this life goes on as it went on for ages before there was intellect to observe it. Muir and Hudson, content with their own observations, permitted the reader to take or leave these as he chose. I chose to take them. Professionally I was identified with man's world: I lived in one of his greatest cities, and my business there was with students and books. But it was a pleasure to place myself outside of it too, and Muir's mountains, like Hudson's Argentina and England, produced a beautiful, vast, ancient world into which I could escape, if only to rest my eyes and ears.

For the same reason I let myself be attracted to the literature of the American Indian. The Bureau of American Ethnology was sending to *The Nation* its annual reports; they were highly technical, and often I was lost in details; but with other books on the subject, notably those of Paul Radin, they filled me with a sense of how good it would be to know all that could be known about the first poets and artists and philosophers of this continent; for among other things they were that, and I had not been aware of it before. I never became proficient in the subject, though in after years I was to meet Paul Radin and have many conversations with him, particularly about the Winnebago Indians he had studied. But in the poem "End of Singing," which Jeffers found too pessimistic, I tried even then to state the difference between a time when all men sang and a time—this time—when only a few do, and are little heeded by the rest. And in *The Mayfield Deer* I was still to remember the Indians who were here before John Richman was.

One of the books I had reviewed for Carl in London was a volume of Thomas Hardy's poems. It was followed until Hardy's death in 1928 by a series of volumes each one of which equaled its predecessor, and I reviewed them all. The spectacle of this man becoming a poet at fifty-five and continuing without any failure of power until he was eighty-eight has perhaps no parallel in the history of the art. The nearest thing to it in modern times is the career of William Butler Yeats, who indeed began as a poet but who turned into a great one after he was fifty. Not only did I review Hardy as he appeared; I read and reread his *Collected Poems;* and eventually I taught a course at Columbia in which only he and Yeats were read. Of the two, Hardy was for me the hero. Yeats is now more celebrated and discussed, and I understand how this can be, for I admire him too; but Hardy is more interesting to me, and so for me the better poet.

The immense, rambling country house of his *Collected Poems* has so many rooms that one could live in it forever. I have heard it called too large a house, with too many low rooms in it where the furniture is old and ugly, and where there is the odor of rats in the wainscot. Too many of Hardy's poems, that is to say, are not "good." And I agree; but I am always changing my mind as to which ones those are; I never tire of opening old doors that resist me a little; and my conclusion is that the building as a whole should be left just as it lies, hugging the dark ground over which Hardy's eyes wandered for decades, peering at every visible shape, human or unbreathing. Yeats never absorbed his ideas in the complete, selfless way of Hardy; they somehow remain his subject matter, as the man does to whom they happened; whereas Hardy, seasoned beyond that point, merely reports upon the world— the chief business of a poet at any time. And his report, while strange, is always musical (with discords) and difficultly true. It even contradicts his theories, which to be sure he is willing to state, but only as propositions to be entertained in the intervals of our own looking. What the reader sees is never Hardy, but the world he saw. There is none of the vanity in him, none of the intellectual pride, that keeps Yeats cold. There is only this world; and by a queer logic it is warmer than he ever says it is. His vision refutes his thought. I have said as much in "Thomas Hardy, Poet":

> With older eyes than any Roman had
> In a stone hole, or Briton under barrow,
> Steadily he gazed; and bleakest worlds
> Grew warm—illicitly grew warm and moved;
> For hope in him was backward, and love narrow.
>
> Belief in him but squinted; God had died
> Of palsy, and mankind, alone with feeling,
> Was a poor skinless thing. Yet maids and squires,
> Ghosts, organists, and gypsies, and small clerks
> Mused in his tales, and oxen kept on kneeling.
>
> It was a late hour and cold when he looked out:
> The last man that remembered country singing.
> And first to call it pitiful. Those folk
> Outstayed themselves, he said. Yet as he listened,
> Wanly, what sweet bell tongues took to swinging!

All of his poems have the air of being stories—an excellent thing in a poet—even when their ostensible form is lyric. But this is simply another way of saying that as a person he had learned how to live with his mind; or without it, if that makes better sense.

I Start to Work: 1920–1928

I have never met a poet who did not feel more or less as I do about Hardy. Professors of poetry prefer Yeats, for he invites commentary. But there is an honesty in the other old man, a fidelity to a vision, which any artist votes for in his secret heart. Two American poets of the generation before mine whose acquaintance I made in the 1920's both confessed to me that Hardy had their devotion too. They were Edwin Arlington Robinson and Robert Frost, who have been paired by literary historians but who are as different from each other as humor is from wit. "Mr. Flood's Party" proves that humor was in Robinson; there is, however, no poem of Frost's that does not derive dimension from it; and the name of that dimension is depth. Wit, the divining rod, has at its best a long reach, and it is wonderful for what it can lead down to; but humor is what is at the bottom waiting to be divined. It is the bigger and older thing. Robinson's wit made all the difference in American poetry when a difference needed to be made. Nor has it lost its edge; nor was it ever without its rich body of reference, its world of feeling through which a fine intelligence traveled, honoring humanity by the attention it bestowed upon tragedy and comedy at work in delicate souls. I reviewed Robinson and I wrote a book about him, and I shall always insist upon his distinction. But I have written about Frost too; and now it seems to me that the things I found to say about him were of the greater personal interest to me. His poetry itself is a kind of person, for the whole of it lives and speaks—with feints, disguises, reticences, and understatements which in the long run surprisingly suggest toughness and strength.

Not that I understood all of this in January, 1928, when I heard from Frost that several poems soon to be published in *West-running Brook* could be printed in *The Nation* if I liked them. I was sure I would, and sent for them. They were "The Armful," "Blood," and "The Bear." Of course I wanted them, and they appeared; but not without changes which he continued to make until the last minute. "It takes a long time," he wrote from Amherst, "for me to make up my mind to part

169

with a poem, longer to part with more than one. Even now I'm not quite ready to let you have these three if for no better reason than that they don't make up into a set to print together. Why don't you choose one and send the rest back?" In the end he let me have all three, though even then he altered them in proof. He entirely rewrote a passage in "Blood," whose title was eventually "The Flood." "You'll notice," he said, "that I hadn't quite parted with [the] poems when I sent them. There were a couple of lines written wrong in Blood [actually, he altered three]. I am still writing them. I hope to have the definitive version before I mail this. Will you see to the alterations in the proof as anxiously as if they were your own?"

A few years back I had seen Frost with Carl, and on that occasion he had told us several stories of New England people who would reappear in *New Hampshire*. And more recently I had seen him with Dorothy, to whom he now sent his regards. "I'd like your son," he added, "to meet our grandson." In the same letter he delivered himself of a devastating sentiment about the profession we shared. "Most teaching is mere correcting mistakes just as most loving is mere folly. Lud sing cuccu." I had found him, as nobody ever failed to do, a mixture of simple and complex, a man who simultaneously gave and withdrew himself: one, in brief, who could hide behind the very charm of his openness, his generosity in speech and act. So I could not be altogether surprised by a brief difference between us in May of this same year, when I wrote him for permission to use two poems in the *Anthology of World Poetry*. Back came at once this note from South Shaftsbury, Vermont: "I confess a choice so perfunctory and slighting hurts my feelings. It simply hurts them: I don't think it hardens them. . . . What do you say if I stay out of this anthology and turn my thoughts elsewhere?" I replied, explaining how the scale of the work precluded the use of many poems by one author, but saying that upon second thought I was glad of an opportunity to ask for more from him, as indeed I was. And here was his answer: "I'm too touchy—

particularly with friends. Treat me well and you'll be expected to treat me better. That's all the pay you'll get for treating *me* well. Such I am, though I don't usually give myself away or get found out because I live too far off in the country to speak on impulse and I'm too lazy to write."

Of course I should have explained in the first place. But I am not sorry I neglected to do so, for this correspondence occurred. In subsequent years nothing from him has revealed him any better, or in my mind to better advantage. Robinson's courtesy, impeccable and exquisite, concealed as much pride, I have no doubt, but concealed it completely, so that one could not guess of what simples it was compounded. Neither in conversation nor in letters did he drop his guard. Frost, even more reluctant to "get found out," nevertheless could allow the thing to happen. Or, it is truer to say, in his case it sometimes simply happened. And then he was gone again.

It was something like the fear he once expressed to me of the notes he was tempted to make for a poem that had yet to be written. Better, he said, no notes at all; or at best, a single word or phrase on a piece of paper. Otherwise the thing got put down in prose, and then the poem was unnecessary— except of course that the thing, if important, could not be said in prose and so would never be said at all. Writing the poem ought to involve the discovery of what it had been in the first place. Writing poems is getting feelings off the chest. Until then they should remain feelings, however perilous or powerful. The feelings of Robert Frost have never been less than that.

City and Country

1928–1933

AS the 1920's drew to their close I might have remarked, though I did not, that I was indebted to them for a number of good things: employment, a wife and children, a place in the country, many new friends, and the freedom withal to write and publish three books of poems. If I made no such remark, the reason must have been that I was too busy to count the years, let alone the decades, that flowed then into one another as if there were no great difference between them—certainly no such dramatic difference as history, and for that matter my own present memories, can tell me was distinctly there. For practical purposes the end of this decade came melodramatically in October, 1929, when Wall Street crashed. I had nothing to do with Wall Street, and so I did not crash; except that a year before the *Anthology of World Poetry* had made enough money so that Dorothy and I could buy a house in the city. We bought one in February, 1929; and nine months later it could not have been sold for a song, my own or anybody else's. Not that we wanted to sell it; it was where we lived; but as an investment it was nothing, either then or through a decade to come. Soon enough we decided not to consider it as such; we settled into it to stay; and for our two sons it was home until they were grown.

It was on Bleecker Street, at the west end of a long block whose interior was made over during the summer of 1929 into a garden for us and a dozen other families. We bought our houses together, demolished back fences and outbuildings at one stroke, paved the space thus opened up, planted the edges of it with shrubs and trees, and there was Bleecker Gardens, an oasis of green peace over which all of our rear windows looked out. Yet if "oasis" suggests "desert," I must hasten to deny that the rest of New York was such a thing to me. Nor has it ever been. I love the country, but I love the city too. Indeed I have never known how to compare them. In either one I can forget the other. By "country" I have come of course to mean Cornwall Hollow, but by "city" I have always meant New York, one of whose innumerable charms, for me at any rate, is its leisure. I have learned how to live in it as if it were a quiet place. For many it is not quiet, but they have not penetrated to that mysterious part of it where multiplicity, pleased with itself, lies down and dreams that it is one thing after all. Where anything can happen, nothing does. The variety of New York is so endless that monotony is there at last: a deep monotony, that daily refreshes the spirit.

So, far from being a desert, the New York our front windows exposed us to was something of which I for one could never tire. A New York street—even Bleecker Street, which I would not dare to call distinguished—is like a stage set for a play. There is no play, no coherence in the scenes, but always there are scenes: people come and go, some of them familiar, most of them strange, as if they had been sent, though that cannot be true either, for they do not look up at any audience. There is no audience, just as there are no actors; yet it is a drama, as without words or music the country is a lyric. And soon I was to learn how rich a lyric that can be. Meanwhile, however, there was New York; and a house in it that once had been a tenement. Of four stories we occupied three and rented one. The third story was Mrs. Graffe's and mine: an apartment for her and a study for me. On 9th Street she had suffered an illness, a breakdown of the heart, that pretty well confined her here; though she went downstairs to see the boys whenever they did not go up to see her, which most of the time they did. I remember saying once that the first thing Charlie did on

Bleecker Street was to fall downstairs. But this must have been when Johnny was old enough—I think he was three—to impress Mortimer Adler with his logical powers. "No," he insisted; "the first thing was, he went *up*stairs." Mortimer had plans in those days to train our younger son in formal logic. Or he said he did. It was one of his infinite jests.

Mortimer left New York in 1930 to join Robert Hutchins at the University of Chicago, where the two of them were to become famous—some said infamous—for the way they thought and talked about higher education in America; and not only thought and talked, but acted. Their revolution was in one sense only an extension of John Erskine's at Columbia, for the basis of it was a belief that great books are the best teachers; yet it was more formal, more philosophical than that, and more far-reaching in its consequences, since in the end it amounted to an assault upon the entire elective system. The weaknesses of this system had for some time been apparent, but no such drastic cure as theirs had been proposed; nor was it palatable when proposed, since it called upon teachers to re-educate themselves. The elective system, stated in its simplest terms, was perhaps no system at all; courses were "offered," and the students "took" those they thought they would like best—or as Hutchins put it, were permitted to "wander at will through the higher learning." The revolution consisted in saying that a college should decide what things its students ought to study and then should see to it that they did so, whether or not they knew beforehand that these things were best. Ignorance in students was excusable, but in teachers it was not. What were teachers for if they were not expected to distinguish between the important and the unimportant; and after that, to seek out the essential? The very question seemed impertinent to some, as to others it sounded authoritarian and dogmatic. To me it was merely sensible; but even then I could see more trouble ahead for Mortimer than he guessed when he went so gaily to Chicago.

Nor was he my only friend who left New York at the turn of

the decade. Scott Buchanan moved to the University of Virginia to teach philosophy. And Allen Tate "retired" to a house near Clarksville, Tennessee, which he named Benfolly for his brother who had helped him buy it. It was not far from the part of Kentucky he and Caroline Gordon knew best; it was on the Cumberland River; it was handsome, I heard, and Allen had hopes of its being a permanent escape from a literary scene which both stimulated and distressed him, and left him, everybody thought, too little strength for poetry. He was not to stay there many years, nor was Scott to stay in Charlottesville much longer.

But we continued to see the Buchanans. We went south every winter or spring to visit them, and they spent several summers in a house across from ours in Cornwall Hollow. Mortimer, who had married Helen Boynton before he left New York, came with her to Cornwall too, and enlivened the whole landscape with dialectical orations and preposterous songs. His spirits, higher than ever, contrasted quaintly with Scott's sober-sounding humor. A few years before this they had published their first books: Scott his *Possibility* in 1926 and Mortimer his *Dialectic* in 1927; and John Dewey had reviewed them for me in *The Nation*. The difference between the books still expressed itself in the authors. If Mortimer's strong point was logic and the development of positions, Scott's was the feeling out of analogies. Not that Scott dispensed with logic; nobody can; but it interested him less, particularly when it was systematic, than what he recognized as "the intellectual imagination," a faculty he would return to in *Poetry and Mathematics*. Perhaps it was during one of these summers that the difference between them stated itself in a fashion I cannot forget. Mortimer remarked that the conversation of philosophers was like a game played with rules. Scott agreed; but added that the game was played best when there were no rules. Then *that* became the argument between them, as in one way or another it has continued to be. The difference bore fruit in later years of controversy and collaboration. For me it bore immediate fruit: as a bystander I learned from both.

Carl and the Krutches, my original friends, were also less accessible now than they had been, but for reasons that were not at all the same. The Krutches' removal to Redding, although it did not mean that we ceased to see them, meant that we saw them less easily and less often. It meant that visits had to be arranged, in winter as well as summer because Redding was their only home. Joe published *The Modern Temper* in 1929 and *Five Masters* (dedicated to me) in 1930. *The Modern Temper,* his best-known book of that period, said in its way what Scott and Mortimer were saying in theirs, though I could never get any of the three to see this as clearly as I thought I did. It seemed to me that all of them were concerned with setbacks the modern mind had suffered because its connection with the past was broken. Scott and Mortimer were digging up ancient and medieval ideas that were valid though forgotten, powerful though despised. Joe was lamenting man's loss of his dignity and greatness through the very humanism that had isolated him on earth and made him think he was its master; he was no longer, said Joe, even his own master. And Joe was called a pessimist for this. To me again he was merely sensible, and a true historian. From all three I borrowed something I have never since mislaid: a sense of the danger that threatens any man who repudiates either his own past or the past of his people. I learned that no thought, no feeling, is to be rejected for the simple reason that it is old. Or because it is new. The truth of it, if one can find that out, is all that matters.

As for Carl, I should try to be content with his own touching account in *Three Worlds* of the private depression he suffered during those days of a public depression so widespread and so demoralizing that even the fortunate could not ignore it. If his account is not as particular as it might be, I have no desire to amplify it, even assuming that I could. And I cannot, for I never understood it. Close as we were, we did not discuss the despair that I could see in his very eyes and hear in his very voice—as kind as ever, and one might think as hearty, but it simply did not communicate the secret things that haunted him. One of these things I am sure was the terrible disappointment he felt at last in the poems and the stories he had written: the poems early, the stories late, but he said to himself that he had failed at both. Perhaps he should not have said this; perhaps he should have kept on with fiction at least; but his pride could not live with the modest success of *Other Provinces* and *The Ninth Wave,* and doubtless the fact that he did give up has an inescapable importance.

"Apparently frank, actually impenetrable"—Carl wrote these words of me, but I can write them of him too. I wonder if they are not true of everybody. Certainly if there was any person in whom he was licensed to confide, I like to believe I was that person. But it never happened, and I conclude that it was impossible; and conclude further that the deepest reserves are found in the oldest friends. Nor do I suppose that literary disappointment was the only cause of his despair— which in any case he recovered from soon enough, so that his remaining years were among the happiest he had. And even in these days of which I speak he was about to put such disappointments far behind him. The writing of his *Swift,* not to speak of the *Benjamin Franklin* in its time, was all the cure he needed. He has not exaggerated the personal importance of the *Swift,* either to him or to anyone who reads it now. The very rage it comprehends, and to that extent subdues, had been his as well as Swift's. It was a document no less than a masterpiece.

II

Meanwhile I was occupied with a long poem in which I took more satisfaction, even as I wrote it, than I had taken in its predecessors ten years before. *Jonathan Gentry,* published in

1931, had three parts: "Ohio River 1800," "Civil War," and "Foreclosure." These parts were held together by heredity, so to speak: their respective heroes, all of them bearing the same name, represented the first, third, and fifth generations of a family whose origin was England but whose destiny was Illinois. And each part gave me an occasion to deal with something I had long been interested in—so long and so deeply that if I had not treated it here I would have treated it elsewhere, in other poems; and the fact is that I have done so, for *Jonathan Gentry* did not exhaust my interest in its several themes.

The first part, as the date in its title indicates, celebrated a historical event which has always fascinated me: the settlement of interior America by way of the great river, the Ohio, that cuts across it to the Mississippi. The Ohio, however, begins beyond the Allegheny Mountains, so that an arduous journey over dry land preceded the relatively easy voyage downstream in flatboats or "arks" to whatever places in Ohio, Kentucky, Indiana, or Illinois the settlers were headed for. The Erie Canal was eventually to pour a larger stream of pioneers into the Middle West by a more northerly, more comfortable route; and when the railroads came there was no further problem at all, as in this century I knew by my own experience. But in 1800 it had been hard for the first Jonathan Gentry to reach Illinois; also, the trip was picturesque, as George Caleb Bingham's famous print, "The Jolly Flatboatmen," had often told me. So the Ohio River was really my concern in Part I of the poem: the river itself, and the great new world beyond its banks which Audubon had explored as if it were Paradise. This interested me too, as I wanted to say it had interested the first Gentry, bent upon starting life again in a vast, remote meadow free from the errors that had made Europe ugly. The experiment would not succeed, but that was another story, to be told in Part III. Meanwhile, here was this river, for the particulars of whose course I consulted a little book by Reuben Gold Thwaites—he had made the voyage himself in modern times—before I began my poem. I had decided to employ a variety of meters, and to intersperse the narrative with songs; and to use free verse for passages where the movement of the river, or of Gentry's mind, seemed to call for that:

> The horses leaned;
> The wagon, gritting its last gravel,
> Groaned, and they zigzagged up.
> Too steep, the driver said, and so they rested
> Where a bright spring, refusing to go further,
> Tumbled down past them backward, laughing loudly
> At labor and all good purpose. But they left it,
> Took a long breath and toiled, and wound thrice more
> Right upward, till the trees
> Opened; the mountain stopped; and all their faces
> Fell on the broad Ohio, soft below.
>
> Like a white dream this beautiful of rivers
> Lay in its forest folds, and if it moved there
> None of them knew it now. They too were moveless—
> High, little gods of momentary stone—
> They too were dreams the mountain dreamed, old father
> Of flocks of dreams that circled each day and fell. . . .
>
> So thirteen days and nights, and the rough hills
> Grew gentler, and the willows
> Waved at the edge of meadows whose deep grass
> Was walked on by a wind of falling flowers.
> Some days the mountains sharpened, and the shadows
> Stood with an awful stiffness.
> Then the mild slopes again, and opening sky.
> Once, where the river widened,
> Suddenly dogs barked; cabins smoked in a clearing,
> And children in a low line by the shore
> Stretched like a fringe of weeds, and would have hailed them;
> But nothing could be heard beyond small cries
> And piping little laughter, that the ring
> Of axes in the forest and deep bells
> Of happy-throated dogs, and idle screams
> Of jays and redbirds mingled with and lost.

"Civil War" and "Foreclosure," continuing the history of the Gentrys, showed their new world growing old as all of man's worlds do. The tragedy of Lincoln's war I had already treated in the poem which Robinson Jeffers told me "filled a whole continent with its weirdness":

The country is no country I have seen,
And no man goes there who is now alive, and no man
Ever is going to leave there. But they try:
Waving a million beards that on pale faces
Blacken with time and spread.
It is a field of bodies of blue boys,
And gray boys, grown half way into the ground.
The wind is dark that sways them;
All of them bending with it, south or north,
All of them straining here; but no one knowing
Of any fellow by who gazes too.
It is a field of legless bearded boys
With bright unnecessary buttons on their breasts,
And skirts of coats that hold them in the sod.
The bodies twist,
The circular, small eyes are mad with being;
A million mouths fly open without sound;
But none can tear his coat up, that must come
With roots and worms or come not up at all.

Away in Carolina, Maine, Wisconsin,
Boys who kept their legs walked long and long.
They set their feet in furrows, or in aisles;
They strolled with girls, were taken, and were fathers;
Had old companionship; and last were covered
Quietly with smooth boards, and grass, and stone.
Stiffly now they hold society;
Forever thus they lie without a want.

In the forbidden country where the sod
Grows down and down, with restless blue roots, gray roots,
In the dark windy land no one can leave,
Separate necks yearn homeward;
Separate hungry shoulders pull and pull.
Wind, oh wind, I did not come to stay;
I must be there tomorrow, not to miss—
But the dark wind is earless, and the day
Is endless, and the grasses hiss and hiss.

This war has persisted for me, as it has for innumerable Americans, in being the one war that is wonderful in all of its dimensions and details; everything about it is obsessively important; still unable to understand it, we find that we cannot turn our faces away from even its most grisly features. In Part II I sent Jonathan Gentry Third and his younger brother Charlie across the Ohio, which for their grandfather had been a highway of peace, into the southern segment of the paradise he had imagined. Remembering, as I have said, what I had learned from Allen Tate about the resemblances as well as the differences between North and South beyond the mountains, I sought to render Charlie Gentry's death in battle as the death of a brother in more senses than one. And the song at the end, when Jonathan comes home alone, I thought of as my contribution (but there would be others) to the poetry of return which all wars, from Homer's on, have made so natural a thing to write:

> Rolling home, rolling home,
> Rolling home across the corn;
> Rolling up, rolling up,
> To the place where I was born.
> Black, black between the green;
> Plenty, plenty, blow your horn.
>   War, war,
>   Go away
>   And never come
>   Another day.
>
> Through the gate, through the gate,
> Through the gate, and what I see?
> Through the gate, through the gate,
> They are coming out to me.
> Well, well, well, well,
> Hello, hello, and how you be?
>   War, war,
>   Go away
>   And never come
>   Another day.

City and Country: 1928–1933

For Part III I needed no more than the experience of Frank and my father with the agricultural depression then in its depths. But I generalized this depression, perhaps not altogether licitly, so as to make it mean at last a change in the whole of American life: the change, by now commonplace to everybody, from a culture of farms to a culture of factories, from an emphasis on the country to an emphasis on the city. Jonathan Gentry Fifth has married a girl who is in love with cities, and for that reason as well as others the ancestral structure in which he had thought to spend his days falls in ruin about his feet. The only voice he hears out of the old days is that of Tom, a homeless wanderer from all over who sings back-country songs such as Laura, enamored of her phonograph, is bound to detest:

> Rain crow, rain crow,
> Heard the saddest rain crow
> Ever, ever seen
> Since the world was green.
>
> Rain crow, rain crow,
> Moanin' like a rain crow:
> Never turtle dove
> Lost such a love. . . .
>
> Rain crow, rain crow,
> Mortifyin' rain crow,
> Who, who's gone,
> And left you all alone?

Jonathan Gentry was my first poem with anything like epic substance. It was ambitious as *Simple Cymon* and *Agatha* had not been. Those were idyls, were anecdotes; this aimed at breadth and depth, and the very aim, I confess, gave me pleasure.

Another book I published in the same year with *Jonathan Gentry* was as different from it as one book can be from another. It was for children, and I called it *Dick and Tom;* it had perhaps a hundred times as many readers as the poem did, for it was about two ponies, and apparently that subject could not fail. Certainly it had not failed with Charlie, to whom during the winter of 1930–1931 I told every night a story of how his Uncle Frank and I had owned and ridden Dick and Tom when we were boys at Hope. Tom was invented for the purpose; we had had only Dick, and even he was Carl's and Guy's more than he was ours. But with two ponies there could be joint trips, as when for instance both boys went for the doctor; and there was even a third pony, a magical white one, a country Pegasus from somewhere else. It was only after I had told Charlie, who insisted on them nightly, dozens of these tales, and after I noticed that Johnny in spite of his being only two was listening as if he understood them, that it occurred to me to put them in a book. But which ones out of so many would be best? I solved this quite simply. One night I asked the boys which stories they remembered—quick, without thinking—and I had my answer. The handful they named became the book. There was a sequel to it next year. *Dick and Tom in Town* shifted the scene to a place like Urbana. And I thought it just as interesting. But no great number of children agreed.

III

In the summer of 1931 we built another house in Cornwall, beside the brook a little more than halfway down the road to Bailey's. It was for Mrs. Graffe, who would be happy in it during the last years of her life. We modeled it after our own house, though of course it was smaller. Dorothy drew the plans; George Crosby proceeded to put it up; and within an astonishingly short time it looked as if it had been there as long as most other things on the place. Since we had to borrow money to build it, I went to a bank in Litchfield; but when I told the banker I wrote books he refused to give me a mortgage. Writers, he said, were not to be trusted with money.

If I had said I was a teacher there would have been no difficulty. I said as much in Torrington and got the loan.

But in August, while the rooms were taking shape, I went out to visit Guy and Paul. In Chicago I found Paul ready for a vacation himself; he proposed a week's trip in his car through Wisconsin and Michigan, and nothing could have suited me better. We left Jessie with Peter, who was four, while we went west across Illinois, north along the Mississippi to Prairie du Chien, northeast and east through Eau Claire and Wausau to Green Bay and Escanaba, then on around Lake Michigan and down the east side of it to Chicago again. All of this country, most of it cut-over pine land, was strange and exciting to me; I have not seen it since, but the great cool lakes still lie in my memory as they lay then, with locks and falls connecting them at Sault Sainte Marie. Then I took a train down to the familiar universe of Urbana and Villa Grove.

I found my mother tired and my father cheerful but not well. There was no way for me to know that he had only two more years to live. If he knew it, as he may have because he was a doctor, he said nothing. At Villa Grove I heard from Frank a story that reminded me of the minister's cat Deborah in the book we read as children at Hope. Deborah had walked through miles of snow to bring her kittens back, one by one, to the house where she thought they belonged. Well, so had Chocolate Drop, a faithful old cat of whom Frank and Grace were fond. During the winter they had left her at a house two miles north of them while they went away for a few days. She was to have kittens, and Grace thought she would be better off in a warm place. But when four kittens were born she carried them home, also one by one, through snow in which she left tracks indicating a total journey of fourteen miles. Now she sat there and blinked at us, her offspring long since weaned and forgotten, and listened without interest to our praise. As a matter of fact she was only one of several animals on Frank's place who then or later expressed a singular devotion to it. Once when he shipped a carload of hogs to Chicago he was notified that one of them was missing upon arrival; somehow it had got out of the car and disappeared. Frank could not understand this; but days later a sow, pitifully lean from lack of food and water, walked into the barnyard, dropped down, and died. Another pig, overwhelmed by a strawstack that had fallen over on it, ate its way through to the open air. This took days, for the pig went in the wrong direction, ahead instead of back; and since straw is poor nourishment, and there was no water, it nearly starved. Yet it survived.

From Villa Grove I took another train to Benfolly, to see the Tates. Allen, Caroline, and Nancy received me in a handsome house where certain of their kin were visitors too. The Cumberland River, muddy and slow, was downhill through trees; Clarksville was nearby; and across the state line in Kentucky there were hospitable relatives of Caroline to whom I was taken. Allen drove me one day to Nashville, and another day to Fort Donelson on the Tennessee, where we saw the gun emplacements of 1862, carved out of clay banks to threaten the boats that Grant had ordered up the river. It seemed to me that the Tates had found at Benfolly the one piece of ground intended for them. This was not to be, but I went home with the warmth of their welcome lasting me all the way.

At Columbia I had started a new course. In the late spring of 1930 Professor Thorndike walked over to Hamilton Hall in search of someone to teach Shakespeare in the College; Professor Lawrence, he said, wanted to stop doing it, and he wondered who of us might take his place. He found me in my office, where I stood by a window fingering the cord that hung down from the shade, and I distinctly remember my sudden interest in this cord as I considered whether I might suggest myself. Finally I did so, and Professor Thorndike, who had perhaps been expecting it all along, consented. So in the fall I began, with eighty-two students who included Maxwell Geismar, Donald Keene, and Robert Caldwell. It was the beginning not only of a new course but of a new life for me. There is no subject like Shakespeare. It embraces the world. I was so sure of this last that I decided to assign all of the plays so that no pleasure would be missed, no line or character overlooked. The plan was radical, but I never departed from it through sixteen happy years. The students, then and later, I thought of as my collaborators in a discussion of what Shakespeare, play by play, had done. They taught me, with Shakespeare's help, as much as I taught them.

To speak of Robert Caldwell, who would graduate the next year, is to be reminded by contrast of a student who had recently graduated. He was as little like Caldwell as a man can be. Caldwell, big of frame and lively of mind, was to become powerful in the world of newspapers, and even now he was impressive for the practical, immediate relation he established with Shakespeare. He was subtle and sensitive, but this did not handicap him by making it difficult for him to talk: whereas the other student, beginning in these years, was to grow in shyness—not of people so much as of thoughts and things, of the very world itself—until he could write me (this was more than two decades later): "I go for six months—for six years—without saying a word." Nor has he been unique in my experience as a teacher. And I have wondered whether this was anybody's fault: my own, for instance. Doubtless it is nobody's fault, and doubtless it was not even college that did it—college, that place where an exquisite brain can be overwhelmed by tremendous things poured in at too swift a pace, so that something like permanent panic results; or if not that, irresolution so deep that action is henceforth impossible. But for Caldwell, equally exquisite and acute, there has never been a comparable problem.

IV

The time now came for my first sabbatical. It came, that is, in the spring of 1932, when I could choose between two forms of freedom from Columbia: half of the ensuing year on full pay, or the whole of it on half pay. With Dorothy's consent I made the second choice; she would be absent from *The Nation* too, and a year seemed long for that—or rather, since there would be two summers, sixteen months; but she was game, and she found that she could manage the leave. The question then was, where we should spend the sixteen months. We thought of Europe, we thought of Mexico. But the boys were only six and four, and either of those places sounded difficult, not to say expensive. Our last choice was Cornwall. This now seems strange in view of the happiness that awaited us there; but the future is never clear, and for the most important things it is most cloudy. At any rate we made our plans. We had never used the house except in summer and for weekends in the spring and fall. A winter. Snow and ice. Snowbound! And the boys would miss a year of school; they were going now to the City and Country School on 12th Street in New York, and this was the year when Charlie would be taught to read. Dorothy, consulting the school, was told she could teach him herself, and she said she would do that. But snow and ice, and temperatures under zero: we knew that a hundred miles north of New York, and a thousand feet above it, the thermometer could drop to thirty below. And all we had for heat was a fireplace in the living room and a wood stove in the kitchen. So a furnace was indicated. When we moved up in June we would see about that.

The furnace we got was a so-called pipeless one, a big cylindrical affair with a single vent through which heat ascended into the living room above it, then circulated as best it could through the remainder of the house. It would burn either coal or wood; we decided on wood, since we had a hundred acres of trees. In the fall I engaged Louis Jasmin, who tended Dr. Lieb's house across the Hollow, to lay in our winter's supply of fuel. French in origin—the Jasmin family had come from Belfort—Louis was expert with the saw and ax. First he came over to select with me the trees he would cut down and split up; then, with help from his brothers and friends, he devoted weeks to filling our basement entirely full of chunks—maple, oak, hickory, birch—that would fit into the firebox of the furnace. The boys watched this work, as I did, with the greatest admiration for him who did it; and in their case I was glad of this, since one of my ambitions for them was that they should become familiar with tools and learn how to use them; in time they were to become good carpenters, gardeners, and (most necessary thing) mowers of lawns. Now they were too young to do anything but watch. They were absorbed in all of our preparations. There had to be a mountain, too, of small wood for the stove. Will Bailey, who could do anything, took care of that. Across the brook northeast of the house there was a thicket of young maple trees, tall and slender, that needed thinning. We had a bridge built so that the poles could be brought up to the house and there sawed into short lengths; then the boys helped me pile as many of these under cover as there was room for in the tool house and the woodshed behind the kitchen wing. I think it was then that I contracted my passion for piling wood; Dorothy tells me I do it as if I were once more building with blocks.

Mr. Bailey, as we always called him, was one of our discoveries this year. We had seen him every summer—Mrs. Bailey too, as plump as he was thin and spry—and he had helped us in a hundred ways. He had mowed with his scythe, an ancient instrument which he wielded like a razor (he cut his lawn with it), many a corner where Felix Jasmin's horses would not go. He had dug a quarter-mile of ditch up to the spring when Lawrence Sturges laid the new pipe that was necessary; Sturges said he was the best man in town for the job; he moved through sod without stopping, like a mole. But now I learned how well he knew the Bradford place where he had lived so many of his years. He belonged to it as the stone walls did, or the juniper bushes. He had worked for Jim and John; he was familiar with every inch of every field. He had, too, a fund of knowledge I have never found in anybody else. It was medieval knowledge, of plants and their properties.

One day when he was scything in the lower orchard—this was before Mrs. Graffe's house was built, and it was precisely at that spot—I saw him bend over to examine something. "Come here," he said. I went, and he held up a long, stringy growth which looked to me like most of the hay around it. "I'll save this," he said. "It's black kohosh. Good for the kidneys." And sure enough, in an old English herbal Dorothy was to acquire we found the name, and learned that the property of the plant was diuretic. Mr. Bailey introduced me to wormwood, too; gave me a leaf of the lacy stuff and told me to taste it; and laughed at the bitter face I made. He could pick blackberries like nobody else. He knew where they grew, and would come back with two milkpails full of them, walking slowly, each level burden motionless at his side. He never hurried, just as he never took off his hat. And his hand, when he reached it to shake yours, felt like a block of wood: square, hard, and surprisingly broad, as I have indicated in "Bailey's Hands":

> The right one that he gave me—
> I could have shut my eyes
> And heard all seventy summers
> Rasping at their scythes.
>
> The left one that he lifted,
> Tightening his hat—
> I could have seen the cut groves
> Lie fallen, green and flat;
>
> Or seen a row of handles,
> Ash-white and knuckle-worn,
> Run back as far as boyhood
> And the first field of thorn. . . .
>
> So by his hands' old hardness,
> And the slow way they waved,
> I understood the story:
> Snath-written, helve-engraved.

He was skillful at caning chairs. He would go into a swamp, bring home a pole of black ash, leave it to season awhile, then pound it with his ax until a cylinder of sapwood was loose;

this he slipped off and cut into strips; and the strips became a seat. I can still see him in his kitchen, ribbons of ash wood curled about him like so many snakes, braiding them patiently into a pattern he had learned in his youth. He did the work for money, but one such chair he presented to us gratis. He had spoken of it many times; it was once John Bradford's, and he thought it belonged of rights in our house, even though John had given it to him. I always protested, saying he should keep it; but one day as I was driving past his door he came out with the chair, a new seat shining in it, and said to me in his high, not very vigorous voice: "I said I would give you this, and by God, I'm going to do it." Of course I took the chair. For one thing, he had sworn. He had no status in the town, and so was not a church member. He always pronounced those two words as if they were one, and put a good deal of scorn into it: his implication was that chúrchmembers were not to be trusted. But he might have had his God—one, of course, who knew what plants were for. Or animals. Yet it was Mrs. Bailey who paid attention to pets: cats and dogs, of whom she kept great numbers, spoiling them with a diet of cake, baked potatoes, and tea. She had many children and grandchildren, all by a former husband. She was motherly to them and to us, whom she adopted too. She spoke, it seemed to me, a perfect English: old-fashioned, correct, and very clear.

The Baileys were glad, I think, that we had come to stay all winter. They never went anywhere, and must have thought it best for others to stay put. So were the neighbors glad—the Hurlburts, the Hallaways, the Jasmins, the Whitfords, and the Ocains—though I am sure they had secret doubts of our capacity to live here like natives to the place, which indeed we have never become in their opinion. Felix Jasmin, who continued to cut our hay, may or may not have approved of something I did one hot afternoon when he was driving the last load home to his own barn. He had said he would pay me $20 for the crop, so now he stopped his horses and reached down to put into my hand a bill of that denomination. But he was so tired, and the weeks of work had been so back-breaking, that I said: "No, forget it." He took me at my word; yet he may have thought me foolish, and his grin—a French grin, half mirthful, half melancholy—may have dismissed me from the small company he knew of sensible people. He was always, however, a fine friend; as his small wrinkled wife was —she worked as hard as he did, but in addition kept beds of flowers (he called them posies)—and as his daughter Margaret was, who in these days came over to help with our children, but then in time, married to Gail Whitford, had five boys and girls of her own.

V

It was not until the end of September that we really felt our year beginning. Every other year we had gone back then to New York, and our friends were going now. But we were staying. And soon enough the difference came home to us. There was the cellar, odorous with its wood; and along the north wall, near the stairs, Dorothy with her mother's help had stored provisions of food: jellies, preserves, pickles, and jars of tomatoes, corn, and what not from the garden. The garden was my responsibility, but the putting up of the harvest was hers. My weakness as a gardener is that I take too much interest in useless products: gourds, sunflowers, morning glories, horse-radish, and the like. This year, however, I cheer-fully raised the things we needed; and I built an extra bin for potatoes, beyond which, when it turned cold, I filled four barrels with apples from the orchard. It turned cold only gradually. After the first frost or two we had many beautiful warm days, and the boys wondered where winter was. Even then, of course, it was coming. The leaves turned and fell; the gray November rains came down; every night, even if we did not notice it, was a little longer, a little more serious; and before too many weeks there was iron in the ground. Then snow. Never enough snow, we said at first; it was not hip-deep; it did not bury us. But in time we had all we could use: enough, certainly, to give us a sense of the house as a snug place, good to be in, after supper when the kerosene lights added their warmth to that which rose from the big register over the furnace.

The house became our world, particularly by night. By day we left it for many reasons: the mail, the milk, to shop in West Cornwall, Torrington, or Canaan, to visit Grandma Graffe in her house, to walk, to run, to slide and skate, to bring in wood for the stove, or simply to be out, in all kinds of weather foul or fair. Yet even then, from ten to twelve in the morning, there was the school that Dorothy regularly kept in the front room we called the library. Charlie did learn to read, and Johnny played the games his mother prescribed; or else he made remarks of a sort that Mortimer Adler should have been present to hear. One day he used the word "born" in such a way as to make his mother doubt that he knew its meaning. He established that he did by saying: "Born is the first name of Dead." When I heard this I wondered if he needed any further education. There were naps, too, and at dusk there was tea with toast. But then the precious hours began, the long evening hours when Dorothy and I read what we liked— I especially liked that winter the detective tales of Sherlock Holmes and Dr. Thorndike—or entertained ourselves with the boys before they went upstairs to bed. They had their own diversions, of course: marbles, picture books, and bagatelle. Or they played with our two kittens, who perhaps that day had waded with us through the snow; though Snippy, the sister, was less sure than brother Snappy that this was good to do, so that sometimes she sat in one of our footprints and cried till he came back and conducted her home.

Then we had Sam, a dignified and intelligent police dog who was not so much a playmate as a guest in the house. We called him "the gentleman," and meant it. I have never known a nobler dog. He had been lent to us by Eli and Dorothy

Nathan, New York friends who had a country house beyond Torrington, in New Hartford. He was seven that winter, but his manners made him ageless; except, to be sure, that he was no puppy to romp with—he preferred to lie by the fire, or when that got too hot to seek out the coldest corner of the living-room floor. He was an excellent friend of Mrs. Hall, a relative by marriage of the Jasmins; she liked to have him with her in the kitchen, perhaps behind the stove where she said he cooked his brains. She was Irish and had many superstitions, but one of these was not that animals are unclean; at least domestic animals, or as Joe Krutch was to say at a later time, civilized ones. Mrs. Hall did think, however, that long icicles foretold a long winter, and that any unusual noise might mean a ghost. She would tell us at breakfast about such noises during the night just past; she had a musician's ear for them, capable of distinguishing thumps from rustles; we listened carefully while we ate her buckwheat pancakes, bitter and wonderful, made out of batter which she kept going, a sacred mess, on the back of the stove.

Dorothy Nathan did us the further favor of lending us a horse, a solemn, good-natured mare named Blackberry, whom Dorothy Van Doren rode. During the summer we had made over the big barn below the house so that it now contained a stall for such a beast as this perpetually hungry and thirsty old girl whom it was my job to feed. I enjoyed doing so; it reminded me of Hope and Villa Grove; but on icy days I found it perilous to carry two pails of water downhill to her from the house. Once in a while she would whinny for a third, and I would go and get it, only to have her swing her head away from it after a single sniff. She pulled hay from the slats of a feeder I had contrived at one corner of the stall, and at another corner she slobbered oats in a box whose bottom and sides grew smooth as the months went by. What she most wanted to do when she was not eating or drinking was to join the two Shetland ponies we had brought from Litchfield for the boys— a mistake, because the boys were too young to ride them, and anyway they were not Dick and Tom. But Blackberry did not consider them a mistake. She seemed to think she was their mother. We kept them in another part of the barn where she could not see them; but of course she smelled them, and if they went out into the pasture before she did she was frantic until she could be there too. She was hard-mouthed, Dorothy said, when she was ridden; she would stubbornly climb banks for tall grass beside the road. But there was never any trouble about getting her home. The ponies pulled her like a magnet.

Indoors by lamplight we did not have to think of Blackberry unless we chose. On the coldest nights I did think of her, and went down in my sheepskin coat to throw a blanket over her. She seemed to like this, though her hair already stood up so thick and long that she wore, one could say, her own comforter. She blinked at the lantern I hung on a nail, and sometimes she nosed me over the partition of the stall as if to suggest my staying with her longer than she knew I would. Back in the house, however, I put her out of mind. The house was all. It was a den where we hibernated, pleased with the very monotony that made every evening like the ones before and after. It was such a time, I reflected, as would never come again, though years would pass before I said so in "Family Prime":

> Our golden age was then, when lamp and rug
> Were one and warm, were globe against the indifferent
> Million of cold things a world contains.
> None there. A light shone inward, shutting out
> All that was not corn yellow and love young.

If anything marred our golden age it was the thing known as my temper, which often was too short. My father said to me once that he had had one too, but somehow had "got over it." He did not say how, nor did I ask; I probably knew that time would have to be the cure. As the winter went on I suspected, however, that one trouble with me was that I had written nothing. I had supposed it would be a prolific year, but the business of living in all of its branches now absorbed my whole attention. I was considering this one late afternoon when the sun, just about to set, flooded the living room where I sat with an amber light that startled me by its beauty: a sudden beauty, suddenly sent, as if the day about to die were speaking some last word. A few days after this, still thinking of how I had been startled, I went upstairs during the school hour and wrote "This Amber Sunstream":

> This amber sunstream, with an hour to live,
> Flows carelessly, and does not save itself;
> Nor recognizes any entered room—
> This room; nor hears the clock upon a shelf,
> Declaring the lone hour; for where it goes
> All space in a great silence ever flows.
>
> No living man may know it till this hour,
> When the clear sunstream, thickening to amber,
> Moves like a sea, and the sunk hulls of houses
> Let it come slowly through, as divers clamber,
> Feeling for gold. So now into this room
> Peer the large eyes, unopen to their doom.
>
> Another hour and nothing will be here.
> Even upon themselves the eyes will close.
> Nor will this bulk, withdrawing, die outdoors
> In night, that from another silence flows.
> No living man in any western room
> But sits at amber sunset round a tomb.

And daily from then on I repeated the experiment, sometimes without success but always with the pleasure that hides itself cunningly in what Cowper calls "poetic pains," a phrase I would never use myself, yet I am glad he did.

We had visitors from New York and elsewhere. Carl came up as often as he could, and in the spring Paul came—he had moved to New York, or rather to Millburn, New Jersey, not long after his trip with me among the Lakes, and now he took a weekend off to see how we were doing. He came alone as I remember; Jessie was occupied with her daughter Paula, their second child. The weekend Paul picked was an odd one as things turned out. It was when the banks closed, and he started back to Wall Street Monday morning with no notion of what had happened. The Buchanans drove up from Charlottesville for Christmas. And one day in January Uncle Walter surprised us by appearing just before dark with my cousin Earl. He said he had left Champaign with the intention of seeing Herbert Hoover, who for some weeks would still be President, about the situation of the farmers. He had not been able to see Hoover, or even the Secretary of Agriculture; but he had talked to an assistant secretary, and now he and Earl were here to look at our scenery. It was too dark to see it then; and since he spoke of having to leave early in the morning I suspected that his interest in it was not acute. He was here to see us.

We spent a remarkable evening. I mentioned chess, saying that Dorothy and I had been trying to learn how to play it from the Encyclopaedia Britannica. "That's no way," he said. "Bring out your board." He made short work of us; then I suggested that he play Earl. He gave Earl a castle but paid little attention to the game, for he talked all the time, until Earl took his queen. "Well!" he said, turning back to the board; and mated my cousin in three moves. His real concern was about the trip home. Could they make it, he wondered, in one day and night? He did not like hotels—an unnecessary expense. He never bought oil for his car; he applied at filling stations for oil that other people had drained out of theirs; it was good enough. The night before I had asked him if he had enough alcohol in his motor to keep it from freezing. He smelled the radiator—there was no cap—and said he thought he did. I drained it, having doubts, into a dishpan; and next morning the contents of the pan were solid ice. This merely amused Uncle Walter, as did the fact that his car had some-thing the matter with its transmission so that it was unable to back. We had pushed it around last night and headed it down-hill; now he sailed off as if there were no cares in the world. And for him there were next to none. He did not look at our scenery, either. He had noticed the country coming here; it was nice. The boys thought him wonderful.

We discovered other people in Cornwall before the winter was over. Chard Powers Smith had bought a house from the Hurlburts, a mile away; he was writing poetry. Merrill Prentice, having nothing to do as an architect until building began again, had bought the Krutches' house. And on Great Hill there was Armin Landeck, recently returned from Europe. We slowly made the acquaintance of these men and their families, and in Armin's case first learned of his surpassing skill as an etcher; he would take up painting later. Armin struck me as soon as I saw him. He was younger than I, but he seemed to have lived more. Keen-faced, cadaverous, amused, he had a strange way of living, so to speak, in others; he knew a great deal about his numerous friends, and spoke of them as if their bad or good fortunes were his own. He took people seriously, and did not judge them. I have described him in "Samaritan":

> Lugubrious, his legs
> Bore tragedy for burden;
> But such a one as shepherds,
> At sunset, on their shoulders,
>
> Hopelessly, uphill,
> Bring home to fire and udder;
> Except he never came there
> And put it down and rested.
>
> There was no mountain fold,
> No thatch for what he carried.
> Lugubrious, a great plain,
> Ahead of him forever,
>
> Was lamb cote, was crib,
> Was where there must be comfort;
> Except he never, halting,
> Abdicated kindness.

VI

Most of the winter, though, we were alone. This was what we had planned; and so our solitude, far from seeming enforced, was a daily blessing. The only trouble was that it could not last forever. Spring would come. And spring did come: the ancient miracle, but for me that year it was a kind of death. It killed our winter in whose routine I had discovered, it seemed to me, the very secret of repose. In ordinary years I am as glad of April as Chaucer was; now I dreaded it, or at any rate begrudged it all its charm and power. To put off warm clothes, to see the days lengthen, to be aware of buds on trees, to stop worrying lest the car refuse to start, to know that the ground would not be white again for months, to let the furnace fire die out: these were not privileges. They were sentences, heartlessly pronounced.

I got over the perverse feeling soon enough, and June relaxed me as it always does. Yet even then I missed the season that was gone. I began to fear I would not remember it; would some day not have it, intact and clear, where I could look at it again. Memory is a miser; it loves to unlock and finger its treasures. Or so mine wanted to do then, somewhat as it had wanted in the spring of 1919 to count over the army days I had left behind me in what I thought was a sealed chamber. Now once more I could not rest until I had put a piece of my past into some suitable box where I could find it when I chose. So I decided to write, this time in verse, a diary after the event: not a real diary, for no such thing had been kept, but a fictitious one which might be all the truer because nothing essential was omitted. I went every morning, then, to my study by the pond and composed *A Winter Diary*, in heroic couplets which at the moment I supposed nobody but Dorothy would ever see and read, for they were not addressed to strangers. I put in every detail I naturally and immediately remembered, and then I finished with these lines:

> Now even the rain is gone, that kept us grey;
> Even the rain, preserving darkness too.
> After the flood dry weather, hot and blue,
> Washed every stain of winter off, and brightly
> Gave us this world, so changeable and sightly:
> Grass upon the mountains; smokeless-green
> May fire that will not languish till the lean,
> Brown, bitten earth, monotonous with stone,
> Hides under hotness, leafy and alone;
> Shade everywhere—as here beneath the crab,
> Where Snippy lies, and rumors of Queen Mab
> Bring bees to set the blossoms in a roar
> While marvelling children pace the petalled floor;
> Shade then for her, the borrowed Tabby, lying
> With three new kittens, curious and crying:
> The summer's offspring, not to be confused
> With those somehow more brave that March misused.
> Now the sleek mare is shod again, and trots
> Each day beneath her mistress, over lots
> Green-rising, or along a sandy road:
> Each of them glad, the bearer and the load;
> But I that walk to meet them down the lawn
> Remember lazy mornings lost and gone:
> Remember the cold, remember the lantern, hanging
> There by her nose at night, and blizzards banging
> Somewhere a shabby door; and my decision
> Goes to the old, the February vision.
> How old it is now, only a rake and spade;
> Only a coatless, an oblivious pair
> Of boys for whom all days to come are fair;
> Only her warm hand, patting down the seed
> Where sunlight lingers and the frost is freed;
> Only the hay-land, live again with snakes,
> Only these things can say what memory aches—
> Oh, vainly—to recapture; only such
> Can tell of the holy time our blood will touch—
> Oh, never again, and never; only June,
> That sings of something over deathly soon.
> Already the mind's forgetfulness has blended
> Music with music; and the months are ended.

Nannette Smith, who heard about the *Diary* and asked to read the manuscript, remarked after she had done so that it must have been painful to write of such personal things. My answer was that it would have been more painful not to. Merrill Prentice, reading it next, approved in the main but pointed to some rhymes which he said were forced and artificial. I explained that all rhymes are artificial; but in my own mind I knew that none should seem so, and I removed the worst offenders. Armin Landeck, going through the poem in his turn, said he was tempted to illustrate it. He never has, but he is still the artist I would select. Two years later the *Diary* was published. I decided not to keep it secret after all. And a famous paradox expressed itself once more: something I had thought too private to be understood by others was understood by everybody who read it. I have been told by a lady in Kentucky that it still makes her homesick for a place she has never seen. St.-John Perse, who is French but who has lived in many countries besides his own, tells me it is true for each of those countries. But nothing pleased me more than this letter that came to me at Columbia:

I liked being where you were in your Winter Diary, and could wish I never had to be or go anywhere else. I believe I saw how you got every turn of phrase and word-shift in it. I delighted in the way you took your rhymes. . . .

I must throw you back some snow for your snow. Be on your guard.

Always of your persuasion

Robert Frost

Amherst December 1 1935

VII

I wish my father could have read the *Diary* too, for nobody knew better than he did what it was about. But he died a few months after it was written, in October, 1933. He was seventy-six. My mother had let us know that the other doctors in

Urbana said he could not live; so I went out alone that summer to see him. I should have taken Dorothy and the boys, for he inquired about them with particular concern. As a result the boys do not remember him, and I am sorry for this. To be sure they would not have seen him as I now do, before he was wasted. He had cancer of the liver, and jaundice had turned his face a bright orange. But his eyes were of course the same; except that they seemed larger, as if they were the chief thing he had left, and indeed they were. Once when I was alone with him in the small room off the living room where my mother kept him so that he could be aware of what went on, he smiled at me as if he knew we shared a secret. "You came," he said, "to see me while you could." I could not deny it, though even then I was thinking: Those huge eyes. Two years later, when E. A. Robinson was dying in New York and Chard Smith went to pay him a final call, Chard's impression was identical with mine this day in Urbana. "I walked into the room," he said, "and there was nothing to see but those huge eyes."

All of his sons went to the funeral, and each of them had his private thoughts. It was not a depressing time, as Carl has said in his *Three Worlds*. We remembered too well the person in our father who could not die; and it was moving to witness how many people—old patients from Hope, friends old and young from everywhere—came to pay their respects; some of them said quite simply that they had never known a more lovable man. But over and over I was saying to myself: "The intensity of his existence, the intensity of his existence!" The words spoke themselves, like words engraved in air, for only me to hear and see. For I saw them as well as heard them; and I wondered if he did not. They were for him; I was telling him at last that I knew how much difference he had made to the world by being in it, and how much difference in return the world had made to him. He loved it in all its parts, the great, the small. Nothing was small for him, and nothing was great; every person, every thing, deserved to exist. I was also trying to tell him, I suppose, that nothing is more important in any man's life than the death of his father. After that the wind blows straight into his face: no oak groves, ash groves, nothing. "The intensity of his existence!" A poor phrase, but it would have to do. It did do until a year had passed and I could write "Here Then He Lay":

Where mild men gathered he was half at home,
Though none of him was there in hostile guise.
Yet even then the swifter half went on;
And still it goes, and still the curving skies
Contain the soundless footfalls of a man
Whose moving part our obsequies outran.

Here then he lay, and stationary flowers
Were like the words of good men come to see:
All pure, all nodding whiteness; final proof
Of wonder—save the last, the far degree.
Already, while the compliments uncurled,
He gathered with the dark ones of the world;

Came noiseless up, and shed the afternoon
Like a thin shoe behind him; so he stands
Eternally in twilight, and the rest
Acknowledge nothing alien in his hands,
That hour by hour acknowledge nothing there
Save the full dusk and the sufficient air.

It was the eyes that brought him; so he stays
Despite the something different in his walk.
Round, round he moves among them, and each one
Is different: more the panther, more the hawk,
More the slow-treading dove; yet no disguise
May alter their unburiable eyes.

Both sun and shade are in them, pair by pair,
Both everlasting day and boundless dark.
This is the field to which the few have come;
These are the visions death could never mark.
There was no way to deepen such a gaze
Save from this dusk, abstracted from all days.

There now his feet fall silently, and now
He is both old and young, his hope the same:

Ranging the mild world, sowing it with pride,
And leaving not a meadow of it tame;
Praising all men that have the quenchless eye;
Yet loving the unlustred who will die.

We praised him for the kindness of his talk,
And a meek heart mortality had kissed.
We might have sung the justice of a glance
Wherein not even littleness was missed.
Then, then we should have added his desire
For the great few and the unburning fire.

We told a tale of charity, and hands
Long practiced in the banishment of pain.
We knew his mind's ambition, and his tongue's
Swift temper, and his wisdom to refrain.
We should have known how nothing held him back
From the great dusk and from the trodden track.

He treads it now, and he is never tired.
There where he goes, intensity is ease.
No strict requirement but of old was met;
The world at last is single that he sees.
All one, the world is round him that he saw
When he looked past us, innocent of awe.

But ten years passed before I wrote, in "Aetat 50," what I must have understood that day without knowing I did. It seemed to me then that life itself had died; and yet the contrary of this was just as clear. Only one man had died, and even about that there was a question. Assuming he had, however, here were the living to say so with music, speech, and flowers. For the first time I understood ritual, the function of which is to say with beauty that true things are somehow good, even the death of an indispensable man. We learn about life by being told what we knew already: told in idioms ancient before our time. The last gift of my father to me was therefore this: that now I myself was licensed to grow old.

Will it be more of this that century day,
If day at all, if number, if I live,
Will it be this and better: what I know now

City and Country: 1928–1933

Doubled at least? I say it must, the learner
Willing. But there is chance, and damp decay,
And horrible dry eld. I know, I know;

But these things too have I, sometimes unwillingly,
Learned. Shall I rehearse them, or do all men,
Halfway between the crying and the cracking,
Honor with me the school a boyhood scorned?
No matter. It is my account, beginning
With ritual's beauty, learned at my father's grave.

No apple cheeks, no pouting, but a full
Brown figure that refuses to grow old,
Having no age; except it is not young
Nor tattered; it is all that sweeps between,
As the sea does, adding its salt to raindrops,
Then sweetening earth's crust from shore to shore.

Ritual, in repetition's colors,
Borrowing the brown, the sometimes gray,
Ritual, in repetition's language,
Borrowing that monotone, declares
How wise it is between our woeful boundaries,
The coming and the going; and how clear.

Ritual, the numberer, the namer,
Diagonals that wilderness; and where,
Passionate, lines cross that it has graven,
Upon that point a standing man is watch tower
To the whole waste; as I, when music sounded
Over my father's goodness, seen as one.

The beautiful full figure, life as lasting
All of the way, intense, across a square—
A circle, for the fierce line of the West
Bends to the East, go tirelessly enough—
The brown, the leather guardian, the gray
Unkillable tall person of our wisdom:

Him, at a death, a funeral, I witnessed
Where he looked on, careless if I mistook.
Younger, I would have; old, been too familiar
With the composite eyes. Which now I carry
Outward of mine, and pray that as I wither
The words too, commencing, will be long.

Before the War

1933–1940

*

THE little world of *A Winter Diary* was something to be homesick for during the seven years that followed its events—or its lack of them, according as such things are judged. The great world to which we returned had no doubt in its own mind that deep and dangerous events were taking place, at points so far apart that an all but universal anxiety seemed in order. The disaster of a second and more terrible world war was not to be avoided; or at any rate, as history went, it was not avoided. Meanwhile, however, there were only tremblings of it here and there: in Germany, Italy, and Spain; in Africa, in China. And at home in America there was the continuing depression, with threats of social war that every sensitive person responded to in his own way. I shared of course in the common sense of doomful things impending. Yet I could forget them too, somewhat as Milton counseled his friend Cyriack Skinner to forget whenever he could the politics of the 1650's:

> To measure life learn thou betimes, and know
> Toward solid good what leads the nearest way;
> For other things mild Heaven a time ordains,
> And disapproves that care, though wise in show,
> That with superfluous burden loads the day,
> And, when God sends a cheerful hour, refrains.

Back at our base on Bleecker Street the boys resumed their school, Dorothy took up new duties at *The Nation,* and all of us began the arduous task of living with Anna Grant, who now came to us as cook and household maid. She was to be our delight and terror for exactly twenty years. We did not know this then, for almost daily she announced that she was leaving; but perhaps we should have known that nothing so natural and good as her regard for us—whatever our failings, and she was eloquent about those, though not to others, as eventually we learned—could terminate this side of death. Anna was colored, was middle-aged, was ample in construction; and was quite as intelligent as she was strong. She took charge of us at once, and that was that. When we went to Cornwall she went there too; she had two homes as we did, and to the many friends who visited her she confided that she loved us. Never to us; we must not be spoiled; sarcasm, delivered in a high voice, was the proper idiom in our case. Yet our own friends were hers as well, so that she grew famous in the world we inhabited with them. "Mr. Carl" admired her as we did, and was not only admired but made welcome in return. She accepted in the same way our old friend Hedwig Koenig, now about to become a physician. Hedwig lived with us the next winter in New York, and in future years was to be with us much in Cornwall. "The Doctor" was promptly added to the number Anna knew, sometimes with sighs, she had in charge.

Back at Columbia I continued to teach Shakespeare—all of him—to students who more and more impressed me, in their talking and their writing, as masters of the thing in him that mattered: his incomparable self. If I should ever write a book about him, it would have their contributions in it, strengthening my own; but this could wait, for I was bound to gain by the delay. I am glad, for instance, that I waited until one student, Frederic Howard Meisel, wrote a paper on the "wailing women" of *Henry VI* and *Richard III*—on their voices, wild in chorus, which ever since I have heard as he described them.

Another course, in the literature of the seventeenth century, confirmed my faith that no better lyric verse has ever been written than was written then by Jonson, Donne, Herrick,

Herbert, Carew, Lovelace, Milton, and Marvell. My first introduction to these masters had been through Thoreau and Emerson, who imitated them with exciting results; and in some sense they had never ceased to be my favorites. But now there were T. S. Eliot's essays on them to reinforce my devotion; and once again I was helped to completer understanding by a student, this time a graduate student, Ivria Adlerblum, who in a paper I still keep by me analyzed their peculiar virtue. She called this virtue "lightness," by which she meant some such thing as Schiller meant when he said that playfulness was the final sign of genius in any poet. Good art weighs nothing; it is full of light; it knows its way among the mysteries of wit and humor; it is serious as air and water are, as love and morning. It is skillful in measuring the force of its exaggerations. Art exaggerates, but never successfully so except when it laughs at being caught in the act: its reference to truth is its smile. Ivria Adlerblum said this and more, and in saying all that she said put the "metaphysical" for me in its right perspective. The criticism of the 1930's went heavily in for that misnomer of Dr. Johnson's, and dredged up difficulties out of Donne, for example, that had better been left buried. Here, in the lightness I was taught to adore, the very secret of a century seemed to be solved. In several essays of my own I tried the theory out: in "What Is Poetry?," and in a paper I read at Richmond, Virginia, before a meeting of the Modern Language Association to which Allen Tate and John Crowe Ransom came. They agreed, but suspected me I thought of being a bit cavalier toward the famous difficulties. My commitment, however, was to ease; and so it has ever been. The best poetry, I still think, does not *seem* hard. Its coming to birth is of course as hard as it is rare; but the poets responsible for it prefer to sound like men who happily, luckily, had those things to say. The poet is first and last a man, and is not different from other men except in his occupation. I said this once in *The Nation,* in a piece called "What Is a Poet?," and was supposed by some readers not to be serious.

Mark Van Doren

Ivria Adlerblum, as I have said, was a graduate student; so I should not have known her if I had not begun, as I did in 1936, to give graduate lectures. I called my course The Art of Poetry, and invited its students, of whom Ivria was one, to read with me the best long or short poems we could find and consider why they were the best. I continued at this for ten years; but my emphasis soon shifted to the long poem, and in the end that was our only subject matter. My reason was personal: I still had ambitions to write such a poem myself, one that would satisfy me, and I thought I could learn by living with masterpieces. Also, I could not doubt that the students would benefit from a purely professional view of Homer, Virgil, Milton, Lucretius, Dante, Spenser, Byron, Wordsworth, and Chaucer. For these became our poets, and we read them whenever necessary in translation. It was not their language that we discussed; it was their themes, their visions, their fables, and their wisdom—or the want of it—in their management of these great things. The art of poetry I conceived to be the art of telling stories or otherwise rendering account of the single world all men inhabit. There was no literary history in the course; there was only criticism, and this was as serious as I could make it. I asked such practical questions as Aristotle had, and did not care how the answers came out. If Homer, Dante, and Chaucer went up and Milton, Lucretius, Spenser, Wordsworth, and Byron went down—relatively down—I had to say so, and I did say so with more and more confidence as time moved on. The outcome was to be a book, *The Noble Voice,* as in the case of the short poems (but these I took back to the College for more intimate examination) the outcome would be another book, *Introduction to Poetry.*

Then in 1937 we started giving in the College a course called Humanities: a course like Erskine's General Honors, but now it was prescribed for freshmen, whose privilege it would be to read and discuss in small sections, meeting four days a week, about twenty-five great books in the Western tradition. I helped to plan the course, and taught it for fifteen years; and nothing I ever did with students was more fun. Homer, Herodotus, Thucydides, Aeschylus, Sophocles, Euripides, Aristophanes, Plato, Aristotle, the Bible, Lucretius, Virgil, St. Augustine, Dante, Rabelais, Montaigne, Shakespeare, Milton, Molière, Swift, Voltaire, Goethe, and the rest: these proved, as Erskine had predicted, to be wise friends for freshmen. Also for their teachers, who if nothing else were grateful for the abundance of matter made available for discourse. Important questions raised themselves again and again; and the freshmen were astonished by their own competence to deal with them. Freshmen have had more experience than they are given credit for. They have been born, had parents, had brothers and sisters and friends, been in love, been jealous, been angry, been ambitious, been tired, been hungry, been happy and unhappy, been aware of justice and injustice. Well, these authors handled just such things; and they did so in the basic human language men must use whenever they feel and think. The result, if no teacher prevented its happening, was that the freshmen learned about themselves. And so did the teachers, at least if they read and talked like men of this world, simply and humbly, without assumptions of academic superiority.

In those days, of course, there were upperclassmen too in whom I took deep interest. This has never failed to be so, but the peculiar difficulty of the time—the depression at home, the brutal fanaticisms abroad—now seemed to increase their number.

John Berryman was first and last a literary youth: all of his thought sank into poetry, which he studied and wrote as if there were no other exercise for the human brain. Slender, abstracted, courteous, he lived one life alone, and walked with verse as in a trance.

Not so with Thomas Merton, who to my knowledge at the moment had no obsessions. Both merry and sober, he came in and out of my view at times of his own choosing. He wrote poems as Berryman did, but they appeared to be by-products of some rich life he kept a secret. His blue eyes twinkled when he overheard a witty remark, or when he uttered one himself, as often he did. I considered him a charming friend, yet I remained unaware of the problems which his own account of them was later to make famous. He was to solve his problems by becoming a Catholic and by entering a Trappist monastery; Communism tempted him but the Church won out. There was no way then for me to have foreknowledge of these things. When they happened he came and told me, and they seemed right to me because they did to him. But the last thing I suspected was that he thought of me as having helped him to make up his mind. It was so much his own mind that my utmost responsibility, I would have said if asked, was to admire it.

His friend Robert Lax, who followed him into the church but not into the monastery, was so uncommunicative and so shy that even if I had tried I could have uncovered none of his secrets. His chief secret, I have since decided, was a sort of bliss he could do nothing about. Least of all could he express it. Merton has described his long, lugubrious, humorous face, and has said of it that it seemed then to be the countenance of one who contemplated "some incomprehensible woe." The woe, I now believe, was that Lax could not state his bliss: his love of the world and all things, all persons in it.

He continues to try. Regularly since his student days he has sent me from various places, in envelopes of various sizes, pieces of verse or prose—once they were sections of a journal, but latterly they are jottings, perhaps a single sentence, a single line of verse—which by a certain fugitive felicity suggest that he may succeed before he dies. Here is one, for example: "Love is the light air and emanation of power and wisdom at play." To think such things and say them has been his only occupation. He has no profession, and lives in no place long. He has traveled with a circus, a little one whose clowns and acrobats he knows as he would know so many brothers and sisters, and loves with a devotion that shines in his eyes whenever he speaks their names. He has been here, been there, in Europe and America; and sometimes he settles in New York. But not for long, since one place merely fills him with the wish to see another. I have put him into a poem whose title, "Woe, Woe," takes its cue from Merton's portrait of his own best friend:

> Woe, woe. The long face,
> Patiently, in hoarse wind,
> Meditates, meditates,
> Without a word that men hear.
>
> When they do, and I have,
> What a seeing, what a song.
> Not a thought but thanks God
> For bird and leaf and Sunday morning. . . .
>
> Good, good: how get it said
> In man's time? God is long.
> Maybe that: he really mourns.
> The night comes. So much unmentioned.

If anyone supposes that the depression produced only bitterness in students, and savagery, and wrath, such cases as Berryman and Merton and Lax refute the supposition, or at least modify its force. There were bitter cases, granted; though again there was Robert Giroux, whose nature was as noticeably sweet as that of Merton or Lax, and as modest and as charitable. Giroux, who was destined to become a publisher of books, thought then that he would never be interested in anything but movies. He saw all the films, and made sure that I saw the best of them; scarcely a week passed without his coming in to tell me of one I must not miss. He lived in Jersey City, next to Bayonne where Robert Caldwell was about to establish himself as a newspaperman.

Caldwell, who had graduated in the deepest year of the depression, the year *A Winter Diary* begins, might have grown cynical because of what he saw; but in him too, for all the indignation he assembled against venal or pig-headed politicians, there lived on the pure temper that distinguished his student days. The uses of adversity, while not invariably sweet, still exercised their function in the 1930's; remembering which, I once wrote this about him:

> Massive the man, massive the wrath;
> He girds at public liars, thieves;
> Unreason so enrages him
> He trembles like a tree, with leaves,
> And might come down; except his strength
> Is delicate, both breadth and length.

II

In 1936 Scott Buchanan left the University of Virginia to be a member at the University of Chicago of a Committee on the Liberal Arts. Robert Hutchins had created such a committee because he wanted more knowledge for himself of the intellectual arts whose names survive without much meaning in the degrees conferred annually upon thousands of bachelors and masters; also, he hoped that a wiser college curriculum might result. One did, for the committee's deliberations had a profound effect, on many campuses and in many lives including mine. Scott's old Oxford friend, Stringfellow Barr, went with him from Virginia, and at Chicago Mortimer Adler and Richard McKeon were waiting to make their own characteristic contributions. The committee sat through the spring of 1937, its various members informing me at times of what they had discovered.

But nothing at the moment moved me half so much as a long letter from Scott, dated April 9, in which he told how he and his family had driven down to see my mother in Urbana. I had urged them to go, and prepared my mother for the visit; then here it was, with a generosity of detail that satisfied my hungriest curiosity. Frank and Grace came up with Martha the second afternoon. "Miriam and Douglas," Scott wrote me, "were ravished with Frank's likeness to you in both manner and appearance, and I found myself chattering to him as I do automatically with you." My mother told them things about me they had never heard; they told her things about me she had never heard; they talked of my father; they laughed about the reputations all Van Dorens have of being liars (tellers of tall tales); Scott began to feel as if he were my mother's sixth son; there were wonderful meals of "milk gravy, hot biscuits, coffee, apple pie, eggs fried in water"; and there was a side trip out to Hope.

"What shall I say about Hope?" said Scott. "One should begin like a medieval traveller and talk about the meaning of the name. It would apply and make a nice pastoral essay with both romance and pathos in it. It stands so open, innocent, and brave on a comparative height as you approach it, as if the ground had sighed and stayed that way just for the Van Dorens to be born, or rather for the Butzes and the Van Dorens to find each other. Those little towns are so eloquent with only a suggestion of their history, the groves that your grandfather planted, the house that burned down after your mother left it, the schoolhouse that Carl's book had already made familiar, the little church, and the real Van Doren house on another bulge in the bosom, all this shot in the middle by the concrete road that has carried the people away to town. We drove up and stopped at each place, made comments, asked questions, recorded changes, and rode back, I at least with curious images of the doctor in his saddle bags, picking the direction for the horse to pick his steps through the mud. The deep ditch on the left of the road as you drive back tells by its depth and width the story of the mud that was there once. May I say that I now know very vividly why you once wanted to be and are now a poet. These things throw the mind into a coction; they almost sing themselves, and they are already stories. My mind is singing with them now. We came through Hope on our way back, took some pictures, and looked again, last at the groves as we cruising-geared the hill."

It had been just twenty years since I plowed corn at Hope and waited for the war to come and take me. Twenty years before that I had played in the front yard, hauling coal and swearing for Frank's amusement. Scott's letter collapsed forty years into one brilliant second of insight. No wonder I was moved, and being moved was grateful to my medieval traveler from Chicago.

The conclusion and fruit of this year for Scott was a new college which he as dean and Stringfellow Barr as president were called upon to create during the summer of 1937 in Annapolis. St. John's was in fact an old college, but it badly needed making over. The two men made it over by building from the ground up a curriculum whose rationale they had discovered at Chicago; or rediscovered, for the thought of the committee had traveled back along the track of the liberal arts to points in medieval practice and, farther yet, in Plato's mind where a strong light played upon their special meaning. St. John's revolutionized itself, and soon enough had revolutionized liberal education in America. This last was seldom admitted, and indeed the example of St. John's was nowhere followed out to the end of a strict resemblance. The experiment was generally dismissed as at once too radical and too ancient for the modern world. But it was for that world and no other and it left its traces everywhere upon it, as did the Humanities course at Columbia, begun in the same year. I am glad that I was involved in both.

I was involved in St. John's as a friend of its chief conceiver, as an occasional lecturer for twenty years, as a member for ten years of its board of visitors and governors, and as the father of two of its students. This may sound like a deep involvement, but it was not: I never worked my way down to the bottom of the structure. To have done that would have meant going there and staying; and furthermore it would have meant reeducating myself. Any true member of the community, whether student or teacher, did what the others did: disciplined himself simultaneously in mathematics, science, metaphysics, phi-

losophy, theology, music, language, and literature. It was a
strenuous way of life; there was only one curriculum, and
all were expected to master it to the best of their several abil-
ities. My own education had been largely literary and it still
is that. And when Scott invited me to lecture on certain
Friday nights he recognized the limitation. My subjects were
Homer, the Greek dramatists and historians, Aristotle's *Poetics,*
Virgil, St. Augustine's *Confessions,* Dante, Montaigne, Cervantes, Shakespeare, Milton, Pascal, lyric poetry, and the like.
They were never mathematical.

Yet I was welcome for whatever I could say, and gradually I
carried away with me more than anyone save Scott could have
been aware of. The love of great books which I had shared
with Carl and with Joe Krutch was somehow made more
serious, systematic, and exciting. To lecture at St. John's was
itself a discipline—and to be questioned by the students later,
in another room of the college, for perhaps two hours. They
all knew the same things; in seminars, tutorials, and laboratory
sessions they had considered as one person the central problems of the mind; and if I remained an amateur in most of
these problems, at least I talked in an atmosphere where
poetry, for example, took on an immediate, practical importance. Great books, the core of the curriculum, not only included poetry; they illuminated it, and were illuminated by it
in return. I saw now as never before why Scott like Mortimer
Adler had spoken of it as one of the basic things. As only one,
to be sure; but elsewhere it was usually not spoken of as even
that; it was an indulged art, whose function most critics had
forgotten; it was not a form of knowledge. At St. John's it was
never condescended to, though it was not exalted beyond its
deserts, as sometimes it is by those in our day who have lost
the skill to see it in perspective. As a reader, a teacher, a
critic, and a poet I learned at St. John's more than I can say.
For one thing, these occupations suddenly became one. They
always had been, but now I ceased to care which of them came
first. They all came first; they were one life; they were my life,

and henceforth I lived it, I like to believe, more naturally, more completely, than before.

The year 1937 was notable again for the return that fall of Joe Krutch to Columbia, this time as professor. He continued to live at Redding, whence he came by train or car to his classes and to an office in Hamilton Hall adjoining mine. He was pleased to be there, as I certainly was pleased to be once more in a situation where I could see him regularly and resume our conversation. Raymond Weaver, almost as ancient a friend of Joe's, took a third part in this conversation; but indeed there were many who did, for who could resist so seasoned a mind and so prodigal a wit?

It was a time, with war not very long away, when other old friends became visible too. The Tates spent the summer of 1938 in Cornwall, in a house not far from ours, and we saw them daily; none of us has forgotten how Allen set up the boys' blackboard on our lawn one afternoon and diagramed the battle of Gettysburg, explaining every move the armies made. Toward the end of that summer, just before the hurricane that devastated New England, we drove up to Marlboro, New Hampshire, where the Adlers had spent their vacation. They had an infant son and his name was Mark; but try as I did, I could never surprise them into a confession that he had been named for me.

Then in October, back in New York, Whittaker Chambers showed up. He called from the Pennsylvania Station one evening to say he must see me—alone, for he was in danger. What sort of danger? He would tell me when he came. Dorothy was at home, and Hedwig Koenig had been with us for dinner; but I must take him directly upstairs to my study on the third floor, where he would make everything clear. What he told me was that he had left the Communist Party, which because he had left it, and because he knew so many of its secrets—its plots, its murders, its misdeeds of every kind—was after him to kill him. What I could do for him was this: I could help him to become known again in the world out of which he had disappeared ten years before—from my sight, as I have said, and from the sight of everyone I knew. Now he was anonymous, so that if murdered he would not be missed. Even one review in a reputable paper would reinstate him in society; I must write a letter for him, recommending him to literary editors. He was so mysterious about all this, and overstated things, I thought, so laughably in the old way, that I teased him a little, reminding him among other things that as a result of his dark life for a decade I knew nothing about him. I ended up, however, by writing such a letter and giving it to him; he slipped downstairs; and I never saw his face again until it appeared in the photographs which every reader of newspapers was to be familiar with after ten more years had passed.

III

Carl's *Three Worlds* had appeared in 1936. He wrote it in Urbana, at my mother's house, and it cured him in large part of his private depression. Its success was good for him too; the beginning of it, reprinted as *An Illinois Boyhood,* soon became a classic account of Middle Western country manners at the end of the last century, seen now by accurate yet charitable eyes, and understood in the powerful way Carl took of understanding any complex human scene. He was free then to go ahead with the biography of Benjamin Franklin he had for years been ambitious to write. Franklin to him was not merely a great statesman and diplomat; he was a great writer, and in the final view he was a great man, universal in his curiosity and impeccable in his wisdom. I have never seen anybody more absorbed in a subject than Carl was in Franklin. Sometimes he seemed to think he should apologize for referring so often to the man he literally lived with day and night. We did not agree. For one thing, he was always telling us delicious things, and smiling over sentences he had found in letters or reports.

For another thing, he *was* smiling. Franklin was the company Carl needed. The serenity in that sage, triumphing over so many troubles, was itself an education in the art of life, a difficult art at any time, but Carl had come close to despairing lest it no longer be possible to practice. The immense success of the book when it appeared in 1938 was among other things a decisive tribute to Carl's achievement of his own equilibrium. Not that he talked of this on any page, for as always he honored his subject by sticking to it. His subject was Franklin. But Franklin lives as he does in the book because Carl was happy that he had lived at all. Unique and Olympian, he smiles there in the certainty that a biographer has at last comprehended him. Carl was the company he needed.

Through most of the decade now passing I wrote reviews for *The Nation;* and for three years (1935–1938) I was its movie critic. This began accidentally, and more or less in fun. I happened to be about one day when the editors were wondering what successor might be found to William Troy, who had tired of the work. "Why not me?" I said. "Think of being paid to see movies!" Before I knew it I was hired; and I must say that I have relished few duties more. With or without Dorothy I went almost nightly—but sometimes it was in the afternoon, or even in the morning if no classes conflicted—into movie houses of all sizes and descriptions, looking for films or parts of films that I could write nine hundred words about. Alfred Hitchcock's melodramas, French and Russian masterpieces, British pictures and American, documentaries and musicals: I tried them all, frequently without result but always in search of principles worth stating. I was helped not only by Robert Giroux, with whom I discussed my reviews, but by Mortimer Adler, long an addict to the art but now in process of writing his own book, *Art and Prudence,* on the subject of its censors. I cannot claim that I elucidated any fundamental principles; but then I had never been serious in the expectation that I should. At the most I enjoyed my excursion, just as I enjoyed the end of it when it came. For I too grew tired of the work when I realized that it was work.

I was tiring, to be truthful, of criticism in all its branches; of periodical criticism, which is to say reviewing, at any rate. For nearly twenty years I had kept at it; but now, quite suddenly, I was through. I would still write critical books, and they would be of great personal importance to me; but no more assignments from editors, I said. It was a wonderful release. I am not sorry that I spent the time and strength I did when I seemed to have them; neither am I sorry that thenceforth I read on my own, for reasons no longer requiring explanation, and with results in my own life that were nobody else's business. I became, as I was to say in 1942, a "private reader": the kind of reader for whom authors really write. They will never hear from him, but they continue in the confidence that he understands their every sentence, every word. For them the reader is the world; and like the world, is most himself when he is wise and silent. Such was the virtue I decided to assume.

Dorothy left *The Nation* in 1936, after seventeen years of editorial labor in more than one of its departments. And soon she was at another novel, one that dealt as I have already said with her own childhood in Brooklyn. *Those First Affections* (1938), taking its title from Wordsworth's famous Ode, is a true book, however, for other reasons than its fidelity to a thousand recollected details. If these details are moving, the explanation is that they serve a deeper purpose than autobiography. Dorothy has always said that no novel can be purely autobiographical anyhow: fiction is better than fact, and it comes into its own when the novelist remembers to be an artist. The little girl who is the heroine of *Those First Affections* is viewed at last like any child; is happy, is unhappy, for reasons any reader may comprehend; and when she fails her parents, as Sarah does at the school exhibition by not being on hand to share in their pride and pleasure, she is authentically a case, touching and clear for anyone to see, of youth that sins by omission just as age did in its time; as all people do in spite of their hope that they never will. From *Those First Affections* I learned a great deal about Dorothy that I had not known before. I learned for the first time, too, what her father had been like: amusing, gentle, proud, and kind. His death, coming so soon after the exhibition that amends in his case could not be made, shook me as few things have in any book. But the final thing I learned was the power that Dorothy had as a novelist.

IV

When I published *A Winter Diary* in 1935 I had many shorter poems to put with it, for several years had passed since *Now the Sky*. There were the "psychological lyrics," as Allen Tate called them, which I had written in the same winter with the *Diary*, but there were others too: love poems, "Here Then He Lay," lyrics descriptive of people, a group that analyzed, somewhat in the manner of Spinoza, the human emotions, and a further group suggesting that individuals who heretofore had lived for themselves might now "return to ritual"—by which I meant, participate in the affairs, the joys and the agonies, common to their species. The volume in other words was a record of my own mind since 1928. I did not need to be told, or perhaps I did, what Allen told me in the review he wrote for *The Nation*, namely, that such records had in modern times gone out of date, along with the "limpidity" and "ease of expression" that make them possible. Poetry had not been used for such a purpose since the age of Dryden, when it was "an objective art with the properties of rhyme and meter, and an expected level of diction as well. It was not a specific experience. Any kind of experience could go into it; the whole range of thought and feeling, from emotion at high tension to casual observation, naturally went into verse. . . . Poetry is no longer an objective art; we are not satisfied with a mere high level of technical performance; we deny that the properties of such a performance have any force in themselves, or that the means of the performance, taken alone, exist." The statement could scarcely have been more brilliant. I admired it for its precision, and stubbornly decided to go on deserving it in future volumes. Allen had ended by saying of "This Amber Sunstream," which he thought the best piece in the book: "We cannot decide absolutely how good it is; but if it is good, it is clear that it will be as good in 1980 as it is today." I made up my mind to keep on trying to meet that condition; and, fashionably or no, to continue with the record of my thoughts and feelings—always, of course, more interesting to me than any technical performance of which I might be capable.

Within two years I had another volume ready. I dedicated *The Last Look* to Scott Buchanan, who received his copy in Annapolis, on a hot day in late summer when he must have been exhausted by his efforts to get St. John's College going. He read it that night and wrote me about it the next day— generously, I need not specify. I have often wondered what he really thought of the first poem in the book. There he was hammering out a curriculum designed to promote in students the skill to designate the things of this world and to order them in terms of their importance; and here I was saying in "Axle Song" that the world had grown weary of such attentions from man the numberer, the namer:

> That any thing should be—
> Place, time, earth, error—
> And a round eye in man to see:
> That was the terror.
>
> And a true mind to try
> Cube, sphere, deep, short, and long:
> That was the burden of the sky's
> Hoarse axle song.
>
> Improbable the stoat,
> The mouse, toad, worm, wolf, tiger;

Unthinkable the stallion's trot,
Behemoth's swagger.

Unspeakable; yet worse—
Name, look, feel, memory, and number;
Man there with his perverse
Power not to slumber.

Let things created sleep;
Rock, beast, rain, sand, and sliding river.
So growled the earth's revolving heap;
And will forever.

The body of the book consisted largely of lyrics with a narrative cast—ballads, I might have called them—treating actual or imagined persons in crises that revealed their natures. But there were poems too about my grandparents, my father and mother, my children ("Boy Dressing" and "Like Son"), and many darker beings I had known or now made up, as ghosts if necessary: walkers over the grave of my own meditations. In a final poem, "The End," I sought to say what all of the volume had been about; and trusted the reader to hear Robert Herrick in its lines, of course with a certain sinister, even macabre difference:

I sing of ghosts and people under ground,
Or if they live, absented from green sound.
Not that I dote on death or being still;
But what men would is seldom what they will,
And there is farthest meaning in an end
Past the wild power of any word to mend.
The telltale stalk, and silence at the close,
Is most that may be read of man or rose.
Death is our outline, and a stillness seals
Even the living heart that loudest feels.
I am in love with joy, but find it wrapped
In a queer earth, at languages unapt;
With shadows sprinkled over, and no mind
To speak for them and prove they are designed.
I sing of men and shadows, and the light
That none the less shines under them by night.
Then lest I be dog enemy of day,

Before the War: 1933–1940

I add old women talking by the way;
And, not to grow insensible to noise,
Add gossip girls and western-throated boys.

And within another two years I published my *Collected Poems*. I omitted some poems, I shortened others, and still it was a copious volume—too copious, I heard soon enough, for all save those who were willing that its record of my thoughts and feelings go unabridged. I made the book even a bit longer by writing for it, because I wanted it to contain new matter, and because I had the idea in any case, a series of poems which I called "America's Mythology." There was much talk at the time of our poverty in myth. We had no gods. But we did, the series aimed to say. Our gods bore no ancient names, even no proper names; yet they were with us every day, in the ways we thought and felt and took things for granted.

Gigantic on the path, they never speak.
Unwitnessed, they are walked through every hour.

They were our folkways, our habits of which we were unaware: the unacknowledged forms of our very life as we lived it. Then I offered examples: the god of front porches, of barn driveways, of strange towns entered by night, of cherry-picking, of sickbeds, of gardens, of knowing the directions, of crowds, of horses, of birds, of flowers, of homesickness for history, of night fear, of the tall tale, of anger, of ghosts, of the wheel, of the schoolroom, of cemeteries, of song. I did not write any more short poems until the war that was coming called them forth.

Well before that, in the middle of this decade, I had written two novels. A better name for them would have been tales; and eventually, accepting the term as appropriate for me, I was to follow them with tales indeed: more than a hundred such, which I called short stories. But now, very rapidly, I wrote *The Transients* and *Windless Cabins;* and learned from Joe Krutch when he read them that they were more alike than I had thought. In each of them, he said, I was concerned with knowledge shared in secret by a man and woman; in the second case, by a boy and girl; and in future stories he was to point out further parallels. The knowledge shared by John Bole and Margaret Shade, transients on man's earth for a little while, was of the eternal place, or order of being, they had abandoned to come here. And they would return; but Margaret would do so unwillingly because she had fallen mortally in love with Bole, and would try in vain to keep him in a deserted house (like several such on the road between Cornwall Hollow and Canaan) which she had neatened into a nest. They were angels caught in the net of time: perfect creatures trying out our imperfection, and fascinated by it in their differing degrees. Here was perhaps my favorite subject. I had dealt with it in "Report of Angels":

"Nothing for envy there"—
Folding their dustless wings—
"Nothing, beyond this pair
Of impossible things:

"Love, wherein their limbs,
Trembling, desire to die;
And sleep, that darkly swims,
Drowning each brain and eye.

"Nothing is there for us,
Who may not cease to know;
But heaven was merciless,
Fixing our eyelids so;

"Whereon no tide may run,
Rolling its night ahead;
Where love is a labor done,
And death long since was dead."

And I was to deal with it many times again. As a teacher, discussing *Paradise Lost* with students, I had tried to make them see that Eden was not necessarily a dull place; we only think it is because having left it we can no longer understand it. We flatter ourselves in the mirror of our consequent depravity. So, at any rate, John Bole insists; and he has the last word in *The Transients.*

Windless Cabins had difficulty in finding a publisher, and so did not appear until five years after *The Transients,* in 1940. The trouble seems to have been that its hero was a murderer who went unpunished. He was a good boy who killed a bad man—without premeditation, too—yet as many as twenty-five publishers stuck at my letting him off. Ray and Lucy keep the knowledge of the murder to themselves: that is the substance of the story, whose setting is a colony of tourist cabins where Ray works, and where Lucy is threatened by a stranger, a guest in one of the cabins. Having killed the stranger with one blow of his fist, Ray buries him in the woods, in such terror and with such haste that he does not retrieve the flashlight which falls, still shining, into the grave. If he is punished at all, and I suggested that he was in a thousand ways, it is by his memory of this buried spark, this telltale brilliance underground. In any case he is never apprehended by the law, nor does he go and confess to the police. He will live, though, forever with his victim, as Hawthorne's hero, Septimius Felton, is unable to forget the beautiful young English officer he killed at Concord. I dedicated the book to Armin Landeck and Septimius Felton; but I never bothered to tell anybody that the name I gave the cabins, Windless, had its origin by contraries in Hurricane, West Virginia, where I had stayed one night with Dorothy and the boys on one of our trips by car to Illinois.

The summer of 1938 I devoted in Cornwall to the writing of *Shakespeare,* a book which Raymond Weaver, with whom I regularly discussed the subject, had been telling me for years was overdue. So when it was done I dedicated it to him and even presented him with the manuscript; but it was not done without intense and tiring effort. This was the summer the Tates spent in Cornwall, and Allen often remarked that I showed the strain. But once I had begun I could not stop; wound up to state if I could the essence of a given play, I could not relax until that chapter was finished. The plan was simple: a chapter for each play, with no words to be wasted because the subject was vast and there was always more to come. I had my students constantly in mind: things they had said to me, things I had said to them, and things they now might learn for the first time as I myself was learning them. I had Stuart Sherman in mind as well, and Lete Flaningam, and numberless other readers, dead or alive, who I knew had been where I was, deep in the riddle of Shakespeare's art—or, and it is exactly the same thing, deep in the facts of human feeling. Carl, who read the manuscript at once, said I had made each play seem different in some fresh way from all of its fellows. My explanation was that I habitually thought of them as creature things, and therefore as individuals, almost as animals, with grace and strength peculiar to themselves. Perhaps there is no better figure for Shakespeare the creator, the poet who as he imitates life seems to show it for the first time in its full natural glory.

V

We had no trouble deciding where our second sabbatical should be spent. In Cornwall, of course, where we had been so happy seven years ago. And there was no other place, in the summer of 1939, that promised peace. The rumors of war were not to be doubted any longer. Nobody knew then how much of the world would be involved; the United States might become this time the battleground; but Cornwall in that case would be one of the last sectors of disturbance, and anyway it was where we wanted to wait out the year. Yet we determined to start off with a trip by car to California: a quick trip, which nevertheless would give us all our first sight of the country west of Illinois. We had driven there many times, and then no farther. It was time, Dorothy and I agreed, that the boys should cross the Mississippi. They were thirteen and eleven, and they would not forget the experience.

We left early in June, and our first stop naturally was Urbana. But I had written my Uncle Mark Butz in Wapanucka, Oklahoma, that I was now prepared to accept his invitation of twenty-four years ago; he had replied at once that he and Aunt Cora would be waiting for us; so we set out southwest from my mother's house with the intention of arriving on the 13th—a nice coincidence, I thought, since it was on this date that I had been given my uncle's name just forty-five years ago. We crossed into Missouri, went on through a corner of Kansas, and early in the afternoon of the expected day found ourselves at a filling station on the edge of Wapanucka—at one end, that is to say, of its single wide, hot street where few people were walking.

Uncle Mark had meant this filling station, I thought, when he advised me to get out and ask how to reach his place, which was four miles north of town. But the attendant surprised me. "Mark Butz?" he said. "Why, he's in town today." "He is? Where can I find him?" "Oh, anywhere. Just ask." I left Dorothy and the boys sitting in the car while I began the search. Almost at once a fat man in overalls, staring as I approached him, stopped dead in front of me and said: "Are you Mark Butz's nephew?" "Why, yes." "Well, he's in town. He's looking for you." "Where?" "Oh, down a ways. Might try the drugstore." I found the drugstore and pushed open its screen door, letting in some flies. From the rear a voice said: "You Mark Butz's nephew?" "Yes." "Well, he's in town. Been here all day. He's looking for you." "Where?" "Oh, he'll be down the street. You'll see him." I went out and kept on, aware now that all of Wapanucka had been alerted; Uncle Mark must have driven in at dawn and told every inhabitant who was coming. And soon enough I found him. On a bench in front of a store four or five men were sitting, and one of them stood up, the tallest of them, grinning at me as he put

out his hand. "Well, you're here!" I said I was, and the blue
eyes in the leather face blazed with pride and pleasure as we
walked back to the rest of my family.

He took the boys into his old Ford and told Dorothy and
me to follow. There had been a rain the night before, and the
ruts were muddy. He splashed through them as if they were
not there; we bounced after him; and then, up a sudden road
to the left, there was a square cement-block house from whose
porch Aunt Cora waved. She was a little woman, merry and
warm, and there could be no doubt that she was glad to see us.
And she was proud of this house that Uncle Mark had built for
her. The log cabin was gone. It had been a legend with me, and
I missed it, but of course I said nothing of that. Frank had seen
it once and told me about it; there was a fireplace at each end
of its one room, and a shotgun hung where Uncle Mark could
snatch it easily when he wanted meat for dinner. His chickens
roosted in the trees, and he shot one of them for him and
Frank; it was tough, Frank said, but tasty. That had been, however, when Uncle Mark was a bachelor. Now he had what he
considered a modern house, built off one corner of the abandoned cabin, which he had not bothered to tear down all at
once; gradually its logs had been used up, for fence rails or for
fires. He did everything slowly. Aunt Cora told us she had
expected to marry him when they were young; but he never
got around to asking her, so she married someone else. Eventually she was a widow, and still Uncle Mark did not ask her;
therefore she asked him. He agreed, grinning, that this was the
way it had been; and then he wanted to know how long we
could stay. I was almost ashamed to tell him that our schedule
called for moving on tomorrow morning. Both of them protested; but so I thought it had to be; and the only question
now was how we all might make the most of our afternoon
and night together.

The most was certainly made of it. We walked over the
farm, unconscious of the chiggers in the weeds—we would
have them with us for a week—then came back in for talk that

lasted after supper until midnight: about Shakespeare among other things, for Uncle Mark admired him too, and said he must read my book, which he was glad I had written. But also we talked of Illinois—Potomac and Urbana—and the boys learned things they had not known before. Once during the night I woke up and saw a crack of light under the door of the bedroom which our hosts, displacing themselves, had assigned to us. I got up and found Uncle Mark on a cot in the living room, upright under a droplight, reading. He was too excited, he said, to sleep. Also, he had to be on hand to get us up in the morning. He did that, early enough, and after a breakfast of pancakes we were off. He insisted on driving ahead of us until we reached the concrete pavement that would take us west. He told us good-by there, and none of us ever saw him again. I put the entire story, with no changes, into a poem, "The Uncle I Was Named For," which I wrote and published twelve years later.

We went on across Oklahoma, Texas, New Mexico, and Arizona to California, then up through the great sequoias to San Francisco; after that, north along the Pacific to Eureka, where we started east again: Nevada, Idaho, Wyoming, Nebraska, and so straight home through Michigan, where we visited Guy's. The whole trip had taken only a month, which meant that we drove steadily and fast, and doubtless stopped too seldom. But we loved the continual change, or at least I did; and at night we cheerfully took our chances in whatever tourist house, cabin, or motel showed up when we were weary of motion. It was such a trip as thousands of American families take every year. This, however, was a special year; and its special event was Wapanucka.

Back in Cornwall I busied myself with making over for winter use the study by the pond where I had written every summer for fourteen years. In 1938 the pond itself had been dredged out and restored to its original state by two neighbor boys, Harvey and Lester Whitford; there was now a stone dam at its lower end, and water spilled noisily outside my windows. The same water had once been conveyed by a flume to an opening in the building through which it poured and turned a ponderous wooden wheel, built for the Bradfords in 1901 by Abram Palmer, and ultimately operated a saw. I did not repair the wheel, whose axle was broken, though I protected it with a new roof. I let the stream fall and run under the building as I had found it doing when I came. But the room where I wrote would not be warm after September; so I lined it with old boards, put down a second floor, and installed a sheet-iron stove with a store of kindling piled nearby. There was plenty of kindling. The pond and the study were at the edge of a forest several miles in depth, and enough dry wood dropped annually to support ten thousand fires. Across the pond, in a glade which two large maples had kept clear of underbrush for many years, the boys and I built a fireplace suitable for picnics that same summer. We have used it ever since, and as I say in "Gift of Kindling," there has always been a supply of sticks to burn:

> Between the pond and brook
> A table of fern land,
> A sweet, surprising lawn
> Where two trees stand:
>
> Wolf maples, that were cause,
> Deep shaders, that could bring
> This miracle to pass,
> This delicate wood ring
>
> Whose center now is hearth;
> We laid those lichened stones;
> And many a summer night
> We picnic on the bones
>
> Of that old buck, the silence,
> Or of that fawn, the fear;
> We burn whatever creature
> Is immemorial here.
>
> Yet with the glade's forgiveness.
> For not a time has been

Before the War: 1933–1940

But dry limbs, dropping,
Have said, let smoke begin.

The boys were going to local schools that year: Charlie to
the new regional high school in Falls Village, and Johnny to
the Cornwall consolidated grammar school. This would leave
me free most of each day to come over the field to my warm
study. We had no horse, though we did have Sam again: Sam
the gentleman, now fourteen years old and a little stiff in his
hindquarters, but as handsome and companionable as ever.
If it is true that he ran back to Torrington a few days after
we brought him to stay with us, it is also true that when we
returned for him he was frantic with joy at seeing us, and
never ran off again. The old Italian who kept him over the
winter told us he was merely obeying a sound instinct to
make sure he could find his way home if he had to.

The Buchanans had given the boys two puppies for themselves. But Sam (named for our Sam) had been killed by a car
in Litchfield, and Mike, whom Johnny adored, developed as
this winter wore on a fatal compulsion to chase deer in the
woods. The dog warden said he would have to shoot him the
next time he found him doing it, and advised us to dispose of
him, for the habit could not be cured. We tied him up for
several weeks, but confinement was such agony for him that I
decided to take the warden's advice. The morning of the day
I did so—I left him with a vet—I wondered whether I should
tell Johnny what was going to happen. On the theory that he
would bear the news better that night, I waited till he came
home from school, then told him Mike was gone for good.
Without a word he walked to the tool house and made some
kind of marker—no one ever saw it—for an imaginary grave.
With this under his coat he went alone to the woods and put
it somewhere that seemed right; I never learned where, though
several times I looked. He never spoke of Mike again. I should
have told him in the morning.

While the summer lasted I played baseball with the boys—
grounders on the lawn—or walked with them and Dorothy

233

over the farm, sometimes with Anna too, since she liked to look for ferns and wildflowers in the woods. I had recently written another children's book, *The Transparent Tree;* it was about certain beauties of the Bradford place I thought the boys were indifferent to. I invented a stranger, Slim Jim, who tricked two brothers like Charlie and Johnny into seeing things they had never seen, and even into praising them. But I now know they did not need the lesson, any more than Will Bailey did who had spent so many intimate years with objects I myself would never have the wit to see. He was still here that fall, with Mrs. Bailey in the house at the foot of the road. As for the farm itself, happily it was in the good hands of our neighbor Allyn Hurlburt, who treated it as an extension of his own acres so that I no longer had to worry about its appearance or its care.

VI

My project for the winter was a long poem. At last I had a subject—which is to say, a story, for the poem must be narrative; I was interested in nothing else. I had considered many heroes, many fables, many settings, but none of them had satisfied me; I could not imagine their further development. One of the heroes, Lincoln, baffled all of my attempts to see him in concentration; he would wait ten years until I did. Then by good luck a subject came. Two or three summers back I had gone with Dorothy to visit Frank and Grace in Tuscola, and one morning I dropped into the office where Grace worked. She put in my hands a big subscription history of Douglas County, saying I might find a few items of interest there; I turned the pages, expecting little, but suddenly I was lost in "A personal sketch by Dr. H. Rutherford, Oakland, Illinois," which the editors had reprinted from the Transactions of the Illinois State Historical Society for 1907. The title of the sketch was "John Richman, a Typical Backwoodsman," and these were the paragraphs I was never to forget:

It was back in February, 1841, that a settler on Brush Creek, three miles of Oakland, had a sale. He had had hard luck as he termed it. He had followed the rainbow to Illinois, but now the bow of promise was in Missouri, resting over the new Platte Purchase. There was snow on the ground, and taking a seat in a friend's sleigh, we made our way through the jack-oak brush to the place of sale. . . .

The sale of old barrels and other trumpery went slowly on. People cared more to group and gossip. A man in one of the groups near me, looking up the road, enquired, "Who's that?" No one knew the strange looking person approaching. Captain Bagley being appealed to, said: "That's old John Richman." Mr. Richman was a man of sixty years, six feet high, strongly built and in vigorous health. He carried a long rifle—a deer gun—with a leather guard over the lock. His rig and costume was unique and picturesque even for that day; a full hunter's outfit. He wore no hat, but instead a knitted woollen cap of white, red and green bands, with a white tassel at the top. His hunting shirt was of walnut jeans fringed along the seams and skirts, and around the neck and cape. His pants, of the same material, were held up by a draw string and secured at the ankles by deer leather leggings, bound by cross thongs fastened to his moccasins. He wore a leather belt in which was stuck a small tomahawk. To his shoulder strap was attached a pouch, a powder horn and a small butcher knife in a sheath. His moccasins had sole leather bottoms fastened by thongs. He was clean shaved, and his shirt and clothing were bright and clean; a cleanly man by the way, and I never saw him in any other condition.

After greeting, he stated that one of his pet deer had escaped from his park three weeks ago. He had expected it to return, but, instead, found it gone down the timber. He was sure it would come back in four weeks time, but fearing somebody might shoot the "critter," he had started out to find it and bring it back if alive. He had staid last night with his friend, Andrew Gwinn, and hearing of this sale, he had come by, hoping to hear of it. It was a doe with a red flannel band on its neck and with a small brass bell held by a leather strap. He added "If I could only hear one tinkle of that bell, I'd know it." No one had seen or heard of it,

Mark Van Doren

but all assured him that nobody would kill it, knowing from the band that it was a pet. Some one suggested that as the truant was going down the river, she might still be on the tramp, and by this time be in Jasper County. He shook his head with a decisive "No! She will not go more than two miles below here." He gave no reason for the opinion, but he no doubt knew what we did not know, that the range limit for the deer was twenty miles from the place of birth and breeding. . . . Some one else inquired, "How will you find that deer among the brush, the thickets, and the long grass?" Holding up a turkey call-bone he said, "Every day when I brought her her feed, I called her up with that bone; if ever she hears it again she will know it and come to me. She will know me, too, and let me lead her home. If she is alive I will find her and find her down there." Pointing to the southwest. I had read with the ardor of youth "Gertrude of Wyoming" and the Leather Stocking Tales. I had heard of Mr. Richman before and now realized there stood before me a type of a mountain hunter, more perfect perhaps than any that fiction had ever made. Shouldering his gun, he went on his way. We watched him with interest till he disappeared among the trees in his loving search for the lost doe.

It subsequently transpired that he made his way to the neighborhood of St. Omar, two miles north of Ashmore. Here, he decided, was the deer's boundary limits, here he began his search, as I was told afterwards by several of the residents. He staid two days roaming over the barrens and river bluffs, sounding his call-bone as he went, but no doe ever came to him. He became convinced that some one had killed it, and the wretch who had done it lived near by. In his anger he told several people what he thought and that if he ever found out who did it, he would put a bullet through him if it was seven years afterwards. He made and repeated this savage declaration in the house of David Golliday, Sr., unaware of the fact that at that time the band and bell of this doe was then hidden within a few feet of him. A few days previous one of the Golliday boys had brought in the dead body of the truant doe, with the red band and bell on it; knowing how mean and dirty the act was, the family kept it secret. The old man's threats terrified them so much that the bell was kept in hiding for several years, till it was known that the ferocious old hunter was dead. . . .

One day in November, '44, Mr. Richman appeared at my house. . . . He staid with me two days and told me a hundred of his hunting, mining and ghost stories. Brim full of superstitions, he

236

was what the scriptures call a "natural man." Without moral or religious training, he did not know one letter from another, and to him the reading of a printed page was a mystery. His youth and manhood had been spent in the mountains of Virginia, living a wild and savage life. He told me he had never worn a shoe or a boot nor ever had an overcoat on his back. Roaming over the country in search of game, in those days when the prairie was a wilderness and the settler was found only at distant points of timber, it was his habit when night was coming down, to make his way to the nearest cabin in sight. . . . Without a knock, he lifted the latch, walked in and made himself at home. To the lonely settler he was always a welcome guest, a God-send in fact. In his dialectal vernacular he repeated to his eager listeners his old time adventures—a light sleeper, he literally "sat by the fire and talked the night away."

From the late Andrew Gwinn I learned that his father was a woodsman by profession, what the French term a Courier de Bois. As a scout he served under Lord Dunmore and fought the Indians under Cornstalk at the battle of Point Pleasant. John was his eldest son, and had the good fortune to marry a woman of exceptional wisdom and patience. It was said of her that no other woman could control his passionate fits. They were energetic, industrious and prosperous. Deciding to live in the Wabash country, they spent a year in preparation. Two great poplar trees made two large canoes. These dug-outs were launched on New River, placed catamaran fashion, a deck was built over them, and pitching his tent on top, with his family inside, the craft floated down the river. Down the Kanawha, down the Ohio to the mouth of the Wabash. In the low water of summer he and his sons pushed that flotilla up stream, day after day, till they reached Eugene. They staid there a couple of years, as I have understood, living in the tent, and in the spring of 1829, moved to the Ambraw. Mr. Richman has ever since carried the distinction of being the first settler in Douglas County. The exact date is to me unknown. . . .

The Richman boys were quite peaceable men, much like their mother in disposition. John and David had her dark hair and personally resembled her. All had more or less of their father's disposition. . . . Of his five sons, I thought Lewis, the youngest, resembled his father the most. . . . Alike in size and build, both had sandy hair, the same piping voice and the same wild staring look.

There could be no doubt about it. Here was my story. The red band, the bell, the call-bone were objects of such startling, irreducible importance that I believed I could make the wheels of narrative turn upon them as the wheels of a watch turn on its jewels. They were hard and bright, and would not wear out. They had been actual—Oakland was only a few miles off— but by some miraculous chance they seemed mythical too: history in them for once was poetry, as if an artist had con- trolled events. I could not know then that they were not quite what they seemed. In the summer of 1940, after I had finished my poem, I was to sit on Armin Landeck's lawn in Cornwall and hear his grandfather, Charles Maulick, tell this identical story in the belief that it had happened within his hearing when he was a boy on the Wisconsin frontier. It was legend, therefore, not history. Dr. Rutherford had read "Gertrude of Wyoming" and Cooper indeed. And in the end this made no difference to me, except to be sure that I could think of the incidents as arch-incidents, with origins immemorially old, and be all the fonder of them for that. But now it was better to be ignorant of such dimensions in them: to think of them as really having happened, as possibly they had, in Douglas County, a hundred years before my poem would be published, and as having involved the Ambraw River which I myself had waded in at Villa Grove. There was a secret pleasure for me in the thought that I had surprised my native country into revealing a hidden poetry which I could now make known.

I had supposed I would remember all of Dr. Rutherford's details. But back in New York, finding that some escaped me, I wrote Grace for a copy of the document. She typed it out, and I kept it by me steadily until now in October, 1939, I was prepared to start my poem. Meanwhile, naturally, the story had grown. For it touched upon many matters that had long been in my mind. John Richman—a real enough person, by the way, still remembered in the county—remained what I had found him: a primitive, a hunter out of old time, a human savage whom civilization could not absorb. But I developed his family, a dead wife and three living sons, in directions more suitable to me than the document suggested. I populated the village of Oakland, whose name I changed to Mayfield, with Gollidays and Emersons. I conceived in Seth Golliday and Nancy Emerson a boy and girl whom Joe Krutch would of course identify as one more of my couples joined in love by the sharing of unconfessed guilt: Seth had killed the deer in order to give Nancy its ornaments which he knew she coveted. And I wholly invented Thorsten, an old Norwegian storekeeper who would be necessary in the resolution of the later action. For there were to be two violent deaths. Richman would murder Seth because he had killed the deer, and David Golliday would kill Richman because he had killed the boy. I contrived, that is to say, a hopeless feud; then ended it with Dandy Richman's decision not to murder David. Here my legend touched the legend of Agamemnon and his family, whose feud could not be ended save by divine intervention. Pallas Athene, not to speak of Apollo and Zeus, had been the final actor in the tale as Aeschylus told it.

I had, however, no gods whom I could use. Or was that true? I wanted some badly, since one of my convictions had always been that no story can be ultimately powerful unless it finds room for the supernatural, and makes that natural too, as Homer did. Yet I could not pretend that the Greek deities had survived to concern themselves with an obscure tragedy in the New World. And neither did I see how Christian mythology, even if I understood it better than I did, could apply at any point; I could not imagine Christ in Mayfield, or any of God's angels. Of course there were the nameless, faceless gods of "America's Mythology." But that was it: they had no form, no will, and so could not affect the action.

In the end I settled for something like them after all: "near gods," intelligences in the air, whom I represented as hovering over the persons of my story and watching them with pity, fury, or if nothing else suspense. They were, I suppose, blood relatives of Hardy's spirits in *The Dynasts*. Or bloodless, one might better say; for although I hinted that a hierarchy of them existed, and that at the top there was one far mind into which all their perceptions fed—a being not unlike God, except that he had no other than a supreme observer's function, and again did not control events—I was unable, in spite of some eloquent passages in which I described them, to fill them with the authority they needed in order to be effective epic agents. For one thing, they were invisible. They were merely the best rendering I could devise of knowledge as medieval theology had personified it: in orders and degrees, and in the classes of lesser or greater angels. They were bodiless configurations of the truth, which I spoke of as existing somewhere without personality or voice, and with no special interest in individuals who erred.

Scott Buchanan, reading *The Mayfield Deer* next summer, pointed out the weakness in this celestial machinery: it had no work to do. When I reminded him that no better gods had been available, he shook his head; a poet's job, he said, was to look for strong gods and find them. I published the story as it stood, with admirable illustrations by Armin Landeck, and only fifteen years later admitted to myself that Scott was right. No gods at all would be better than these; so I took these out, reversing the experiment of Pope when he rewrote *The Rape of the Lock* to insert in it a race of sylphs. I remembered now that none of Armin's illustrations had contained even so much as the shadow of a god—logically, since without bodies they could cast no shadows.

The poem in its new and leaner form had only the people in it; and the landscape; and some Indian lore I had borrowed out of books for purposes of temporal enrichment. My original desire had been to lend the story every possible importance, and one way to do this was to give it depth in time; so I searched out parallels in Indian life, a still more primitive thing than John Richman's. Some of those remained, as did everything I had had to say about horses, oxen, birds, the Ambraw, rustling corn, and deer. My leading symbol had always been John Richman's doe—the creature itself, and his fanatical attachment to it. The deer of Cornwall were my introduction to the species. As many as four of them might suddenly appear at the upper end of the orchard, grazing without sound, moving slowly through the long grass, listening for danger, lifting their heads when there was movement near the house. There were too many of them, the neighbors told me; and I was not happy when they killed my young apple trees. But I could never have killed one of them, any more than Richman was able to bear the thought of finding Nelly dead. Nine years later I was still thinking of her when I wrote the sonnet "A Deer Is Feeding":

> A deer is feeding in the orchard grass:
> A doe, with young ears, maybe, watching her
> From the pine thicket southward; not to stir
> Until she starts; and then the two will pass,
> On amber ankles, delicate as glass,
> Among great stones and trees, by dust and burr
> Unbothered; or by me—oh, foreigner
> Forever, and most terrible, alas.
>
> See how she looks and fears me, all her skin
> Atremble. But her eyes—I know them best,
> From some that I saw dying once. Within,
> How dark, without, how moist. What agony,
> What dew of old despair, that even we
> Who love them cannot ever burn to rest.

The writing that winter of *The Mayfield Deer* was difficult, as anything worth doing is, but the difficulty was pleasurable. I came every day to my study and added some lines to a penciled manuscript which finally filled three black and red ledgers I had purchased for the project. I kept these in a steel box where mice could not nibble them overnight. The only permanent residents of the building are deer mice. Their long ears, bright eyes, and snow-white bellies were attractive, but I did not let them have the ledgers. When Armin, to provide himself with objects he could draw, bought a small brass bell and a ribbon of red flannel, and cut a notch in a turkey bone so that it resembled a whistle, I begged him to give me these as soon as he was through; he did so, and I dropped them into the steel box where the bell still tinkles if shaken. But that was the next year. This winter I wrote on in silence broken only by a waterfall, the roaring of my stove, and sometimes a northwest wind that beat at the building whose stout walls I was glad to think were double. Most mornings I had read bad news in the paper. But I persisted at my task, thankful to it because it shut out even war; and by late spring it was finished.

A few weeks before that, on the first of May, Will Bailey died. The abandoned church in the Hollow was opened for a funeral service to which relatives and neighbors came. I do not know what he would have thought of the words that were spoken over him, but I cannot doubt that he approved of his burial place: across the road, in a section of the Hollow cemetery which Mrs. Bailey could see out of her kitchen window. She sat there more and more as the days of her widowhood increased. She was a fat woman, built so that her lap seemed one long slope from floor to chin. Her cats walked up this slope to caress her, or to notify her when they were hungry. She stirred as seldom as possible out of her chair between the window and the wood stove she could reach and tend without too great an effort. We kept a supply of fuel at her feet; she had a poker handy; and out of nearby bags and boxes she could even feed her pets, including an obese dog, Pooch, who was scarcely more active than herself. A clock ticked on a shelf overhead, and on the table in front of her were newspapers, balls of yarn, and an old book in which she kept records of birthdays; for each of us was faithfully remembered with a card. When we thanked her the next day we were in her debt again for the way she called us "Dear." Our only name was "Dear," pronounced, I thought, as it might have been in the old country centuries ago. What she said to herself when she looked out at her husband's grave I shall not presume

242

to guess. But once I did describe her where she sat, in "Bailey's Widow":

> Still there, as if the weathered house
> Were tomb and low memorial; no shaft,
> No sky thing, but a hugger of such earth
> As he with horizontal craft
> Knew webwise; we remember how he kneeled
> And studied every silver herb afield.
>
> Still kitchen table bound, by windows
> Wiped to keep the headstones far and clear;
> Still huge among her trinkets: catalogues,
> Gilt cards, rag balls, and cooking gear,
> She sits, the clock a goddess overhead
> Less watched than watching, like the distant dead:
>
> An old man under gravel, sidewise
> Peering; and she rubs the pane to see.
> Yet more that he may feel how still the cats
> Prowl round her, blinking up; how three
> Small dogs dispute the blessing of her lap;
> And how she sometimes nods to him by nap.

Another thing she kept on the floor where she could reach it was a can of kerosene. Electricity had come our way in 1936, but she would have none of it, any more than she would have a telephone or plumbing. Fire and water belonged outdoors in her opinion; except, of course, for the necessary stove and lamp and water pail, which last we filled for her from a well beyond the front door that operated by a wheel and a rusty chain. Her lamp she was strangely careless with. Its chimney was always black with soot, and one day I offered to clean it for her; but she said she preferred it so because a strong light hurt her eyes, which might have been red, I said to myself, for the very reason that she gave them too little help. The terrifying thing, however, was the way she filled the lamp. She would tilt it, still burning, a column of mixed flame and smoke pouring out at its top, almost singeing her hair, and let kerosene run into it out of the uplifted can. I exclaimed more than once that this was dangerous, but she only laughed: "No, dear, I've always done it that way, and no harm." It crossed my mind that maybe she wanted to burn herself up, or at least would not mind if she did. It never happened, but I took the liberty of imagining it in "Lady of Where She Lived":

> The round old lady with the little eyes—
> Lady of where she lived, of the split shingle
> Walls, and the warped door that let four cat feet,
> Cat feet in—the white old one, she perished
> Even as planned. For where she lived she was lady,
> And the lamp knew it that she tilted over:
> Tilted, and it poured obedient flame
> Due upward till the cupboard papers caught.
> There must have been more oil in secret places,
> For the first valley warning was the last;
> The windows were too bright, then not at all
> In the one peak of red, the pyramid
> She built, this queer old queen, to shrivel under.
> The cat feet, cat feet fled among the highway
> Asters, and they never felt again
> For the gone door she must have heard them pressing
> Till the warp freed them. They are wild now,
> As she is, but they were not sacrificed.
> She ended it alone. And lives alone
> In the one place of which she could be lady,
> The wild place of weeds; and of these clockworks,
> Melted at the hour, the little minute,
> He the lean one left her years ago.

Perhaps I wrote the poem to forestall the fact: if the holocaust had occurred, it could not occur again. But Mrs. Bailey survived her lean old man six years in any case.

The house we built for Mrs. Graffe was not far up the road, as I have said, on the way to ours. She had enjoyed it for nine years, even with a heart that prevented much exertion; but little exertion was necessary, since the house had been planned with that in view, and some day in fact it will be convenient for Dorothy and me. Mrs. Graffe loved of course to visit back and forth, and particularly to have Anna bring the boys down for a picnic by the brook—even in the brook, for during low water they used to cook on a pile of stones midway between the banks. The house itself grew more and more to look as if it had always been where now it stood. For Mrs. Graffe it was a dream come true: her own place, in beautiful country near her daughter and her grandsons. A moving epilogue, I sometimes told myself, to *Those First Affections.* Her brother George drove up at least once every year to see her, and it was her special delight to cook for him; he was a big man still, and he entirely filled the rooms. But she would not be there after this summer of 1940. Her weakness grew worse, so that in September, when our year was up, we took her to a nursing home in Winsted, twenty miles away. Here in December she died. She was buried in the Hollow cemetery, where subsequently Dorothy arranged to have her father's body buried too. A second epilogue to *Those First Affections,* with annual geraniums saying the last word of all.

My mother, myself, Guy, Frank, Carl, my father. A family group, with Paul quite naturally missing

Guy, Frank, Paul, Mark, Carl. On the front porch of the High Street house in Urbana, 1900

Jeremiah and Rebecca Butz, by
their giant Canna lilies at Potomac

My Grandfather and
Grandmother Van Doren

Kimber & Evans   Kankakee, I

Carl at 21

Mark and Frank at 2 and 4

Paul at 6

Joe and Marcelle Krutch,
sometime in the laughing 20's

Armin Landeck with Charlie
and Johnny, 8 and 6, on the
lawn in Cornwall

On the day of my father's funeral in Urbana, 1933. Carl, Frank, my
mother, myself, Paul, Guy

Charlie and Johnny, 12 and 10, photographed with their father in Cornwall by Joe Krutch

Cornwall, 1942. The author, with hoe. By Helen Taylor

Dorothy in 1942

Charlie and Johnny, 13 and 11, with their mother in Cornwall

Cornwall, 1942. I sit with Dorothy in front of her flowers. By Helen Taylor

Marcelle and Joe Krutch at their house in Tucson, 1954

Christmas in Cornwall, 1954. Dorothy and I contemplate my cat Walter.

Our Lady Peace

1940–1945

THE anxieties of 1940 are impossible in retrospect to overstate. So far the war remained distant, but only as thunder does when the storm of which it is a symptom has been
diagnosed as "general." Sooner or later it may be overhead;
and soon enough this was true for all those Americans—certainly I was one of them—who felt that the very conditions of
human life as they had known it were in danger of disappearing. And the chief source of the danger was Germany, whose
man Hitler was not only mad but strong: he worshiped power,
and seemed to want a universal war which would give it to him
in unlimited amounts. There was Italy, too, and Spain; and on
the other side of the world, Japan. And after everything was
over there would be Russia. But in 1940 it was Germany, moving swiftly through Norway, France, and the Low Countries,
of which most people were afraid. They were afraid for England, whose danger seemed their own. As year followed year
the center of anxiety shifted; there were indeed to be many
centers; the war did become universal; but now it was London, battered and burning, that seemed to matter most.

If this has been forgotten, it was nevertheless true then,
just as it was true that the absence of fear in one Englishman,
Winston Churchill, suddenly made all the difference. I remember when I myself became aware of his courage. We were
visiting Guy's; Carl was there too. It was in June, 1940, and
Carl had invited us all to have dinner with him in Clinton,
two and a half miles east of Guy's house. As we sat at noon in

the little hotel on Main Street we became conscious of a voice on the proprietor's radio. We listened; and Churchill was telling the world that England, at whatever cost, would take care of itself. To me it was incredible; yet I was convinced. I said to myself that if I could believe this I could believe anything; and within a year I had put my sense of the miracle into a poem, "The Single Hero":

This man kept courage when the map of fear
Was continents, was paleness to the poles,
Was Jupiter milk-white, was Venus burning.
The very stones lay liquid with despair,
And the firm earth was bottomless. This man

Could walk upon that water; nay, he stamped
Till the drops graveled, till a sound returned
Of pillars underheel, of granite growing.
This man, alone on seas, was not afraid.
So continents came back. So color widened:

Bands upon blankness. So the other men,
The millions, lifted feet and let them down;
And the soil held. So courage's cartographer,
Having his globe again, restored each mass,
Each meadow. And grasshoppers sang to him.

During the five years that followed I could not have forgotten the war if I had tried. Perhaps I did try at times; but the attempt itself was evidence that nothing was the same as it had been. The most singular aspect of the period, looked back at now from the narrowest possible point of view, my own and nobody else's, was the intense activity it stimulated in me. I was never in the war, yet I was of it in numerous ways; then I continued teaching, and I wrote as many as five books. Indeed I published six; but *The Mayfield Deer*, which appeared in 1941, exactly a hundred years after Dr. Rutherford said the events in it happened, had already been written. It was not successful, though by some individuals it was praised. Scott's explanation of this, as good as anyone's, I was not prepared at the moment to accept; I was simply disappointed.

The contents of *The Private Reader*, a collection of critical

pieces—articles, papers, reviews of books and movies—which
appeared a year later, were also in fact from an earlier time;
and the preface suggested that this time would never come
again, as it has not. I said good-by to reviewing: "partly because in the normal course of things I am done with the desire,
but partly because I have come to certain conclusions about
contemporary criticism, a house in which I no longer feel at
home, even—or especially—in its finest rooms." I then proceeded to lament the disappearance from the literary scene of
what I called natural critics, or as T. S. Eliot called them on
another occasion, normal ones: artists, I said, not would-be
scientists, not torturers of the word, not pedants obsessed with
one thing, language. Doubtless I exaggerated, and I know I
hurt some feelings here and there; yet it still seems clear to
me that Carl and Joe Krutch, to whom I dedicated the volume
because so much of it had been written for them in *The
Nation,* were cases of the critic whom intellectual fashion can
underrate merely because he is a sensible, wise man who "says
what he sees," briefly and—God willing—wittily, then is done.
At any rate I forthwith ceased to consider myself in any con-
fining sense a member of the literary profession. I preferred
the company "of those nameless strangers with whom writers
dream that they communicate."

Without any question, however, the contents of *Our Lady
Peace* were new. This pamphlet of war poems, published in
1942, included of course "The Single Hero," along with
twenty-six other lyrics in which I had sought to render the
very complex response I found I was making to the war. I
loathed it as the calamity it was; I knew how many blunders
as well as how much evil had made it possible; I thought I
understood the terror, the despair, the sickness of heart it
caused in countless other persons than myself. At the same
time I saw the necessity of its being ended on the best terms
thinkable, and I doubted the morality of those who would let
it take its course as if it were an extrahuman event, a doom
without form, a massacre without meaning. Yet it was those

things for me too. It was a nightmare from which, try as one might, it was impossible to wake up. Nightly, daily, it deadened the nerves of thought. It was a bully, abominable and obscene. It stopped, as the shadow of a hawk stops little birds, those numberless "little wars" which make the world of peace a living place:

The million little wars
Of peace: the sharpened word,
All night the grassy rustle,
All afternoon, absurd,

The games, the leather shouting,
The white lines to cross;
All over earth the tinkle
Of silver win and loss:

The billion little battles
Of peace are like a sea,
Are like a field that ripples;
And so it still would be,

Save for the one, the War,
The hawk wing that reaches,
Suddenly, and stops
Bravest breath; and teaches

No one now to move,
No one here to mar
The death peace, the waiting
On one, the overwar

That would not have us glisten,
That loathes the little waves,
The trillion, the green trembling
Peace returns and saves.

And yet again I despised the doomsters, the connoisseurs of premonition who insisted not merely that neither party to the war was more worth saving than the other but that nothing about the entire conflict meant anything at all. Or else, remembering Milton's sonnet to Cyriack Skinner, I dreamed of holidays from horror: "The Pond in Wartime," "God Sends a Cheerful Hour," and "Invincible," whose reference was rain, the survivor of every disaster, the nurse of earth's worst wounds. In several poems such as "Total War" and "The Lacing" I dealt with the special difficulty of understanding a struggle whose dimensions were those of the earth itself. The title poem represented Our Lady Peace as a "homely goddess," mountainous in bulk, "Grandmother and taskmistress, field and town," who did not dance or smile but simply stood there, immovable, implacable, a grim force calling always for more effort, not less, from those who recognized her in "each other's frown." The whole endeavor of the pamphlet was to get as close as words would go to the truth as one appalled person felt it day by day, contradictions and inconsistencies notwithstanding. Nor did the endeavor cease here. Other poems followed these, finding their places in the next two volumes I published. The subject of the war was never dead.

II

Students in those days came and went with an abruptness to be expected. Louis Simpson, for example, disappeared out of my Shakespeare class and did not return to it until after several years of service in Europe: dangerous service, for he was a paratrooper; he jumped from planes. It was hard for me to think of him, so brilliant, so black-eyed, so intense, doing what he had to do; nor did Louis himself take the full difficulty of it in till he was back, when he suffered shock; but he promptly recovered and resumed his career as a student and then as a novelist and poet. Jack Arbolino, soft-eyed and affectionate, was no less impossible to imagine as a marine in the Pacific; his letters were not about that at all, except to be sure when he was wounded; then, lying in a hospital, he wrote me about the happiness it gave him to "lie here and think of all my friends who are dead"—really think of them, night and day, as they deserved. Barnette de Jarnette, a small, shy student, a child rather than a man, and a poet with the oddest, most touching idiom, as one piece of his will prove—

Stephen were sleeping
When I walked in
And it were a madness to stay
But I had crossed mountain
And I had swum ocean
And it were hopeful to say

O Stephen, a pleasure
I beg you a pleasure
And let me lay in your bed,
And I had crossed mountain
And I had swum ocean
But oh my Stephen were dead—

appeared in my office one day to confess that he was about to "go" and was badly scared, for he supposed he would be killed. I discoursed sagely upon the great number of soldiers who escape death, and he said he felt better; letters came from him too, enclosing poems which I saved; but one of my answers was returned with a stamped message on the envelope: "Deceased." Robert Giroux, who after his graduation had worked for a broadcasting company and then for a publisher, went into the navy and risked his life on a carrier in the Pacific; again I could not think of such a man as doing that, though his letters indicated he did it naturally enough.

José Garcia Villa, a Filipino who had lived in New Mexico before he came to New York, and whose connection with Columbia was never clear to me, though he belonged there in some essential fashion, called on me one morning to introduce himself. He had a completely impassive face, and he moved with a quietness that captivated me. He had brought some of his poems for me to read. When I said that I preferred to read manuscripts at my leisure, to myself, without their authors' eyes upon me, he said in the softest of voices: "You can read these now. This one"—the top one—"is very fine." He handed it to me and of course I read it. The first line justified his claim: "I was not young long. I met the soul early." And so did all of the lines waiting for me on his lap. Raymond Weaver admired them too; they were at once mystical and witty, and like Barnette's "Stephen Song" they did as they pleased with English grammar. In 1942 the first volume of them was published, with a dedication to E. E. Cummings and me; and I never ceased to marvel at both the poet and the man in Villa. The man was a unique combination of gentleness and firmness—"you can read these now." His opinions, not always comprehensible, were stubbornly maintained, as if they were laws, were ancient decrees, not personal to him who held them. When he was married, his first child, Randy, became my godson. Villa never changed. I have said his face was impassive; there could be, however, a subtle play of humor or of pain about the eyes; and this amounted in the end to eloquence, for it expressed, delicately, a thousand reservations. "Like Mice, Like Flowers" refers to those reservations:

> Look. The stone face—
> It is not stone, but the soul's grace
> That he met early (he was not young long),
> Frozen.
>
> Look. Now, years away,
> See the hot subtleties that play
> Like mice, like flowers, like rain, yet never
> Melt it.
>
> Look. Sweet mercy's worm,
> Within him, still cannot make infirm
> His judgment: silver gentle, iron
> Decisive.

There were many other meetings, in and out of the university. One of these, half in, half out, I arranged between two of my friends. Charles Everett, a colleague who in time was to administer our department in the College, happened to remark one day that an aptitude of his might be useful in Washington if only someone there would put it to work. Charles, as an authority on Jeremy Bentham, had read millions of manuscript words and digested them; there must be some office, he thought, where copious documents lay waiting for such treat-ment. I thought of Edward Greenbaum, Dorothy's old friend and now mine too, a lawyer who had gone down to the War Department and become a general in charge among other things of army contracts. I spoke to him when I saw him next, and he sent for Charles; they did need, he said, a practiced mind to go through mountains of reports. Charles went as often as he could, and amused me when he came back by his description of the files. There were nine miles of them, he said, merely in one section of several concerned with contracts. I remembered my own paper work of twenty-five years ago, and was not amazed. For if I had kept a steady stream of copy flowing between Camp Pike and Washington, so had count-less other adjutants or assistant adjutants done the same thing in countless places. I wondered how one capital could hold what this one did.

As for my students, not all of them were young men. Margaret Clark, a high-school teacher in Bayonne where Robert Caldwell edited his paper, came over to attend my graduate lectures on long and short poems. I did not see her often, for she was formal and shy; but seldom has there been a more passionate student, and seldom I think has there been a better teacher, for I have heard from more than one boy she taught. Whenever she could she sent them to St. John's, which she visited herself, impressing Scott Buchanan as she had impressed me by a certain loving seriousness behind every thought she had, whether of books or of people; or of God, for she was completely religious. She did not expect others to be, however. The most she demanded was clarity and light. She found little enough of these in Bayonne public life, par-ticularly in its school system; the politics of the city, gruesome by her description, which outdid Caldwell's, she could not ignore; there were some things she simply did not let happen, however bitterly her "interference" was resented.

She was quite different from another woman, a very old and frail one, who began to write me in 1941. This was

Our Lady Peace: 1940–1945

Cornelia Dike, whose nephew, Donald Dike, I had known as a student in the College. She insisted that she was my student too, though she had graduated from Vassar in its earliest class. She read every word I published and praised me as though I were Shakespeare and Plato pressed into one. "Poet and Philosopher"—the envelopes in which her letters reached Columbia always carried those three words, doubly or triply underlined. When my colleagues smiled, I showed them how exquisitely she wrote; her praise of me, I said, was not the point, nor did I take it to myself; she was a tremulous lady whose last years were being dedicated to letters, to music, to contemplation, and to praise—an art as she practiced it, and a noble art; by sheer accident I had become its theme. She died not long after the war ended, ancient of days and infinite of grace.

James Thurber, who remembers his professors of English at Ohio State University with an affection reserved for them alone, admitted me to their company, if only by adoption, in the summer of 1941. Dorothy and I had gone with the boys to Martha's Vineyard as guests of the Greenbaums—the general, known to us as Eddie, and his wife Dorothea (Dotsy), the sculptor celebrated for her animals and girls. At a party on the beach one night there was Thurber with his wife Helen. So far as I can recall we had nothing special to say to one another; I know I was tongue-tied on the subject of his eyes, the good one of which had undergone several operations for cataract and still threatened him with blindness. But the next afternoon he came where we were, at another house, and asked me to go outdoors with him for a talk. I led him to some chairs on the lawn; he could see nothing, and I remember now the softness of his hand in mine; then suddenly he was asking me whether what had happened to him was not a punishment for the kind of writing he had done. I was astonished; there was no writer I respected more, and as a humorist I knew him to be unique. "I have done nothing," he said, "but make fun of weakness and folly; wisdom, strength, goodness have never

255

Mark Van Doren

been my subjects as they ought to be for anybody—as they are for you. I have been pitiless, trivial, destructive. And now this trouble comes." What I at last thought of saying could have been said by anyone. I said he was a satirist, and the language of satirists is the reverse language of scorn; but all the while they are really serving goodness and strength, whose absence makes them angry, and properly so; their readers accept this anger as a tribute to the very virtues he supposed he had neglected. Somehow it worked. He told me he felt better, and in October he wrote me that he was "all straightened out again."

When he moved to Cornwall, as in a few years he did, he continued to treat me with a kind of awe that was charmingly out of proportion to anything I had done, if I had done anything at all. This was partly because he knew me to be a professor of English; he had a weakness for the species. But it was also because he associated me with the qualities he imagined that day to be deficient in himself. He ceased to worry about them; his eyesight left him, yet he kept all his other powers; and indeed with the passing of more years he has increased those powers.

He is a brainy and passionate man, tall, white-maned, and sometimes wild of tongue; he can look for all the world like a startled Arabian horse, ready to run away. He has never pitied himself for being blind, though his rages—terrible, fantastic —could be traced to the condition. In my own opinion they are a satirist's indignations: savage, like Swift's, and with as deep as source. These rages end as suddenly as they begin, and a great sweetness follows. Thurber is tiger, then is turtle dove. Sometimes I have begged him to get mad at me, if only to prove that I am one of his natural friends; but he refuses. So there is no personal experience behind the poem, "Anger Is, Anger Was," in which I have sketched him:

> The tumult in this shouting man
> Gives way at once to dove's words.
> Anger is, anger was,

256

But half between is holy ghost
Descending out of time gone.

The memory of this hunted man
Is barking wolves, is fool's gold.
But here a wing, and there a wing,
And all within is sleepy peace.
He walks again the good world.

But there is no reference in those lines to the energy with which his brain perpetually works. It is his distinguishing feature after all. His memory would shame the ablest elephant. And nobody knows how he manages to keep up with what happens in the world where others see. In 1944, to give but one example, I was surprised to get a note from him, in the large handwriting he found convenient, that showed how much he knew about some of the company I kept: "Hutchins, take the front door! Buchanan, the rear of the house! Van Doren, fire from the attic! Adler, go for help!"

Thurber once discussed Henry James's *The Ambassadors* with me on the radio program called "Invitation to Learning." He is a tireless reader, and he can be eloquent about books he despises or adores. "Invitation to Learning" was for me an adventure in itself, begun in the early years of the war and prolonged until near its close. I first heard about the program from Scott Buchanan and Stringfellow Barr, who agreed with the Columbia Broadcasting System that great books were a practical subject for popular discussion. They turned out to be of the liveliest public interest. Once a week for half an hour three men would converse without a script about a book of distinction, ancient or modern; and since there is no end to what can be said about such books, the audience seemed never to grow tired of what they heard. Scott's idea that the same three men should pass all the books through their minds was sound, I thought, like his other idea that they should never be specialists in the authors represented. They should be seasoned amateurs, responsive to speculation because they were speculative themselves, but they should not be laden with the kind of scholarship that loves itself and boasts of the minutiae it has mastered. Both ideas were eventually abandoned, and when that happened my own interest waned. Yet for a whole year I met weekly with Allen Tate and Huntington Cairns, and for another with a variety of persons whose conversation I enjoyed. It was a pleasure also to write paragraphs about the books for a pamphlet that was circulated to listeners who asked for it. A paragraph to a masterpiece—it was a challenge I liked, for I have always been intrigued by brevity, the soul of criticism as well as wit. But once on the program brevity showed me a different face. I was discussing Ibsen's *The Wild Duck* with Margaret Webster and John Mason Brown, and after twenty minutes we ran out of things to say. We gestured to one another until we grew hysterical, fighting for time and breath and subject matter. Our conclusion was that *The Wild Duck* should never have been labeled a masterpiece.

III

Dorothy's freedom from *The Nation,* achieved as I have said in 1936, left her after *Those First Affections* with more leisure than she liked. The coming of the war supplied an occupation. I did not understand at first why she was going to libraries and reading the files of old newspapers; she had a project, but she did not discuss it. I might have known it was a novel, for she will never talk of one till it is ready to be written, and even then she is shy of disclosures, having almost a superstition lest the spoken word make the written word superfluous. The newspapers she was reading were those of 1918, beginning with January 1st when her hero, Urian Oakes, and her heroine, Dacey Hamilton, were to meet in the editorial offices of the New York *World,* though Dorothy never called it that. The novel, that is to say, would be about the end of one war while another was beginning. When *Dacey Hamilton* appeared in 1942 it enjoyed a greater success than had come to any of its predecessors, but I am not sure that its topical nature explains this. The lonely newspaper man and the beautiful woman with five children who entered his life on New Year's Eve must have been equal in interest to the events of 1918. Dacey was another of those unfulfilled women whom Dorothy had studied in Emily and Laly. But this time the cause was more explicit and dramatic: a rivalry with her mother for a husband she had not learned how to love. And the outcome was a fulfillment with Urian so complete that nothing short of Armistice Day could express it. The two climaxes are simultaneous in the book: the public joy, the private joy are one, so that document merges perfectly with plot, a consummation rare in historical fiction.

Even as *Dacey Hamilton* was being published, however, Dorothy discovered a second occupation; and this one would outlast the war, for it took all of her energies until June, 1946, when it ended. Early in 1942 she became aware that the government was looking for people experienced in handling news, or otherwise competent in public affairs, to keep in movement a stream of words that would tell the truth about the war as the United States and the other Western nations wanted it told. She volunteered her services, and in April went to work at the office on Madison Avenue of the Coordinator of Information. The name was soon altered to the Office of War Information, and headquarters moved uptown to 57th Street. There Dorothy spent the four busiest years of her life. The hours were long, there was much overtime, and Anna was left in total command at Bleecker Street. Dorothy, efficient, good-natured, humorous, and expert, rose steadily in the OWI until at last she was in charge of all the broadcasts that went out in the English language. She missed the pleasure of writing scripts as she had originally done, but she seems to have behaved like an inspired executive, for I heard from many men who worked under her—hard-bitten journalists, most of them, sometimes older and normally tougher than she—that it was a wonder how any woman could run them as she did. When she resigned they gave her a party, and I learned then, if I had not known it before, how she had ruled them by laughter as well as law: their skits lampooned her authority, and lovingly revealed how amused they had been by her pronunciation, with sarcasm, of the words *"very interesting."* Carl, who came to this party, enjoyed it as much as she and I did. He had often been drafted for broadcasts, on Franklin and other topics, so that he knew all the people who were making merry as they said good-by. He had continued his work as an American historian with *Secret History of the Revolution,* 1941, and *Mutiny in January,* 1943.

Before Dorothy went to Madison Avenue we had both been air wardens on Bleecker Street. The example of London suggested that if any American city was to be bombed—and why not New York?—precautions should be taken against whatever panic could be avoided, and whatever unmanageable fires. So a civilian defense was organized, and wardens with helmets and armbands went by night about the streets. Nobody ever knew how seriously to take this business, and in the end it proved to have been unnecessary, since no bombs fell. But when Dorothy ceased to have time for it and I did it alone, I at least found my neighbors good to know, and I became acquainted with our part of the Village as I had not been before. Davidson Sommers, a charming and cultivated young lawyer who lived on Perry Street, was first in charge; then he went to Washington, and Ralph Millington, an importer with offices in the financial district, took over. He was a huge man, nervous and sensitive but inexhaustible, who spared neither himself nor anybody else in his effort to make our sector the best in the city.

The experience resulted for me in a third novel, *Tilda,* whose heroine was an air warden in New York. But it also provided me with an opportunity to use the story Captain Cooper had told me at Camp Pike about the death of his wife. Not that I used Captain Cooper; Morgan Hood, who meets Tilda Wyatt and tells her the story, derives from himself and has his own concerns. His first view of Tilda, however, is from a balcony like one I had stood on every morning for seven weeks at the studios of the Columbia Broadcasting System, where I read *The Scarlet Letter* over the radio: fifteen minutes of Hawthorne's masterpiece each day. I had been asked to read some novel and I suggested this one; it was a good length, and powerful on every page. Frequently, while the engineer was getting his apparatus ready, I stepped out onto a balcony which overlooked gardens full of ailanthus trees and admired the beauties of a New York morning. I never saw anyone like Tilda, nor so far as I know did anyone down there become aware of my presence; but it seemed the right place for Morgan to fall in love with Tilda, so I used it too. *The Scarlet Letter* manifested its genius every day I read it. I thought I knew every turn of its plot, and indeed I did; but now I knew at close range every turn of its incomparable prose. I was to remember this six years later when I wrote a life of Hawthorne.

In December, 1942, I was called on by Julian Street, Jr., a consultant of the Treasury in Washington, and invited to be chairman of a National Book and Author War Bond Committee. It seemed an odd thing for me to do, but I did it because Pete Street, as everybody called him, was persuasive, and because I was curious as to how the manuscripts of books might be maneuvered into raising money. The scheme was simple, though the details of its working out were many and hectic: groups of authors would visit cities, deliver speeches of any sort they liked, about war, peace, life, death, or anything at all, and assist at last in the auctioning of manuscripts, their own or others', to bidders for war bonds, the highest bidder in each case having then the privilege of presenting the manuscript he had bought to the local library. The enterprise, which went on to the end of the war, soon became enormous and complicated, and before it was done took much of my time; though most of the work was done by Martha Huddleston, Dorothy Pratt, Agnella Gunn, and numerous other women in the New York office who thought of me quite properly as their figurehead, not their boss. I attended rallies in several cities and gave the manuscripts of "America's Mythology," *Liberal Education, Tilda, Windless Cabins,* and *A Winter Diary* to be auctioned. Carl gave *Mutiny in January,* the *Secret History, Swift,* and other things. Hundreds of such gifts were made by as many as 140 writers, including Albert Einstein, Thomas Mann, Eugene O'Neill, Gertrude Stein, Marianne Moore, Sigrid Undset, and among my own friends Thurber, Adler, and Krutch. Nearly $200,000,-000 worth of bonds got sold by this device. But it may have been equally important that works of the mind were treated for once as necessaries of life, not to say monuments worthy of preservation. In Europe the war had devastated libraries; here they were being enriched. When it was over, though, I worried about our having scattered so many manuscripts so far beyond the range through which accident would normally distribute them. They might be dispersed beyond record or recall. So with the help of Louis Bailey a pamphlet was printed, listing them in their new resting places, and Julian Boyd, then librarian of Princeton, wrote a foreword in which he expressed his pleasure that the "grim story" of books in wartime had been reversed. Julian, a scholar with an angel's temper, an old friend of Carl's and like him a member of the special Manuscript Committee which had to be created in 1944 to increase and administer the flood of paper pouring in, now became my friend whom I was to know still better when Carl died.

The Committee, I say, took time. So did teaching and writing, the education of the boys, and the society of our friends. But even then there were nights, particularly when Dorothy was at the OWI, when it appeared that I had nothing to do. I was free, that is, to read. And what did I read? Detective stories—thousands of them, I suddenly think, but it must have been only hundreds at the most. I had long been addicted to the vice. Annually in Cornwall I relived the adventures of Sherlock Holmes, who may well be, as someone has said, the best-known and therefore the best-built character in modern fiction. But now I branched out in every direction from Conan Doyle: Dorothy Sayers, Agatha Christie, Margery Allingham, R. Austin Freeman, Carter Dickson, Rex Stout, Melville Davisson Post, David Frome—the list only begins there, for I read with an undiscriminating appetite, and swallowed more nonsense than I care to recall. At the best, though, it was not nonsense. I do not seriously mean that detective fiction is a vice. It has its limitations, and they are clear; but it has virtues that seemed to me life-saving in those days. It wholly absorbed me, so that I forgot things I wanted to forget; it gave me stories, not the substitutes for stories that fiction of the "better" sort was cultivating; it preferred good people to bad people, a refreshing thing in times when many writers tell us they have done with the distinction; it suggested that law was admirable, and showed it, as Rex Stout once remarked, to be no respecter of persons, for a rich murderer was punished as quickly as a poor one; and—this might have been the main thing—it was a riot of fancy.

The world of crime as detective literature treats it is a fairy world in which anything can happen. Sherlock Holmes, sitting with Watson before his fire in Baker Street while the North Sea sends sheets of rain against his windows, is king of a realm that Scotland Yard in actuality has nothing to do with, nor does anyone suppose it has. A web of invisible lines spreads over the whole of England, and along one of these a message may come at any moment: a duke has been found dead on his estate, and there is something strange about the way his dogs are behaving. There is a train, of course, that starts for there in twenty-eight minutes if a hansom cab can be found to take the master to it; one is found; and so the adventure speeds to its conclusion. The situation, the invented violence, is what draws the reader in; the solution only lets him out to commence another dream. Fancy and imagination are a famous pair, and the second of them is more respected than the first, as doubtless it should be. But without the first there can be no fiction at all; it finds the stuff of story in places where one would have thought no stuff could be; like Dryden's spaniel, it discovers the game; it gives the imagination whatever work it will later do, it assigns the subject, it locates the feeling and the thought. On some of these nights I tried reading stories of pure mystery: tales of horror and the supernatural. But most of them were bores. The fancy in them was stale, was statutory; the conventions they subscribed to never *had* been powerful. No, I preferred the elfin fields of Scotland Yard and Center Street and Nero Wolfe's impenetrable den, where anything could happen, and with luck the most wonderful things did.

IV

Charlie went to college at sixteen and Johnny at fifteen; it was wartime, and schedules were askew. Neither of them finished his four years at the High School of Music and Art, which both had elected because they wanted a taste of public school. They liked the taste, but St. John's would admit them early, and so they went there in 1942 and 1943 respectively. It was better for them, we all agreed, to avoid Columbia where I was. Of course I lectured at St. John's, and the dean was one of their dearest friends; that was no strange place either. But it was their choice—never regretted, they tell me; it was away from home; and there were the intrinsic advantages of its curriculum, which I for one had now to consider with a new seriousness, since I had undertaken to write a book that must touch upon it. The Association of American Colleges was concerned even in 1942 lest when the war was done it would be difficult to restore to liberal education the status it had had before technical training took over in the laboratories and classrooms of the country. Whatever this status had been, a definition of the thing itself seemed desirable; and Gordon Chalmers, president of Kenyon College, asked me to take a term off from Columbia and attempt the definition. The Carnegie Corporation of New York paid my salary for the spring term of 1943, and by June the book was written.

It was a happy four months: happy and hard, for education is a formidable subject—more so, as Jacques Barzun has made clear, than teaching is. It even has the name of being a dull subject. "A treatise on education," Emerson said, "affects us with slight paralysis and a certain yawning of the jaws." And this in the face of the fact that education is an exciting experience. I decided that I would try to make the subject as exciting as the thing—as exciting as Emerson himself, whose ghost became my audience. If I could convince him, I could convince my contemporaries. Readers of *Liberal Education* often spoke of its style. It was Emerson's style, epigrammatic to the point of parody. This could have been because I loved Emerson; but another reason was that the reading I did before I got ready to write—I was ready on the first of May—had turned up all sorts of priceless things, in Plato, Comenius, Whitehead, and everybody. And in Scott Buchanan; for Scott, at Chicago and elsewhere, had written memorandums on the nature of the liberal arts, and these I plundered at my pleasure, finding in them the insights I most needed; though Mortimer Adler's contributions were meaty too, and Robert Hutchins's, and Alexander Meiklejohn's. I had been warned by the sponsors of the book not to let it be overly influenced by what they called "the Chicago school." But the most usable ideas were there, just as St. John's College, when I reviewed it in its whole context, appeared to me the clearest expression of what I wanted to say. The book was not about St. John's; it was about liberal education; but when the two seemed one I said so.

The subject as I saw it grew in beauty as I wrote. Nothing is more human than education. Man does all he does by art. Animals have instincts, but men have arts; and the intellectual arts are those that free them to be themselves. College, where the intellectual arts are encountered, makes more difference in a person than anything else ever does: it turns the child into a man. What subject could be more exciting? None, I told myself, and then proceeded in that faith. Allen Tate, acknowledging his copy of *Liberal Education,* said it was the first of my books to bring together all I knew. If he was right, he could have meant that I wrote it as student, reader, teacher, poet, and person. And as a philosopher, to the extent that Scott and Mortimer had made me one.

The next year, when I was fifty, I published *The Seven Sleepers and Other Poems.* I dedicated it "To St. John's College in Maryland where the Seven are Awake"; for the sleepers were the liberal arts, and the title poem, which Scott read aloud to some of his students and glossed—I wish I had heard him—represented the arts as ancient and neglected, and therefore difficult to rediscover out of the old world east of here where they were born. A further reference was to the famous seven sleepers of Ephesus with whom Gibbon has such fun. The final reference, however, was to the fact, or at any rate the faith, that liberal education is an education in precise disciplines which are hard to master; it is not a state of mind, a sentiment, a gesture. Lionel Trilling, now a colleague at Columbia, exclaimed when he saw the title poem that he would not have supposed any poem could begin as this one did, with three academic words. I told him they were not academic in the doleful sense, and he sweetly agreed.

> The liberal arts lie eastward of this shore.
> Choppy the waves at first. Then the long swells
> And the being lost. Oh, centuries of salt
> Till the surf booms again, and comes more land.
>
> Not even there, except that old men point
> At passes up the mountains. Over which,
> Oh, centuries of soil, with olive trees
> For twisted shade, and helicons for sound.
>
> Then eastward seas, boned with peninsulas.
> Then, orient, the islands; and at last,

Our Lady Peace: 1940–1945

The cave, the seven sleepers. Who will rise
And sing to you in numbers till you know

White magic. Which remember. Do you hear?
Oh, universe of sand that you must cross,
And animal the night. But do not rest.
The centuries are stars, and stud the way.

The poem that ended the volume, "Aetat 50," was about my
father, as I have said; or rather, it was about what I had
learned at his funeral. "How We Shine" was also about death,
despite men's knowledge of which they "brighten bravely."
There were poems about time and eternity, childhood, old
age, and war. I reprinted here the contents of *Our Lady Peace;*
but I was not done with the subject, which a dozen new poems
enlarged. "April, 1942" contemplated the spring leaves of
Cornwall, little and trusting, against the background of a
world that would wither them if it could. "The Unknown
Army" spoke for

   . . . the civil fathers, the poor unnecessary
Clerks of a fair world great death besieges.

"Observation Post" described vigils with my neighbors in a
booth on Hart Hill where planes were listened for by night
and duly reported.

But no such poem came as close as "Matins" did to the
central fact for me about this war: it simply could not be forgotten.

Where do wars go in the night?
How can strong pain disappear?
The fiend that swims unseen in us
Slips to what cave, the torturer?

Biding the hour of sweet sunrise
When we are tempted—ah, but he starts,
He stings us then, as into bliss
Of an old time we think we wake.

Of an old day before this devil,
Finned in our depths, was parasite.

Mark Van Doren

So in his darkness he resumes;
And morning at our face is mocked.

If I ever forgot it, I did so by listening to Mozart's music, the
only equivalent to Shakespeare in the world of art. Harry
Dick, my friend and wise colleague at Columbia, had said this
to me years ago; and more recently I had understood it still
better through Bernard Haggin, who spoke and wrote of
Mozart in such a way as to explain why he never wearied me
as other composers sooner or later do. Now in "Old Style" I
made my bow to the Haffner Symphony—to its minuet and
trio, which always sounds to me like an emperor entering a
hall filled with dancers. And in "Northern Minstrel," to name
another latitude of art, I paid homage to Franz Kafka. Meyer
Schapiro, one morning on the subway to Columbia, had
introduced me to *The Castle,* and I read it at home that night
without stopping for breath. Such is the effect of genius in a
room.

V

In the summer of that same year Thomas Merton published
the first of the many books that would make him famous
around the world. His *Thirty Poems,* most of them written at
Our Lady of Gethsemani, in Kentucky, where he had been
since 1941, I selected out of many more he had sent me for
the purpose or had left with me when he walked out of the
world. He had made me then the custodian of all his manuscripts: not merely poems, but novels, journals, and notes for
unfinished works. His literary ambition, I saw when he
brought me these, had been unbounded; but now, presumably,
it was laid aside along with many another object he could not
take with him. I soon felt uncomfortable with the manuscripts,
which I thought I had no right to keep stored in the closet of
my study on Bleecker Street, and sent them to the library of
St. Bonaventure, at Olean, New York, where Merton had

taught after some graduate study at Columbia. But the poems I held on to, so that now at the suggestion of Robert Lax, and of James Laughlin who wanted to publish them at New Directions, I placed them together with the new ones that had come and went through them all to see, if I could, which thirty were best. It was not easy to do this, but the very labor was enlightening, since it proved to me how excellent a poet Merton had become, how passionate, how rich, and in a subdued, deep fashion how witty too; for his wit, I knew at last, would never die, being a faculty he possessed in a kind of partnership with the poets of the seventeenth century and with the modern poets whose language his more palpably resembled. The very beginnings were auspicious:

When cold November sits among the reeds like an unlucky
    fisher . . .

Sweet brother, if I do not sleep,
My eyes are flowers for your tomb. . . .

Where are the merchants and the money-lenders
Whose love sang in the wires between the seaports and the inland
    granaries? . . .

Because my will is simple as a window
And knows no pride of original earth . . .

No reader, I said, would fail to go on from there. And no reader did, for the book succeeded beyond anybody's expectation, as book after book by its author has done since 1944. A contemplative, vowed to silence in the strictest of all orders, was to find himself a best-seller in the seaports. The predicament, even more in his view than in that of the world, has never ceased to be strange.

And in the fall Joe Krutch published his *Samuel Johnson*. I remember taking the manuscript with me to Cambridge, Massachusetts, and reading it in a hotel there; but I do not remember why I went to Cambridge. It was some sort of meeting, and doubtless it seemed important at the time. Even at that it could not have been all-important, or I should not have had the time to write Joe the long letter I did about his magnificent book. It was such a letter as one dreams of having the leisure to write yet seldom does. At home I would have talked the subject out; or at best, scribbled an enthusiastic note promising more later in the same vein. Now, though, having lived with Johnson as only Joe could make me do it, year by year in the London he and I had seen together a quarter-century ago, I used up all the stationery in my room, and more too, in an attempt to say for once how much I owed him and admired him, not merely for this book but for countless further things as well. Johnson had been a happy subject for him to settle down with; in both men there is a common sense that goes on, the more one sees it, to look massive beyond the possibility of destruction. At the same time they both are exquisite in scruple, capable of fantastic faith, and delicate without end in their dealings with others. Both, that is to say, have characters. And Joe was to reveal his henceforth in subjects no longer literary; he was to become a naturalist, which Johnson himself would have died rather than become, though in his grave I am sure he has forgiven Joe for going to the desert; he was fantastic in forgiving, too. Joe's acknowledgment of my letter ended with a paragraph so perfectly like him, and so agreeable to me, that I cannot leave it out of this record: "Love to Dot and to the boys when you write. Perhaps some day when the remark would not seem so obviously interested I'll say I love you too. Marcelle does. Yours, Joe."

The paragraph before this one referred to the fact that our older son was now in the war, or soon would be. "I know how you must be feeling about Charlie and I won't be impertinent enough to try to say anything about it. The conflict probably makes it worse. It might in some ways be easier if you did not feel as you do—I mean if you could merely resent the necessity and curse everybody." If we did not curse, we certainly did not exult as the day approached when Charlie would enter the Army Air Force, in which he had enlisted with the understanding that he would be called on or after his eighteenth birthday. It was two months after, in the middle of April, when he went off for basic training in Mississippi. He was to spend a year and a half in three southern states without further training. He never became an aviator, because there were more than enough of them already. In Georgia, in Florida, he marked time on the ground, or did "made work" in hangars, until he was discharged. Or he played poker, and sent his winnings home. All this suited us very well, but he said he was not pleased. He had left college only to count bolts and wrenches; he was not even learning to be a mechanic. When I visited him near Sebring, Florida, more than halfway down the peninsula, he said little of what he did there; he preferred seeing me in the town, and was delighted when he got a pass that permitted him to take a train with me to Miami. We loafed and swam, then took another train back through country so strange to me, so full of wild long-legged birds and crazy trees, that when I was in New York again I wrote about them instead of him; or rather, "War's Distance" is a poem about both boy and landscape, seen as one through the transparent wall of strangeness.

Two months after Charlie set off for Mississippi we had a telephone call from Carl in New York: something had gone wrong with his eyes, and the doctor said it was a detached retina. An operation might restore normal vision, but Carl was not sure it would; meanwhile, he professed to be cheerful. I knew he was not, for I heard the familiar anxiety in his voice. The operation was successful. There was a long convalescence, and then I drove down to bring him up with us for a quiet month in Cornwall, since quiet was the main thing he needed. He had it in abundance. On the way from New York, at a point between Sherman and Gaylordsville, I spoke of a maple tree, a vast one with a curving top, that had become famous with us; we always waited for it to come in sight, and we envied the people whose house it covered like a great green cloud; in the fall it rained red leaves. The pinpoint glasses Carl wore did not permit him to see this tree at the moment

I spoke, so at the foot of a hill I turned the car about. There it was, and he admired it in the opulent way that made him so rewarding a man to travel with—Dorothy often says now: "I wish Carl were with us, he would enjoy everything so much." On our lawn, however, there were no further excitements even of that innocent sort. The tall maples there he could take for granted; and we saw to it that little company came. He could sit or lie all day while September passed without so much as a word; though he was a marvelous talker, and most of the time there were words.

One week they were Homer's words. By chance I had brought the *Odyssey* outdoors, in the translation of A. T. Murray, to read Carl a passage that was pertinent to something we had been saying. This was his favorite poem, and suddenly he hankered to hear it all. So I started at the beginning and went through to the end. I shall never forget the excitement we both felt at the high moment of Eurycleia's recognition scene. The old nurse of Odysseus is washing his legs and feet in the presence of Penelope, who has not recognized him yet; nor must she until the proper time has come. There is a scar on one of his legs which he knows Eurycleia will identify if she sees it; so he turns that side of him away from the lamp. But her hand identifies it in the dark—it is an odd-shaped scar, got long ago in a boar hunt—and the basin she has been holding drops; the bronze rings on the stones; the water runs over the floor. And Eurycleia cries out: "My child, I did not know thee until I had felt the entire body of my lord!" Neither of us had ever noticed before how the sentence begins and ends: in the second person as Eurycleia remembers the boy Odysseus had been, and then in the third as she remembers that he is now her master. All the art of the greatest poet, we said, flowering in a lonely exclamation. We laughed too at the way Odysseus seized the old dame by the throat and almost choked her lest she say more and give him away. But what she cried out is what I have never forgotten. Nor have I forgotten the pleasure, second to no pleasure in the world, of sharing a noble poem with a noble friend.

On other days we talked about world government. Mortimer Adler's book *How to Think About War and Peace,* appearing in the spring, had convinced me that world peace would never come by any other method, and now I found that Carl agreed. Both of us were to think and talk world government for years. In 1947 he was to publish *The Great Rehearsal,* suggesting that the union of our states had shown the way. And even before the war ended I lectured on the subject at air force installations over the entire northeastern quarter of the United States. This was done in the name of information and education; I flew from base to base, often in small planes that went over land and water with the pilot and me as the only passengers. My visit to Charlie was incidental to such a trip, except that this time I went by train. But first I had stopped in Washington, at the White House, to be a guest at a luncheon with several hundred other persons who were believed to have helped Franklin Roosevelt be elected President for the fourth time. All I had done was make brief speeches in New York, Albany, and Syracuse; but I was on the list, and an invitation came. On the train from New York I sat with John Gunther, who was equally surprised at having been invited, but who would not have missed going any more than I would. In the long room where the lunch was I watched the President at his small table over which he looked steadily up into the faces of people who passed. I wrote Dorothy that his own face seemed to me beautiful—I remember the word—nor did I see on it any sign that he would be dead in April.

His inauguration was the next day, but I had to be in Georgia then, offering my arguments for world government to weary fliers of Thunderbolts and Fortresses who sat in camp theaters and listened or slept as they chose. The topic was my own; it had not been assigned, but neither was it challenged by any officer in authority. Those who listened seemed to do so with respect for the lecturer; further than this I could not tell how much difference if any my going made. In May my one poem on the subject, "Let There Be Law," was sung at San Francisco while the United Nations was being formed; for me the United Nations was not enough, since it was not a government, but that seemed the time and place to speak of nations under law, and in stanzas as simple as I could make them I pressed the point to its limit. When discussion of world government died down, as it did during those very postwar events which might have kept it alive, I stopped talking too. The arguments of Mortimer Adler and Immanuel Kant would still be good, I said to myself, whenever there were ears to listen. There were not enough ears now. Neither, perhaps, was the world ready to reconsider its age-old and (I granted) fascinating commitment to utter chaos.

Then suddenly that commitment made sense to me in the way it had through most of my life, and as it does now. I am not aware that the world wants to save itself by any of the devices individuals contrive. It was not, of course, that I had wanted to save the world; I would perfectly have agreed with Emery Neff that no man can save another, let alone all men. It had seemed to me rather that I wanted to save myself as a part of the world. The difference finally was that I ceased to consider myself, politically at any rate, as such a part. Franklin Roosevelt's death took away the one man who ever gave me the illusion that I could even in the mildest measure assist in modifying events. As the war drew to its close that illusion died its natural and by no means tragic death.

One day in the spring of 1945 I was called by Henry Rosenthal, my student of the 1920's, and invited to lunch at a hotel in midtown New York. I had seen him in this way several times, and he had no special motive for the meeting now. But an astonishing event grew out of it. In the course of our talk I happened to remark that I was about to finish my twenty-fifth year of teaching at Columbia. He said nothing

then, but a few weeks later Dorothy confided to me at dinner
one evening that a surprise party had been prepared for me
on the 22nd of May, at the Hotel Algonquin, with old students
and friends present, and with Clifton (Kip) Fadiman, famous
for his felicity in the role, acting as master of ceremonies. She
had got Henry's permission to tell me because the shock might
otherwise be too great, and also because she did not know how
to get me there at the scheduled moment unless I knew where
I was going. Johnny would come up from Annapolis, and even
Charlie had been given a furlough from Florida. I stared at
her, and finally said "All right." But my mind was a blank as
to what I should anticipate, or as to whether I could bear it.

I walked that night with Charlie into a room full of so many
familiar faces that the past seemed to be speaking with one
voice. People sat at tables with wine, cheese, nuts, coffee, and
cake—my favorite food and drink—and while I sat at a similar
table they got up one by one, or some of them did, to make
speeches about me. They were introduced by Kip, who now
and then varied the routine by reading a letter from somebody
who had not been able to come. Allen Tate's letter invited me
to have lunch with him in 1965 at the Chinese restaurant
where we had made each other's acquaintance in 1925.
Mortimer Adler's described a session of General Honors in
which I had conducted a discussion of the *Iliad*. Ivria Adlerblum (now Sackton) wrote from Texas that as a teacher I had
made "the difficult attainable through lightness." Miriam
Knowlton (now Corrie) wrote from Urbana about the evenings
when Frank and I had played with her and Beth under the arc
lights on High Street. Frank himself, uncannily corroborating
my own recollections, wrote from Tuscola: "I remember his
first swear words—How he cut off a curl while Mother was
shopping in Danville, and how he hid under a bed when we
saw her coming—His first day at school, when he had to be
carried in by the teacher, red in the face, yelling and kicking
—Playing under the arc lights in Urbana—High School days

—His visits to the farm—His going away to War I and his return." Robert Lax wrote from heaven knows where:

> People who know him
> Have their own ideas
> And you can't tell them anything.

Thomas Merton sent from Gethsemani a letter so long that Kip could not read it all. Reading it myself now, for it was left in my hands, I cannot help wondering whether Merton's best-known book was not born in one of its paragraphs. "This is not the time," that paragraph begins, "for me to be writing a spiritual autobiography; but in 1935 it was an especially good thing that I came in contact with you. . . . With you it was never a matter of trying to use poetry and all that is called English literature as a means to make people admire your gifts; on the contrary you always used your gifts to make people admire and understand poetry and good writing and truth." Since this in effect was what Tom would say in *The Seven-Storey Mountain,* I suspect, unless he was in the middle of that book three years before it was published, that soon thereafter he set about writing a spiritual autobiography in dead earnest.

I sat and listened to such things, and in the intervals between I listened, as I have said, to live voices in the room. It should have been hard, but somehow it was not. I learned then, if I had not known it before, how dearly I love to be praised. Also, the speeches were not ponderous with sentiment. They were weightless, like wit, which on such occasions saves everything. Jim Thurber presented me with one of his drawings: an elaborate one, that unrolled. Frank Adams, or F.P.A., was of course not heavy; he could not have been if he tried. Nor was Carl, nor Joe Krutch, nor Scott Buchanan, nor Henry Rosenthal, nor John Berryman, nor Jacques Barzun, nor Harrison Steeves, nor Stephen Aylward, nor William Sloane my publisher, nor John Gassner, nor Lionel Trilling, nor Rex Stout. Nor was the slender book that Carl had supervised in the printing, with blank pages in it for the signatures of guests and with one beginning page of compliment which of course he had composed—nor was that either anything but a work of grace: as good to read as if it had been about somebody else.

When it was all over, naturally I had to speak. I decided only at the last moment what to say. It was that I accepted their praise. I threw none of it back at them as exaggerated or undeserved. If they loved me I loved them too, and I was not ashamed to admit it. The accepting of gifts and praise exactly in the spirit in which they are offered has always seemed to me one of the chief duties of man. Well, here was my duty, and it was delightful to do it. Then the evening ended, and some of them came down with us to Bleecker Street where we could talk of less personal things than who I was or what, allegedly, I had done since 1920.

I did not see Charlie again until November and the war was over. He telephoned one day from Sebring to report that he would be home soon—just when he did not know, but soon. "He's coming," Dorothy and I said to each other again and again. But when? And—senseless worry—would the train run off the track? After nineteen months of fearing what might happen in the air, here I was imagining what might happen on the ground. I saw trees falling in front of the engine; collisions; washouts; explosions. Absurd; but the result was a poem, "He's Coming," to which we had already given its title:

> He's coming. He just called. Said he was coming,
> Maybe, right away. O southern river,
> Kiss that trestle sweetly,
> Rub that upright gently,
> And keep no train from home.
>
> He's coming. Said all papers would be signed
> By Sunday. O you honeysuckle timber,
> Wrap those tulips, redbuds,
> Hold those oaks from falling
> Down on the right of way.
>
> He's coming. Said expect him. There! what music
> Rails already make, and pounded switches:

Mark Van Doren

Wheels inside the south wind.
Where? O you the south wind,
Keep soft and strong today.

Then all at once he was home, discharged, and ready to go
back to college.

Poems and Stories

1945–1953

❧

THE war had almost filled the gap of time between my second and third sabbaticals. There was only a year to run before Dorothy and I would go to spend our first winter in Cornwall alone. The boys whom she had taught to read and draw were now in college, preparing to graduate together in 1947; and Anna was to take her own sabbatical with friends in California. When our year commenced in June, 1946, we scarcely realized how typical it would be of other years to come. The quiet of Cornwall multiplied itself until it became absolute: a thing so personal to us that we could not describe it to those who wondered how we spent our days. "We live here," my answer was; nor did I not mind if they thought I was joking, for I did not want to sound too serious either. Cornwall had always been for me both work and play, and so it continued to be. I wrote a great deal—poems and stories—and at night I read Dickens: all of him, with mounting excitement, in an edition Dorothy gave me for my fifty-second birthday. Dickens had excited me when I was a boy in Urbana, but I saw now that he was not a children's author; he was comparable (I had not known this) to Shakespeare. And I cut grass or shoveled snow. But I also walked about the place as I always had, in deep woods or down the long slope of stone walls and open fields that does not rest until it reaches the highway along the bottom of the Hollow.

Halfway down this slope is the ancient cemetery of which I have already spoken: the one no longer used for burial, so that its stones, when they survive at all, are difficult to read because of the wind and rain they have weathered, some of them since the third quarter of the eighteenth century. I had always liked to visit these memorials to another time and faith —another world altogether, as the verses declare in an idiom that seems to know it is poorly understood by those like me who poke among the weeds and have to lie down in order to make out a last line buried in the sod. One of the things I did that year was to take paper and pencil there and copy every legible epitaph. Some of them I had to rub, after the manner of scholars in cathedrals, since they would not yield their legends to the naked eye. When I had them all I typed them and deposited them with Emily Marsh in the Cornwall Library. My favorite epitaphs are those of Deacon Benjamin Sedgwick, who died of apoplexy in 1757:

> In an Instant he is Call'd,
> Eternity to view:
> No time to regulate his house
> Nor bid his friends adieu;

of Mr. John Thomson, who died in 1765 at the age of 77 (he had been born while Dryden lived):

> From tiresome days releas'd,
> To rest these weary limbs,
> And rise again Afresh
> When time and nature ends;

and of Abigail Sedgwick, who died in 1783 at the age of seven weeks:

> Why should we mourn her flight
> From this dark wilderness
> To Realms of Joy and Light
> Through our Redeemer's Grace.

Those people meant these things, of course, as I have said in "Oldest Cemetery," which might have been written then but waited instead nine years to be given voice:

> I go downhill some days to a little room
> Where the first people put their souls to sleep,

And where four walls of fallen fieldstone keep
Close rumor of their names, with verses cut
(I lie and read) against forgetful doom.
Remembered, they would rise in fields of rest
As far away as east is from the west;
Or farther, past all compass; for they shut
This wilderness of time, of nature out;
They thought to wake in such a world of light
As no man works for, warned of coming night;
Pure joy and peace it was. And so they put
Each weary soul to bed, with owls and crows
To watch, and weeds to deepen its repose.

Some days I think the end has come and gone.
Sound fell, and they got up, and where they lay
Was nothing now but litter as away
On wings they went and had their dream at last:
The universe was over. Time goes on
As always, and the same birds in the sky
Declare it, but without hope's reason why:
Tick, tick until the finish. Or, no blast
Of horns was heard, no host of angels passed;
It all was childish error, and these stones
But tilt above time's waste. And whose the bones?
The verses tell. I ponder them, steadfast,
Expectant. No, the end is coming still
For such as these, on this forgotten hill.

When Mrs. Bailey died in January, 1947, she was of course not buried here with the old people whom no one now disturbs. The Hollow church was opened again, and she was put beside Mr. Bailey in the place her window still overlooks, though others sit there now and doubtless do not think of her. The circumstances of her last days I cannot forget. One morning in November I stopped as I regularly did, on the way to the mailbox, to see how she was doing. But the house was cold, and I did not see her in her chair. The rope she had installed to guide her across the floor ran into the small bedroom on the right where my first thought was that she had overslept; or worse. I called her name, and was glad to hear the familiar "Dear," though it was feebly spoken. I found her on

the floor by her bed where she had been since yesterday afternoon, unable to get up after a fall. She thought she had
"broken something," but it was only her life. I got Lester
Whitford to help me lift her onto the bed, called Dr. Bradford
Walker, and heard him tell her tenderly that in spite of her
having no fractured bones she still must go to the hospital in
Torrington. This she insisted she would never do. People only
died in hospitals. But when a state trooper came in an ambu-
lance she let me help him transfer her to the stretcher, and off
she went, Dorothy behind her in our car. There was a bright
sun, and the vehicle ahead of us glittered as it sped over the
high ground of Goshen. She had never moved in elegance before, and for that matter had not left home in years. Washed
and petted, she looked almost well when we visited her next
day in the hospital. But she had been right. She *was* dying, and
seven weeks later she was not there to call either one of us by
the epithet she uttered in so distinguished and touching a
fashion.

In June the boys graduated from St. John's, in the same class
because the army had held Charlie back. Dorothy and I went
down for a whole hot week of ceremony and celebration, then
drove home with them across the Eastern Shore of Maryland.
In the fall they became advanced students at Columbia:
Johnny in the Law School, though a year later he suddenly
stood up while he was registering, walked out, and became a
graduate student in American history; and Charlie in the
department of mathematics, though he too abandoned that
choice at the end of his second year and went over to the study
of English. The summer of 1949 they spent together in Europe.
They sailed from Quebec, where Dorothy and I drove them
and saw them off.

Some of their letters from England, Italy, and France
mentioned a new member of the family then only a few
months old. This was a black kitten with white paws whom
they had given Dorothy for her birthday on May 2nd, in New
York. We named him Walter Mitty, after Thurber's hero,

though he has never been called anything but Walter: a preposterous name for a cat, but it consorts with his Egyptian dignity, as does the more domestic name Blackie with a companion we got from Allyn Hurlburt's barn the following summer. The two of them, the city cat, the country cat, soon became inseparable from us. When I need to be flattered, it is done by someone's saying that Walter is my cat. Of the two he is the far-traveler; we do not know where he spends some of his nights. Blackie, plumper and more sociable, more home-keeping, adores his mistress.

II

When I went back to teaching in the fall of 1947 I made a complete break with my past so far as courses were concerned. The Shakespeare class I had given over to Andrew Chiappe for the year I was to be away, and now I told him to keep it. It was too good a thing not to be shared, and he was too good a teacher not to share it. In place of it I invented a course called The Narrative Art, by which I meant that we would read and discuss a few absolute masterpieces of storytelling and see, if we could, why they were that. They turned out to be the *Iliad* and the *Odyssey,* as much of the Old Testament as there was time for and the four Gospels, *The Divine Comedy,* Kafka's *The Castle,* and *Don Quixote.* Why these? Charles Everett, now administering the College department, pointed out that none of them was an English book; not that he cared, but he pointed it out. I had not thought of it, nor did I care either, since I had long thought of myself as a teacher of literature, not of English literature, and found it natural to choose whatever books best suited a particular purpose.

My purpose in this case, and I did not keep it a secret from the class, was to examine the various ways in which the greatest storytellers had put divine things and human things together. The ultimate dimension, I suggested, was given to narrative by the presence in it of gods or their equivalent. In the case of Cervantes I promised that it would be difficult to say what the equivalent was, yet I supposed it was there, or else *Don Quixote* would not be the supreme novel it is. Reading it slowly in preparation for the course, listening to every word of it in Motteux's joyful translation, I had fallen hopelessly in love with it as I continue every year to do. The Bible too became for me a boundless world of wonder, terror, wisdom, and delight. Dante and Kafka, the one finishing his thought, the other unable to do so, I likewise discovered to be bottomless in meaning as well as brilliant with ten thousand details that cannot tarnish. Homer, I need not say, remained for me what Dante said he was, the sovereign poet. In a subsequent year I cut the course in half to fit it into one term instead of two; but I knew from the first that I would never want to stop giving it while I taught at all. One reason was the papers the students wrote. Many of these told me things I could not have learned alone: things never said before, nor said with such beauty and force.

I started again, too, in my graduate lectures. The short poems I once had discussed with the class on mimeographed sheets I taught henceforth in the College only, in a new class called Verse. The long poems I deserted for another subject: tragedy and comedy, which like my gods and men, and for that matter the mysteries of verse, I knew I would never be done with. I think it was Scott Buchanan, in his books and in his conversation, who first convinced me that tragedy and comedy are between them the deepest single subject in the world. But now I have no idea where he left off and I began; nor does it matter, in his mind or mine. I started my lectures tentatively, with little sense of the end they would arrive at. They have never, in fact, arrived at any end. Tragedy and comedy do not; certainly comedy does not; so every May I have left the subject in mid-air. Edward Edelman helped me at first with some masterly Notes on Tragedy and Comedy he wrote out for himself and brought to me; and William Burke and Louis

Simpson, to name no other students, added unforgettable insights. But I know that I shall not live to see the end that Socrates may have seen when he was overheard, as he walked out of the *Symposium,* remarking to Agathon that the genius of tragedy and the genius of comedy are the same.

As for the long poems, I could desert them with a good conscience because I had put my convictions about them into a book. I wrote *The Noble Voice: A Study of Ten Great Poems* in the summer of 1945, and dedicated it to Charlie who at St. John's had heard some of the lectures on which it was based, though most of it derived from The Art of Poetry in Philosophy Hall at Columbia. William Sloane, who was my publisher for twelve years, first as editor in another house and then as master of his own, and who throughout that time was generous beyond description, came to visit us in Cornwall just as the book was done. He insisted upon reading it at once, and did so in my study by the pond while I waited at the house for his verdict. He approved in the warm, intelligent way I was familiar with, but suggested that my title, *Calliope,* be changed; he said most people associated the name with circus organs. Calliope was the muse of epic poetry, and I had begun the preface with a reference to her noble voice. That phrase became the title, though I still think of the book as an examination of the ten poems, beginning with Homer's, in which she might have been most interested.

Beginning with Homer. In a sense I ended with him too, for he remained the sovereign poet to whom all others were but subjects; though Dante came out pre-eminent in his own kingdom of philosophy, and Chaucer I represented as first among comedians. These three were my models by which the others were measured and found wanting more or less. Virgil and Milton, for all of my old love, and I had by no means lost that love, went down on the scale that Homer and his peers established. Even Lucretius did; and certainly Spenser, Wordsworth, and Byron did. Charles Everett told me I had been ruthless in my application of the scale, particularly in the case

of Wordsworth's *Prelude,* which he admired. I told him I
admired it too, as I admired *Don Juan* and *The Faerie
Queene;* I had simply endeavored to explain why none of them
had become a poem of world importance; some dimension was
lacking, and I sought to name the dimension. He understood—
there is no man who more honestly desires that other men do
what they will and say what they mean—but I imagine that
his discomfort has been shared by numerous readers to whom
I could not confide, for instance, that I reread *The Faerie
Queene* with unflagging relish—at home, on subway trains,
on buses, or wherever else I was—before I wrote about it. The
relish was real, but it did not delude me into claiming for
The Faerie Queene the final, the indispensable virtue of perfect wisdom and truth.

I was holding out for the best thing that poetry can ever be:
a report of the world as it is, without exaggeration or make-
believe. Shakespeare gives such a report, but he had no place in
this book. Homer never gives anything else; all that we know
he knew; he is solid and immense, yet delicate too in the details that test his eyesight when he is either close to something
he describes or far away. The ancient conception of the poet
as wiser than other men about the very things all men experience has not been honored lately; it was my conception
here, and it is probably true that my statement of it was ruthless. Nor have I changed my mind upon this point. As long as
poetry is expected to be ignorant, or at best half-wise, it will
meet the expectation and so deserve the contempt that it in-
curs.

My view in *The Noble Voice,* that is to say, was kept very
high, and I know I sounded dogmatic to those who were not
serious in their demand upon the art I discussed. One reviewer
remarked that I had cited no authorities. I was trying to be
one. A dedicated critic does not presume to prove; he merely
says things—and risks appearing a fool if nobody believes him.
If he is believed, that is another matter; but still he has proved

nothing. It cannot be proved that Homer, Dante, and Chaucer are the best narrative poets. One either knows it or does not. My own knowledge, for whatever it was worth, I soon testified to in another fashion. I wrote poems of homage to these men— for example, this one to Chaucer:

> Those waves of understanding that arrived
> Were the least ones. You let the long swells go
> In their own darkness on around the world
> Till they piled high and broke in afterwoe.
>
> For you the choppy ones the sun had wrinkled.
> They had come far too, and they still come on.
> But in you then they rested. You gave forth
> The sound they seek, of old men young at dawn;
>
> Of men that have forgotten nothing woeful,
> Yet at their waking smile. The world is fool
> Forever, and its tears are not to cease.
> But neither is this birdsong, high and cool,
>
> This answer, like your own, to those least waves
> That come with sunwarmth dappled on their crests:
> The ones unseen except by old late men
> And silly larks, up early in their nests.

In the same year with *The Noble Voice* I published a third edition of the *Dryden*. It was out of print again, and Marjorie Nicolson at Columbia, widely known as a seventeenth-century scholar and a powerful person in her own right, was good enough to inform William Sloane that she thought it should be available. He agreed instantly, and I set about revising it— not much, but here and there I found I had used the word "cynical" as a term of praise, and since I no longer thought of it as that I took it out or modified it. In a new preface I spoke of Dryden's mastery in the art of verse, and said I still hoped his example would be followed in the interest of a greater firmness and resonance than modern poetry on the whole possessed. I was aware of no immediate response to the suggestion.

III

Meanwhile I was writing poems on my own account, and I was about to start on a headlong career with stories that still, whenever I think of it, astonishes me. But first as to the poems. One thing I asked William Sloane to do he did with characteristic alacrity, but it was a mistake. I asked him to let me collect all of my poems again in the form of a series that might run to as many as five volumes, each one a unity with respect to subject matter. I proposed to begin with those, including of course *A Winter Diary*, which had to do with the country, whether Connecticut or Illinois. So in 1946 appeared *The Country Year*, with line drawings of the house and lawn at Cornwall, and the study and the pond, which John O'Hara Cosgrave came to make. I still prize the drawings, as I do those of Waldo Peirce for the poems about children that appeared a year later in *The Careless Clock* (the title came from "Boy Dressing"). But by and large the public did not recognize that the volumes were collections of old pieces; and some reviewers, making the same error, were appalled because as a poet I had become so copious. I am copious, but not to the tune of a new book every year. So I abandoned the project, and to make things clear published in 1948 a volume labeled distinctly *New Poems*.

It contained a section of poems about the war—my last—and as had become customary with me there were sections, unnamed, that dealt with ideas, persons, children, the country, and love. But the poems of homage were there too, and at the beginning I placed five pieces of greater or less length that had had their start in my recent reading, or at any rate in my reflection. "The Case Is New" stated the dilemma of democracy: each individual a king, yet what to do with so many kings? Perhaps I came nearer to my true, secret understanding of society in "The Close Clan," which said that among the world's multitude there is a hidden and quite harmless aristocracy of perfect persons who do not know of their perfection but who have it nevertheless, and it makes all the difference:

> Even from themselves they are a secret,
> The like ones that dwell so far asunder:
> So far, and yet the same; for gold is gold
> In any earth, and thunder repeats thunder.
>
> They are the scattered children of what pair,
> What patient pair so long ago extinguished?
> But the flesh lives, in certain ones that wind
> And dust and simple being have distinguished.
>
> Whatever these, and howsoever born,
> They are the ones with perfect-lidded eyes,
> Quieter than time, that yet can burn,
> Can burn in rage and wonder and sunrise.
>
> They are the ones that least of all the people
> Know their own fewness, or the loving fear
> Such lineage commands—that ancient couple,
> And these their growth in grace's afteryear.
>
> In them the world lives chiefly, as gold shines,
> As thunder runs in mountains, and hearts beat.
> They are the ones who comprehend the darkness,
> And carry it all day, and sweeten it.

"The Stranger's Tale" alluded once again to the myth of Plato I had discussed in *The Noble Voice*, in the chapter on Virgil: the myth of a double world, now primitive (the Golden Age), now civilized (the age of Zeus, of effort and of art). The volume ended with poems as simple as these were complicated. My title for the section was Words for Music More or Less, and in it I put six lullabies, five of them for children and one of them, "Sleep, Grandmother," for an old woman in her second childhood:

> Sleep, grandmother, sleep.
> The rocking chair is ready to go,
> And harness bells are hung in a row
> As once you heard them
> In soft snow.

Sleep, grandmother, sleep.
Your sons are little and silly again;
Your daughters are five and seven and ten;
And he that is gone
Was not gone then.

Sleep, grandmother, sleep.
The sleigh comes out of the winter woods
And carries you all in boots and hoods
To town for candy
And white dress goods.

Sleep, grandmother, sleep.
The rocking chair is old as the floor,
But there he nods, at the noisy door,
For you to be dancing
One dance more.

A number of poems in the section were subsequently set to music as I had hoped they would be. Nothing pleases me more than that. If I cannot always fathom the relation between my words and the composer's notes, I do not worry much about it. Poets are traditionally hard to please upon this point, as Milton's sonnet to Henry Lawes makes forever clear.

I was beginning now to read my poems in public. It was not easy at first, partly because I was diffident and partly because I did not subscribe, as indeed I never have, to the notion that the existence of a poem is incomplete until somebody, preferably its author, reads it aloud. The completest existence of a poem is in that inner ear where no sound ever comes. The harmony is in the reader's brain, or better yet, his soul. And if he is a good reader he cannot bear anybody else's voice between him and the words. Elliott Carter's fine setting for "Another Music" gave most of its attention, naturally, to the physical sounds which that poem insists poetry has nothing to do with. Elocution is the enemy of verse. So I was uncomfortable until I learned to talk about my poems before and after I read them, saying where they started and what they were about, and thus to minimize the reading itself, which more and more I came to do in my plainest voice, with emphasis purely upon the surface meaning. I got to enjoying this, and so I think did my audiences, who certainly never minded hearing that the poems were about something. Before I made the discovery I used to read each poem twice, on the theory that once was insufficient for the twofold purpose of placing the subject and pleasing the listener. I did so with "The Case Is New," which I delivered at Harvard one spring as the Phi Beta Kappa poem. I explained my theory beforehand; but President Conant was in the audience and he told me afterward, with a grin, that he had listened very closely and understood it the first time. Once at the University of Toronto, where Kenneth McLean had invited me to come and read, I met E. J. Pratt, the best Canadian poet and one of the best poets anywhere. He is the nearest thing to Homer in our time, and like Homer is full of the sea. On land, however, I found him so congenial and convivial that I did not miss his waves and tossing ships. When he saw me off at the train he slipped a flask into my briefcase. No telling, he said, how thirsty or how lonely a man might get before he reached New York.

I have gone lecturing, too; arrived, delivered my speech, and then been ravenous for food. It is usually provided by kind hosts; if it is not, before I go to bed I prowl the town for sandwiches and milk or coffee. My story "Dollar Bill" begins with a man in such a plight who counts on finding something to eat at the station before he boards a midnight train for home. But the booths are closing at that moment, so he must lie in his berth and fret because the one sure pleasure of his trip has been denied him. I borrowed here the predicament of James Joyce's boy in "Araby." But of course the boy had not been lecturing.

Now as to the stories. They were a tempestuous experience, and I do not pretend to understand it. It began without warning in 1946, on a train bound for Baltimore and Annapolis. I had expected to make notes for a lecture at St. John's, and was supplied with paper for the purpose; but instead I started writing down, in sentences, phrases, or single words, ideas for stories—in prose, I took it for granted, but my thought went no farther than that. And before the train reached Baltimore I had fifty such ideas. Idea here means anything at all: a person or place I remembered, out of my childhood or less long ago; a strong feeling associated with some action I had performed or failed to perform, or witnessed in another; a sharp perception of some truth, forgotten after a while but restored to me now so that it seemed a present thing; a mere conviction about something, based upon instances of it I had never assembled before, but now they fell into form like pieces of colored glass in a kaleidoscope; a generalization about life or death which without knowing it I had arrived at over many years, and which now embodied itself in some action that went on before my eyes; an incident in some great story which I wanted to retell, altering its terms; a sheer fancy, flying in out of nowhere, and perhaps involving magic, or at any rate the supernatural— which I made a resolution never to explain; a god, an angel, a hero out of myth; anything, I say, at all. But the remarkable fact about each one of them was its clarity, its immediate presence in the air about me.

As soon as I could, at home on Bleecker Street and then in Cornwall, I commenced the hard work. The ideas had come without effort, but words never do—entirely so, that is, for many of these did. I wrote on the whole in a kind of dream, and it was seldom difficult to decide what should be told next, for it told itself. Sometimes, however, there was a struggle; and a few of my notes I could no longer make out, the original figure having vanished. I was aware too that no further ideas came. So I hoarded these, and eventually found that I had put as many as forty of them into form—this within little more than two years since the day I got them. After that the process slowed down; new ideas came one at a time, and as soon as I was sure of them were converted into tales, each of which I thought might be the last; but within five years I had written a hundred, and twenty-five more came straggling after those. The prison story, "April Fool," was told me by Frank, to whom it had been told by the warden of a penitentiary in Illinois; Frank was then in charge of the farms that fed the state institutions, and he picked up many a morsel as he went his rounds. It seems to me now that I shall never write another story. This may or may not turn out to be true, but anyhow I consider the adventure, as an adventure, to have written its own end.

I have already mentioned a few of the stories in connection with events in my own life or the lives of people I knew. But there has been no occasion to mention several that were suggested to me in New York as I walked the streets or sat in the apartments of my friends. "The Watchman," except for its development and end, happened to me in Horatio Street: I saw such a young woman through a window, then made up the rest. "Consider Courage" grew out of my fascination with an amusement center at Broadway and 52nd Street; I saw the little Oriental with his bird, and incidentally I was startled by the reappearance of that bird in *The Castle;* Kafka had seen his like, in Berlin or Prague. "Satan's Best Girl" blossomed rather wildly out of the ticket booth I passed every day in front of the Sheridan Theater on 11th Street, near home. "Like What?"—with changes, that is Armin Landeck's studio. "The Uncertain Glory," "The Prism," and one or two others of their kind occurred to me on trains: always a fertile place, for there one is both in company and alone.

I particularly enjoyed writing those stories that came out of other stories by men now dead. Every story, even a fantastic one, has to come from somewhere, though the source may be hard to discover; but a book is as good a source as any, and there is the further excitement of inventing disguises that will make the material feel new. "The Key" I took from Hardy's poem "The Sailor's Mother." But I can confess to further thefts. "Not a Natural Man" comes from the twenty-fourth book of the *Iliad,* as "Night at the Notch" comes from Eurycleia's recognition scene in the *Odyssey;* and "Miss Swallow" is my version of Pallas Athene, the gray-eyed goddess who helped Odysseus out of every scrape, and who sometimes sat on his roof beam like a swallow that had flown there through the smoke. "Still, Still So" makes clear in its text that it derives from Act IV, Scene 4 of *The Winter's Tale*. "I, Tobit" is of course from the *Book of Tobit* in the Apocrypha: one of my favorite narratives, old or new. "The Bees" comes almost intact out of Whittier's poem "Telling the Bees."

Four stories take their start from Hawthorne's *American Notebooks*, where he was in the habit of entering ideas for tales that he would or would not have time to write. "Mr. Hasbrouck," for example, traces back to this: "A rich man left by will his mansion and estate to a poor couple. They remove into it, and find there a darksome servant, whom they are forbidden by will to turn away. He becomes a torment to them; and, in the finale, he turns out to be the former master of the estate." And "The Engine and the Flare" to this: "The scene of a story or sketch to be laid within the light of a street-lantern; the time, when the light is near going out; and the catastrophe to be simultaneous with the last flickering gleam." And "The Quarry" to this: "Two lovers, or other persons, on the most private business, to appoint a meeting in what they supposed to be a place of the utmost solitude, and to find it thronged with people." And "Wander's World" to this: "Stories to be told of a certain person's appearance in public, of his having been seen in various situations, and of his making visits in private circles; but finally, on looking for this person, to come upon his old grave and mossy tombstone." For many years I had been haunted by those *Notebooks* of Hawthorne's, as he was himself: they were a bound volume in which he daily buried a piece of his mind so that he could thenceforth brood over it as if it were dark gold underground. Chekhov kept a similar record, and so did Hardy. But Hawthorne's seemed to me the best; and in these four cases I was sure he had not gone on to write the tales, so that it could seem my agreeable duty to do it for him. In another case, however, I rewrote one he had finished: "Fisk Fogle" is "The Wives of the Dead" brought forward in time to the Civil War. Finished or unfinished, any story can interest me to the point of my wanting to tell it again. I tend to believe whatever I hear. Tall stories take me in; Dorothy says I am gullible. I do not walk out of bad movies, and I read the worst mystery tales to the end. Nor does it matter that these things are only fiction. Only? People move in them, and that is enough for me: I must find out where they are going.

By and large my stories had to be their own reward. Magazine editors were seldom impressed by them, and it took a long time to get them published in books: *The Witch of Ramoth and Other Tales* in 1950, *The Short Stories of Mark Van Doren* in the same year, *Nobody Say a Word* in 1953, and *Home with Hazel* as late as 1957. But this never dampened my desire to write them. It was an authentic desire; it could even have been a secret vice. They are a life I lived for seven years all by myself, a life with its own beginning, its own end, as if I had been another person while it lasted.

One story took shape in verse. Late in the summer of 1947, when I had exhausted my initial ideas and believed I might never have any more, there was still one that bothered me because it was more ambitious than the rest, and had among its persons some divine beings—just which ones I could not make out at the moment, but clearly they were gods. Here perhaps was my last chance to do what I had failed to do in *The Mayfield Deer*. This time, I said, my deities would have names and would be powerful; they would really influence the action. They would, that is, if I could bring the story into focus. It might even be a novel—I wondered a while about that, then rejected the notion. A poem would be better. So *Mortal Summer* resulted, with seven Greek gods in it—Aphrodite, Athene, Hermes, Ares, Artemis, Hephaestus (my old friend), and Apollo—and three great Hebrew angels from across the Mediterranean: Michael, Gabriel, and Raphael. I awakened all ten of them out of their long sleep and brought them to New England, where they interfered in the lives of

Daniel, Dora, and Bruce, three lovers who shared on two levels such a secret as Joe Krutch recognized without difficulty when he read the poem. But the poem did not appear between its own covers for six years, when Carroll Coleman printed it by hand at his Prairie Press in Iowa; in 1950 it had been published with many misprints in *New Directions* for that year.

As for my gods and angels, I enjoyed their company while I had it. They were ten more among the countless characters I lived with in those years—ideally, quite countless, for "The Ballad Singer," which I put last in *Home with Hazel,* truly expresses my feeling about the storytelling art. It is an art that rescues individuals from oblivion. The world is peopled by men, women, and children concerning most of whom no story is ever told. The storyteller considers this multitude even as he singles out one member of it for attention. He loves or hates that one, but he is never unconscious of the rest. They press upon him till they become a burden, almost a pain, that he can do nothing about. In a thousand years he could not do justice to the experience he knows has left its traces in the air. Life is long and art is short.

IV

Our friends continued to move about. We stay put; they come and go. In 1947 Stringfellow Barr and Scott Buchanan left St. John's, to everybody's sorrow there, and labored for more than a year to create a new college near Stockbridge, Massachusetts. The Buchanans lived first in the parsonage at Richmond, near by, then bought a smaller house in the same town where ever since we have gone regularly to visit them, for it is only forty miles from Cornwall. Stockbridge College never came into being. Scott could not assemble a staff. I was one of those he invited, but I refused—after a war within myself—because in spite of my devotion to him I did not care to dislocate my life. I had always resisted change, and even Scott could not uproot me. Mortimer Adler, who would not come either, in 1950 put himself more than ever out of reach by moving to San Francisco where he would found an Institute for Philosophical Research. Since that year we have seen him only between plane flights. He loves the air as much as he used to love the Twentieth Century Limited.

Joe Krutch, having published in 1948 an excellent, wise life of Thoreau, made good its promise of a shift in the direction of his whole thought about the world by publishing next year *The Twelve Seasons*. I suggested the title, but nobody had suggested the book, which surprised such readers as were not aware that Joe had become a student of nature, a Gilbert White of Redding who could absorb himself endlessly in tortoises, snowflakes, mice, cats, weeds, and the stars. He was more, of course, than a Gilbert White. Always a speculative man, and certainly a modern one, he had enlarged all of his views until they embraced the most unrelenting questions: of joy, of survival, and of the probable face truth wears when no one is looking. He was to follow *The Twelve Seasons* with a series of books equally rich in entertainment for the mind, and he would go at last to Arizona where the desert, seen by Marcelle and him on various summer trips, could no longer be withstood. They too moved away while we stayed put.

He had written his *Thoreau* for the American Men of Letters Series, of which like him I was an editor. My own choice of a life to write was easy; it had to be Hawthorne's, since no other American writer touched me half so closely. I spent the winter of 1947–1948 reading the twenty-two volumes my mother had given me when I graduated from college, and of course I went through all the literature I could find about the author of *The Scarlet Letter,* from Henry James's beautiful book—one of his first, and I still think one of his best—on down to monographs and articles containing what are called, by those who read only them, "discoveries." And I thought steadily about this mysterious man who lived at least two lives: the life of wit, of civility, of charm, and the life of terror. My job as I conceived it was not to reconcile the two, for that cannot be done, but to keep them distinct from each other in any reader's perspective; and to note without faltering the penalty Hawthorne himself paid for his failure to understand their relation, or even to admit their existence. When I wrote the book in the summer of 1948 it cost me a good deal because of the tension it kept me under. But excitement is good for the soul, and in this particular case I was happy to endure it. I lived with Hawthorne as one lives with a difficult friend; I did not let him shake me off, or evade me as he evaded most of the people he knew in Salem and Concord. Like Proteus, though he appeared in fewer forms, he was hard to hold down. I must not claim I held him down; but I am sure I never flinched when it came to deciding between his lesser works and his greater. Only a few of them have strength. But when they have it, it is enormous. That was my problem, to state if not to solve.

Thomas Merton stayed put, of course, in his monastery. But in 1948 he reached out from there with a book that the world he had left could not ignore. *The Seven-Storey Mountain* hit me for one like a bolt of lightning. Robert Giroux, its editor at the publishing house, had told me that Merton was writing an autobiography, and when it was about to appear he sent me an advance copy with a letter advising me to look up my name in the index. To my amazement I learned that the classes of mine in which Tom had sat and the conversations we had had —some of these I did not remember—had been of decisive importance to him. No Catholic myself, I had helped him (without knowing it) to decide that he wanted to be one. Providence, he wrote, had used me as an instrument. "The truth is," I read, rubbing my eyes, "that Mark's temper was profoundly scholastic in the sense that his mind looked directly for the quiddities of things, and sought being and substance under the cover of accident and appearances. And for him poetry was, indeed, a virtue of the practical intellect, not simply a vague spilling of the emotions, wasting the soul and perfecting none of our essential powers." I flushed with pleasure at the opinions imputed to me, but then I ransacked my memory for any sign that Tom as a student had seen me in this light. I could recall none whatever. He had kept his thought of me a secret, well hidden behind the twinkle in his eyes. Or else it had developed in him later, so that only upon reflection he now believed these things to have been true—now, but as much too as three years ago, when he wrote his letter to the Algonquin party. My only conclusion could be that what he said about me in his book, moving and beautiful as it was, revealed more of him than it did of me. I did not repudiate his praise, but I assigned it to him as a merit infinitely surpassing those merits that formerly attached me to him. He had grown immensely; and one proof of this was that he could say such things about somebody else. His subsequent books attest to his continuing growth. So do his letters, to me and to his friends. He does not write me in the sublimely antic idiom he reserves for his contemporary Robert Lax, but even to me he is humorous and serious together: one happy man, as light-hearted as he is grave, and much less lost to the world than many who insist they still are in it.

When he was ordained as a priest in 1949 and became Father Louis I could not go down, as Lax and others did, to witness the ceremony. Another old student, Donald Keene, was flying from England for his doctor's examination, and I knew he wanted me to be present. I was supposed to be in any case, for although the dissertation had been written in the department of Chinese and Japanese I was a member of his committee. He was one of my first students in the Humanities course—in the Shakespeare course too, as I have said—and I had not forgotten his erudition even at that age; he seemed to have read everything. During the war he had studied Japanese; now he taught it at Cambridge University; and what he was to be examined on was a translation, with commentary, of an eighteenth-century puppet play, *The Battles of Coxinga,* which when he published it in England carried a preface written at his request by me. I enjoyed the examination, and of course Father Louis understood my absence from Gethsemani. I did not learn until much later that Keene, like Merton, had come to Columbia because I was there. It never occurs to me that such a thing is possible; and of course no student admits it at the time.

Lax kept informing me of his whereabouts by dispatching to me those letters, long or short, which were and are a record of his inimitable thought. He talked more and more about the circus—a small one, named for the Cristiani brothers who performed most of its acts—which he had adopted as a multiple and ever moving friend. He followed it one year to Canada, writing me from there about the unearthly sweetness and grace of the people who had taken him in as a poet and philosopher without portfolio. He spoke particularly of Mogador, a bareback rider whose father, Papa Cristiani, had named him for the place in North Africa where he happened to be born. And one day in New York, when Bob for some reason was there, he invited me to a restaurant so that I might meet Mogador. Mogador was handsome and lithe, but scarcely more articulate than his friend, so that I did most of the talking. But I learned that he studied dancing under Balanchine in order to perfect his balance; and he told me he hoped I could see the circus for myself some time—New England was one of its beats, and it might play near Cornwall.

This did not happen until 1953, when Dorothy saw a notice in the *Lakeville Journal* that the Cristiani Brothers would be in Pittsfield, Massachusetts, on a certain day. Since Richmond, where the Buchanans live, is only a few miles from Pittsfield, we took them too. We went early in the evening so that I could send our names in to Mogador as he had suggested. He bounded out to greet us; assigned us the best seats in the tent; and during the show perpetually bowed and waved to us, so that we felt very important. He even stepped out of the ring three times to come and sit by us and tell us who among the troupe was doing what. His own performance on a plump white horse was as beautiful as Bob had promised it would be. But we were equally interested in the loving attention he gave at other times to a small pretty woman on the slack wire. This was his wife, whom we saw afterwards in their trailer; it contained a baby too, and was visited by the sword-swallower, not to speak of another man who brought Mogador a pile of currency, the night's take; Mogador was treasurer as well as equestrian. When we departed to find our car, the only one left in the parking lot, Mogador walked with us, talking of Lax and of the winter quarters in Florida where we must pay them all a visit as soon as we could. I have forgotten where Bob was that summer—he was not with the circus—but I wrote him about our adventure, and he was so overcome with joy that he could send me back but one word: "Gee!"

Since 1942 or thereabouts Robert Caldwell had been writing me letters of another sort: long ones, on his office typewriter, about the politics of Bayonne, the doings of his wife Mary and their four children, and the difficulties of Greek, which he says I once suggested that he learn so that he might read Plato and Thucydides in their native sentences. A horse for work, he started in on those giants and to this day has never stinted any effort to puzzle out their meaning—in the case of Thucydides, not always easy to be even approximately certain of. The experiment paid off, if at no other point, in a sentence from Thucydides which he recently made a part of the masthead of his paper: "Even though a man prospers, yet if his city goes to ruin he perishes with her." Caldwell's remarkable letters, which it is understood I need not answer unless I have the time (I have more time than he has), never stop coming, nor has their writer ceased to be a power in his own world.

My last years with Raymond Weaver, who died in the spring of 1948, gave me unique pleasure because he himself was unique. We had often disagreed about people and books, but we did so less and less, and finally it was a tacit assumption between us that neither could be wrong. In his thunderous voice—so different from that of Burdette Kinne, a teacher of

French who amused us all with his piping sarcasms and indignations—Raymond would defend even my nonsense; and I was happy to defend his. This is the way of friendship as I see it. I prefer that those I like should think and say whatever they please; it is not for me to change them or—odious image —straighten them out; I am pleased with their outlines, crooked or otherwise, and would not redraw them. So it has been with Joe Krutch, and so in these years it was with Raymond, who stopped writing and gave all of his mind to the classes he taught. His behavior there is still a legend, certain particulars of which I learned only on the day after his death. When word came of that we all dismissed our classes and sat about in our offices talking of Raymond: of his utterly serious devotion to literature, and of the sometimes frightening way he revealed this to his students. According to Joseph Mazzeo, a younger colleague who had been one of those students, and who because of that had already become a distinguished Dante scholar, Raymond could put a question to the rows of faces before him and wait through eternity, or so it seemed, for an answer. The silence while he waited became itself a kind of thunder as beneath his fierce eyebrows he glared at whomever he had invited to utter some tremendous thing. It was not that he doubted the youth's capacity; he simply was willing to wait until the best possible answer could be composed. If it was inadequate, he then might be surprisingly gentle as he proceeded to amplify it. But if it sounded perverse or vain, capital punishment ensued. For my own part I was to remember longest of all the man's exquisite courtesy: natural to begin with, but in the end a work of art which his beloved Renaissance writers had assisted him to finish and perfect.

He disciplined me in courtesy, purely by his example. So did two other men whom I saw frequently at this time. Douglas Southall Freeman's manners were a product, one could say, of Virginia where he lived and wrote the lives of Lee and Washington. But I choose to think of them as quite his own. I first made his acquaintance when we both became directors of the American Academy of Arts and Letters and sat near each other at meetings. His stately compliments, delivered in a resonant voice that called up images of rooms in houses older than the Civil War, delighted me no matter whom they were addressed to; and his discourse, formal on every topic, fascinated me by its union with that formality of a conspicuous, almost studious ease, as if he had long ago mastered the fine art of being natural in all he thought or did. When Dorothy and I were guests at his house in Richmond—I had been invited there to read my poems, and he introduced me to the audience with flourishes I could not fail to admire as well as approve—he and his wife Inez conspired with many of their relatives and friends to treat us like royalty from New York. Once I protested that nobody could mean the nice things they said; and was smiled down so sweetly that I knew I sounded barbarous. I had lived enough in New England, where nobody ever says good things about another, at least to his face, to have forgotten that it is possible to live by amenity alone.

Freeman's *Washington,* then in its fifth volume, inflicted a schedule upon him that would have killed any other man, and did I suppose account for his own death in 1953. He rose at 2:30 and was at work by 4:00, in an upper story of his large house where Mary Wells Ashworth assisted him with his notes and manuscript. At 8:00 he stopped for the day, and after a broadcast to the people of Virginia came down for breakfast with his family. He had gone to bed, of course, at something like 7:30 the evening before, so that he had no society of the conventional sort. One of the days we were there he took us after breakfast in an old car to see Cold Harbor and other battlefields near Richmond. He read the bronze markers with such rapidity and ease that I asked him whether he had not composed their texts. He had, for his knowledge of the Civil War was like the knowledge most people have of their back yards. On the way home I said to him that now I thought I knew why he maintained such an unearthly regimen: he wanted his days free for his friends. He told me I was right.

But that regimen, I think, was something that no man could survive. It had been even crueller when he edited a Richmond paper. Latterly, he liked to say, he took things easy. But among the kinds of ease he valued, sloth was never one.

Archibald MacLeish, my third tutor in the ways of gentleness, I had known slightly since 1928, when he reviewed *Now the Sky* and said among other things that it was not modern. Not long after this he invited me to lunch in New York, and when I offered to pay the check pretended to be deaf. I saw him a few times during the war, when he was busy in Washington, and later I met him as Librarian of Congress. But it was not until the difficult days after the war that I made his intimate acquaintance. Then we drove back and forth between his place in Conway, Massachusetts, and ours in Cornwall for visits the memory of which I would not trade for any other. There is no better host than Archie, unless it be Ada his wife. He is quick in kindness; he is dexterous with wine and a connoisseur of chicken; he is funny, he is serious, he is affectionate all at once, in a fashion I have never encountered elsewhere, and I cannot doubt that it exists only in him. When he was invited to become a professor at Harvard he hastened down to talk with me about teaching. I told him he needed no briefing; of course he did not believe me. Dorothy and I took Carl to Conway with us once, but at all other times we have gone there alone as Archie and Ada have come alone to Cornwall. Occasionally he comes by himself; and after one such trip he sent me this for a thank-you note:

On a day of strong dry wind
In the summer of hatred
I drove a hundred miles to visit you.

Everyone talked of war that summer.
Off to the north
Forests were burning: the sad odor.

You came to the gate of your garden to meet me.
Almost till dusk
We talked of admirable things—

Of great poems, of noble men,
Of the labor of art—
The labor of schools and the difficult victories.

Driving homeward the odor of burning
Was sweet as leaf-smoke.
The whole world was spacious and beautiful.

When Archie published that piece in his *Collected Poems* he changed almost every line. I give it as it came to me, not because it is better thus but because it is different. In either version it expresses the man who could write to me like one old Chinese to another in the days when sages sat on their mountains and exchanged meditations as quiet as a leaf on which some golden butterfly with soundless wings has lit.

V

Courtesy was hardly the trait one found during the postwar days in congressmen who investigated people's opinions. The necessary moves against conspiracy, here and abroad, were augmented by a fanaticism at home that even then was easier to forgive than the cynicism of numerous persons, public or private, who sought to advance themselves by exposing others —not for conspiracy, which there were agencies to detect and deal with quietly behind the scenes where it went on, but for ideas and sentiments allegedly contributory to it. I became aware of this in the late 1940's, so that in the summer of 1949, when I happened to be experimenting with the sonnet form, I had a subject ready to hand. The experiment itself was of a sort that has always intrigued me. It consisted of trying, out of purely technical curiosity, a verse form I had hitherto not used: the Italian sonnet, famous in English through the triumphs of Milton and Wordsworth, to name no others. Allen Tate and I had once agreed that such experiments not only are refreshing but may lead to ponderable results. In his case the mere desire to see what he could do with rhymed trimeter had moved him, at a time when he thought there were no further poems in him, to write "Seasons of the Soul": I had recommended the trial, and he said he was grateful. Of course the poems were in him; they only awaited a mold into which they could be poured; that is the whole point of the matter.

So, I think, with me in the summer of 1949. There was something I wanted to say, yet I scarcely knew what it was because I could not hear it being said. Then by an accident I learned. I had been asked to edit a selection of Wordsworth's poems, and in doing so I became especially interested in his sonnets. Mine so far had been wholly in Shakespeare's form, less intricate, less artificial than the octave and sestet with their serried rhymes. Looking closely to see how Wordsworth did it, I came upon a note by his sister Dorothy telling how he had chanced upon the form: it was through her reading aloud to him the sonnets of Milton. He determined to emulate those, and soon was delivering himself of political judgments (about Napoleon) that otherwise might never have come out. Precisely the same thing happened to me. Before I knew it I had written thirty-three sonnets, and among them were several that bore upon the contemporary madness. "The deepest dream is of mad governors—" one of them began that way. And another one said what I knew I had been thinking: that the best people were now being protected by the worst, or at any rate the better by the none-too-good—Plato's guardians were running amuck.

> The time of martyrs may be come again;
> Yet as of old, no single heart is foul.
> Security, blindfolded, wears the cowl;
> Stupidity sits here and judges men.
> The best are most despised, as they were **then;**
> As long ago they did, the worst ones howl
> Loudest of fair intentions—wolf and owl
> And dark hyena, guarding our great den.

I sent this group to *The Nation*, which printed them under the title Political Sonnets. They also appeared, with others not political, in a pamphlet, *Humanity Unlimited,* published early in 1950 by the College of William and Mary, where I had gone with Dorothy to read them as Phi Beta Kappa poems. And then, in a way that I can only call weird, the past spoke out of its darkness. The conspicuous security case at the moment was that of Alger Hiss, and his accuser was no other than my old student Whittaker Chambers. When the newspapers first reported the accusations, naturally there were photographs of Whittaker; and Dorothy, seeing these, was tempted to think they were not of the person we had known. They were, of course; he had grown older, and his face was fuller. Knowing Whittaker's flair for the dramatic, remembering his numerous plunges into extremes of conviction contrary to one another, and having in mind too his cloak-and-dagger air when he slipped down in 1938 to have me help save him from murderous pursuers, I found I could not believe him now, though I granted that he might very well believe himself.

Before Hiss's first trial, when there was much public interest in his accuser, a journalist called on me one day to discuss Whittaker, concerning whom he proposed to write an article. The article never appeared, but in the course of our conversation I showed him some of Whittaker's letters, and he took them away with him to study. The next thing I knew, they were in the hands of Hiss's lawyers. I had not sent them there, as Whittaker understandably believed; nor was I comfortable when one of the lawyers asked me for permission to use them as evidence in the trial. They were the letters of a student, and one desires to be scrupulous about such things. On the other hand I was advised by lawyers who were my friends that I had no right to withhold documents which might have bearing upon an important issue. I did not see the bearing, nor can I suppose that the one letter placed in evidence made any contribution to the case. Anyhow, early in 1950 Hiss was found guilty of perjury and sentenced to five years in a Federal penitentiary. While he was awaiting sentence somebody who knew him suggested that I send him a copy of the William and

Mary pamphlet. I did so, and on March 6th received an acknowledgment containing these remarkable sentences:

> Yesterday Dr. Shotwell and I found ourselves agreeing that perhaps the things that most need saying—and being heard—can be effectively conveyed only by verse. The spate of articles, speeches and comments has debased almost all exposition and exhortation in prose, so that the best is lost among the voluminous worst. Your sonnets came vividly to mind as an illustration of what might be done.

The nerves of such a man, I said to myself, must be made of more than ordinary iron. Nowhere in his letter did Hiss mention his own predicament, nor use any other voice than that of one whose mind was free to consider the difference between prose and verse. During a subsequent brief period when my own opinions were called in question, though mildly as such things then went—my books, removed from the shelves of a library in Jersey City, were replaced when a committee of citizens protested—I was fortified by the example of one who could think of the whole matter as other than altogether personal to himself.

VI

Meanwhile, by an odd rule of life that makes things simultaneous when they have no conceivable relation to one another, Dorothy was writing *The Country Wife*. This book, for which Charlie supplied the title, revealed her for the first time as the humorist she is. The sketches in it were of our life in Cornwall: its pleasures, its frustrations, its successes, its defeats, and more than anything else its amusing madness wherein imbecility lies down with inspiration and curses hourly alternate with caresses. Many of its particulars I have already told here from my point of view; but when I read *The Country Wife*, which I did chapter by chapter with growing edification and delight, I learned how different Dorothy's view had been. For one thing, I discovered quite a bit about myself. My name in the book is The Professor; and while I am in the habit of saying that he is a fictional character, and she noncommittally assents, I recognize his deeds as mine, as well as his misdeeds and miscalculations. On the whole he is treated tenderly, as befits a fellow, half hero, half ass, who takes for granted the fondness of his wife without remembering regularly enough that she is more intelligent than he is, especially in his tantrums. Dorothy, however, learned something herself when the book, widely read, began to draw responses from its readers. Any number of women wrote that their husbands were just like me. For example, they thought they disliked parties, but when they arrived at one enjoyed themselves more than the poor women did who had dragged them there. Dorothy describes such a party, which I hate to attend and then cannot be induced to leave. "After all," she remarks, "my attitude toward the Joneses has not fluctuated; I was rather calm about going in the first place and I am calm at the thought of going home." So if I gained nothing else from *The Country Wife* beyond the pleasure of reading it and recognizing its truth, I gained the discovery by its author that her husband was not unique.

Two further things, still more unrelated if that is possible, happened together in the summer of 1950. I had set aside the month of July for the writing of a textbook about poetry which William Sloane suggested that I do. It would have to be, I said, a set of commentaries upon single poems; I did not want to discuss poetry in general, or contrive ideas about it; I was weary of such talk, for it led nowhere. Better to talk in my own way of certain poems I knew well and indeed had been going over in my classes; if some theory was implicit therein, so much the better, but I would be the last one ever to state it. Sloane agreed, and I was ready to start the commentaries.

But Carl, whom we had brought to Cornwall with us on my birthday, became ill the next Monday night and was sent by

Dr. Walker to the hospital in Torrington. It was his heart, which all of us thought he had been unnecessarily worried about for the past two years. He was so little of a hypochondriac, or had been throughout a life conspicuous for its superiority to weakness of any sort, that nobody, not even the doctors in New York, had been able to understand this apparently baseless anxiety. I have said he could be anxious, but it was never about his health. One of his daughters, I think Margaret, called to tell us what had happened. He was at Irita's house on Cream Hill—once his house too—and was happy among his grandchildren, whom he adored, when sickness came. Most of us, including myself, believed because we wanted to that Carl would be well in a month. But on July 18th he died, after days when he could see us only one at a time. I took my turns, appalled by his paleness, and said nothing of what was more and more on my mind: the great tree in whose shade I had lived was about to be cut down. It was unthinkable, yet it was true. I pondered it, tried to put it out of reach, then pondered it again. The only way I could put it out of reach for as much as an hour was to return to the commentaries, which I had in fact begun. Stubbornly, whenever I was not at the hospital, I stuck to that enterprise. The *Introduction to Poetry* was composed in the lengthening shadow of death.

Since that death the world has been so changed a place that I date most events as after or before it. For several years on Saturday nights Carl had come to us on Bleecker Street for supper. Often he walked down from his huge apartment on Central Park West, a distance of three miles; for nobody ever liked walking in New York better than he did. His coming never failed to please us. He knew this so well that nothing could have induced him to deny us the pleasure. His genius for friendship meant among other things that he went to see those whom he liked even when it would be more comfortable or convenient to stay at home. It is more blessed to pay calls than to receive them—he said this once to Sinclair Lewis,

whom he loved, in the hearing of Clifton Fadiman who repeated it to me, and I wish I could have been there myself.
Lewis had been complaining about the inconstancy of his
friends. "One thing you may not know about friendship,
Red"—I can hear Carl saying this after all—"is that you have
to work at it. Sometimes your friends will bore you, but you
must not tell them so. At other times you must put yourself
out to go and see them; it is a kindness to interrupt them
even if they don't think so, or you don't." The measure of his
success is the number of individuals who now think he was
their best friend. And he was. For nobody's letters came more
promptly when letters were desired; and when he was with
anybody it seemed to be true that there was no other person
in the world.

Hundreds of people wrote me about his death. Most of them
spoke of how he had loved me, and had said so over and over.
I knew this, yet so much evidence of it all at once, and after
the fact, was overwhelming. My remaining brothers assembled
at Cornwall in September—Paul was about to buy the Hollow
schoolhouse for his summer place, and so to become our
neighbor—and later in New York there was a memorial evening for Carl at which Julian Boyd, Kip Fadiman, and others
described with accuracy the person they had known. As Carl's
literary executor (Paul handled the business side) I sat many
nights in his apartment putting papers and books in order
for their journey to the Princeton Library where Julian was
to see that they were kept. These were ghostly nights—I was
often there till early morning, and the silence of the big rooms
was a dreadful thing—but there was no alternative to my
spending them as I did, and I cannot be anything but glad
because I had them. I found that Carl had saved every word
I ever wrote him; I had kept his letters too, and all of them
went in one box to Princeton. But the paramount fact about
Carl henceforth would be that he was gone. I have never been
able to say to anyone how vast and solid a fact this is for me.
So solid, strangely enough, that he often seems present because

I know him to be absent. The intensity of his existence was equal to my father's, and that is something like an absolute, as I have said. My poem about him, "In Memoriam," tries to do justice to the courage and the love which conquered in him the anxiety, the excitement, and the fear. These were as much a part of him as the self-confidence most people envied in a man whose laughter could reassure them as dawn reassures the grass.

> Look, till all of his years,
> Foreshortened in your gaze,
> Become, as under glass,
> A few intensest days.
>
> See? The courageous head—
> The brown one—the white—
> It flickers like a single
> Star in densest night.
>
> Listen. But no sound.
> Not even glancing here.
> The fever in him flashes:
> The love against the fear.
>
> Anxiety in this man
> Yet could not kill the heart,
> That now is burning coal,
> And his immensest part.
>
> The panic, the distress—
> Oh, brothers, do not cry.
> His love alone is climbing
> The fences of the sky.

VII

My trips to Illinois had never ceased. Usually they were by car, with Dorothy and the boys; my mother, older and frailer now, with a memory that played strange tricks, so that she was not always sure just who had come to see her, nevertheless wanted us to be there when we could. But for two or three years running it chanced that I went alone, on trains which Frank and Grace would meet. The occasion might be a lecture somewhere else, and I would arrive from there; the only real reason for the engagement being that it took me within range of Urbana and Tuscola. Always a lover of trains, I particularly enjoyed them now. They made me young again: a child luxuriating in the peculiar loneliness of a long coach or Pullman whose other inhabitants appeared to have no knowledge of his being among them, nor did the backs of their heads present themselves to him as anything more than detached round objects rolling with the motion of the car. And since to feel young again, or for that matter very old, means for me that poems must be written, I wrote a number now, en route or afterwards at home, about the clandestine pleasures of a train. "To Be On Trains," which José Villa printed in a magazine he was editing, stated these pleasures in their most abstract form:

> To be on trains, perfection of alone:
> The one among the many that the blue cap
> Counts not, sitting in the roar
> Of such a startled stillness as the whistle—
> Where?—unmakes and makes as whirlwinds do
> Necessity of sound. To be this one
> Yet no one that the blue cap, bending, sees.
> To be nowhere but here, and yet not, yet not
> Anywhere by night, by day—which is it,
> Brother in the green seat opposite, sister
> Ahead there, swimming under time's
> Thick water, under firmaments of—oh,
> To be and not be numbered—let it go
> Oh, anywhere, this absolute alone.

Other poems dealt with specific sights seen out of flying windows: the edge of a town in Indiana where a man and woman were planting seeds, a small bird engaged in battle with a big one over woods in the middle distance, an oak tree solitary in a field, and numberless fields themselves as in May

the great machines of the farmers went over them to pulverize
their soil for the reception of corn, soy beans, or oats. A martin
house on a pole near the station at Danville moved me to
write "Civilization"; and a side trip I took, from Lafayette to
Indianapolis, could not be forgotten until I had exactly repro-
duced it in "The Merry Trainman," whose talkative conductor
said just these things:

Apologetic, the old person in the black hat
Fumbles to descend, saying: "Once I could do this faster."
"Can't fool me," fellow in the blue cap answers. "Dancing,
Dancing—you was up all night—I know it—dancing!
Shame on all such girls. Where's Henry?" And the grandchild
Jumps from the top step of the vestibule—clear down
And clings. "Old-timer! Well! Hello! And how is crops?"
They both go comforted. He tilts his dusty cap.
"Indianapolis local! Last chance this morning
To visit the state capital and bring back home
Some silver souvenirs. What's that? Three quarters of a half hour
Late? Not by the sun"—he squints—"but what if so?
Who hurries, and who worries? Up with you, Tom Carson.
Smoking car on the right. But I don't recommend it.
Board! All aboard!" And the coach, creaking among cornfields,
Bears on the summer rails his chosen people, smiling.
Seat by sleepy seat he ministers, this Mercury,
This clown of the blue cloth, while overhead the high planes
Hum, with kings in them, or queens for all he cares.

In the spring there would be newborn animals everywhere in
the pastures. Jessie, Paul's wife, spoke of them once when she
returned by train from Chicago. The next time I went I
looked, and of course they were there, and I said my say about
them in "Spring Birth":

The lord of increase, travelling with me,
Said: "Look! There are more than you will see,
Yet look!" And laughed, and pointed at the small
Pigs bouncing as they ran, and at the tall
Bewildered foals, their four legs wildly braced
Lest the ground heave again; while kittens chased
White butterflies, and calves, all ears and head,
Butted and sucked as their great mothers fed. . . .

When I had enough such poems to print as a collection, I did so in a pamphlet Carroll Coleman had offered to publish at his Prairie Press. The title, *In That Far Land,* I took from the first poem in it, "Only For Me." That land is not so far as trains and planes now measure distance, but for me it is out of this world: I measure it by years, not miles, and have the illusion that their number cannot be counted. Of course they can; but when I am out there, riding perhaps with Frank and Grace along straight roads that never jog until they must do so to keep in line with the meridians that converge upon the North Pole—a long way off, yet it is there to remind highways that the earth is round—I consider myself transported to another existence altogether: not as old as Cornwall, but the earliest one in my chronology, and increasingly precious for that reason. The pamphlet was my tribute to it. "No Word, No Wind" stated the limitations of a life I am unable to go back and live, somewhat as "Midland" had stated them in *The Seven Sleepers;* but also it endeavored to say why one born there might want to die there too. The beauty of the place is the beauty of a still hour in the middle of the night when a south wind is soft among the curtains and sleep has become impossible, yet there is nothing to think about very long or deeply.

In October, 1951, I went on out after a lecture in Ohio to see my mother at Tuscola, where she had been taken after it was clear that she could no longer live alone in Urbana; Dorothy O'Brien, once Dorothy Knight, and Aunt Cora Butz, Uncle Mark's widow, had stayed with her there by turns, but then it got too difficult for anybody. Grace had written me that she was very weak, but I still thought she might know me. I even took a blue wool shawl, just the color of her eyes, that I had bought in New York; its softness pleased me, and surely would please her. But she was too far gone to take note either of me or of her present. Or I think she was. It is never certain what a dying person sees and understands. Or an infant, powerless to utter one word. My mother at eighty-eight was as help-

less as any of the five babies she had borne. I went back and
forth between Frank's house and the nursing home where she
lay, helpless myself to do anything better than regret that I had
not come months ago. My last visit, on Sunday, could last only
half an hour: a terribly short time, and the thought of it filled
me with guilt and grief, nor was I helped as I left by hearing
an organ in the next room that played, of all things, "Abide
With Me." But the proprietress of the home had not selected
the tune with me in mind.

In November Frank telegraphed to Paul and me that she
was dead. We went out on the train together, sitting up all
night both ways, talking more than we slept. The old people
from Hope who came in to the funeral at Urbana were fewer
than had come to see my father buried; eighteen years had
passed, and most of my mother's friends were gone. A generation and a way of life went with her. And in her own person a
pride, a passion, which not too many years back "The Fine
Plan," in *New Poems*, had taken for its subject:

The dust has long been settled that she rode,
A goddess in a buggy, with straight back
And blue ambitious gaze. For she was born
In a wild moment, and at twenty was taken
For better, worse, by husband and by pride.

And one of them is gone, but the other lives
As she does, thin in bed, remembering dust
And the hot horses; and when they were home,
The sons she would assess. For she could measure
By no rule but her own, that rode with her,

Superior to clouds; where now is clearness,
And weeds that have forgotten how she sped.
And strangers in that house. For the sons have scattered.
Only one gaunt lady will remember
What they were to have been, or what she was.

Here now she lies, with one of those she wedded
In the wild hour she fiercely lives again.
Here now she lies, and rages and refuses

All sixty years since that one: all poor time,
All persons, all that tempered the fine plan.

Still farther back in time she had suggested "Nothing But
Death" and "The Visitor," and "The Pair" is a story about her
and her father. But my last word about her was another story,
"Abide With Me," in which I did not depart by as much as a
comma from what I had felt and thought during my half-hour
with her in the nursing home. I have never needed to tell anybody that this story was personal to me. Autobiography in it is
assumed; it must have happened, they say, just so. And truly
it did. Nor was I surprised when Frank, after reading it in
Home with Hazel, wrote me that he would never be able to
read it again.

VIII

Charlie had sailed for England in September, on the same
traveling fellowship from Columbia that Joe Krutch and I
together enjoyed so much in 1919–1920. He was to spend the
winter at Cambridge; but in the spring he went to Paris and
stayed there a full year, returning in 1953 not with a dissertation but with the first chapters of a novel. Johnny kept on with
his study of American history, and I benefited from this by
talks I could have with him about Lincoln, concerning whom
I had begun to think I might write a long poem—at my
leisure, after much reading. I laid in a supply of books and
spent all of my spare time over the next three years with a man
who from my childhood had been for me the richest and
deepest character in a past I could think of as my own. He was
tragic and he was comic; and furthermore, he was from Illinois.
His origin was to diminish in interest as I read on, but not so
the two masks he wore, or the single soul behind them which
his style made audible if not visible to me. In the sequel there
was no poem. Of that, however, at another time.

Mark Van Doren

In the spring of 1953 I published *Spring Birth and Other Poems,* assembling in one volume *Humanity Unlimited* and *In That Far Land,* the rest of the sonnets I had written in 1949, and a number of new pieces. These last included a group of seventeen which *Commentary* had printed in 1950 under the title The People of the Word. They grew out of my consuming curiosity about certain persons whom the Old Testament treats with a brevity so brutal that the imagination thereafter must struggle to amend it and fill out their stories. This cannot be done because it need not be done: the stories are perfect after all, there being no better proof of this than the reader's desire to extend them. Yet the temptation is rarely resisted, and after several years of talking with students about the wives of David, the patriarchs and their families, Joseph and his father, Jephthah and his daughter, Moses, Noah, Samuel, and Sarah of Ecbatana who after the deaths of seven bridegrooms married Tobias, son of Tobit, I found that I too was unable to keep my hands off the Book; and so these poems.

The Final Miracle

1953–1957

❧

I RESIST change, yet in the spring of 1953 I embraced one form of it that promised to be lucky and throughout five years has fulfilled the promise. I half retired from Columbia. I was fifty-nine, and my first thought had been to retire altogether, as Joe Krutch had and as Emery Neff—I talked it over with both of them—was planning to do shortly. Dorothy and I supposed that in such an event we would spend two or three months of the late winter and early spring in New York, leaving Cornwall to its ice and snow; so our scheme was to keep the house on Bleecker Street and live snugly on one floor of it from, say, the end of January to the beginning of April. We did not care to cut all our connections with the city or to give up seeing our friends there. But Marjorie Nicolson, hearing of this, sent word to me that I might as well teach while I was on hand to do so; New York, she said, would not be what I remembered it if I became one of its idle citizens—it was a poor place to do nothing in. I had not intended to do nothing, yet she had a point, and in the end I did as she suggested. She said too that I would miss teaching, and I had never doubted that this was true. Yet some day I would have to stop, and my notion, like Emery's, was to do it sooner rather than later. The more leisure after sixty, surely, the better. It would mean more time to write, and between spells of that to be as lazy as I liked. Laziness is good too, as wasting time is.

> If I could only waste it all.
> But, temporal, nobody can.

So I found myself saying after the change was made.

Mark Van Doren

I was to be free each year, then, from June to February. I might have chosen to teach in the fall term, but I remembered how much I liked being in Cornwall while the vegetation died, the leaves fell, the colors deepened, the days shortened, the shadows lengthened, the ground hardened, and cold came. The excitement of spring is fine, but the excitement of a year's end is more than words have ever stated, though many of mine have tried, as witness "Dance of Death":

> Fall is a crazy dancer—
> Look, how he whirls in leaves;
> How happy Death is to be stamping with him—
> There, on the stricken body
> Of grass, of mortal green.
>
> Down with it all: he dances,
> And look, she laughs in his arms;
> Wicked, the bright wind is funeral music
> For long days—remember?—
> And hot dark, and flowers.
>
> Death is a wild partner;
> But look, she is not young.
> She is the eldest daughter; she has danced
> Forever, without wedding
> Any warm one.

In any case, such was our decision, and in June we went to the country for twenty months: a sabbatical year was due, and after that would come my first half-year of truancy. Moving to the third floor on Bleecker Street meant that I must dispose of a great many books. I did so cheerfully, selecting only the essential ones, the ones I knew I would reread, to take with me to the new study I was making out of our smallest guest room in Cornwall.

But there were other changes as well. Dorothy's kitchen was made prettier and more convenient than it had been, and more commodious to boot; and for the old pipeless furnace we substituted an oil burner. The most radical change, however, had to do with Anna, who when we discussed the future with her announced that she was retiring too: she would live with a

The Final Miracle: 1953–1957

friend in Sharon, the next town to the west, and come to see us
as often as we pleased. It was just twenty years since she had
come in the first place, and of course she was one of us. But
she was firm in this as in all of her resolutions, our only comfort when she left lying in the thought that we would be alone
as we had been seven years ago while she wintered in California: alone to keep what hours we liked, and to live in every
other respect the life that lay ahead. We could not have foreseen, of course, that Anna would die in December. She was
driving her car through Lakeville when she suffered a heart
attack and barely had time to pull over to the curb. She did
that, shifted the engine out of gear, and breathed her last
breath. Then we saw her room in Sharon, which she had insisted we put off inspecting until it was furnished to the final
inch. As we walked into it we could not help noticing first of
all the photographs of the boys she had hung in every available
space. Her old room in our house—it still is Anna's room—
became as time went on the favorite of many guests, notably
Paul when he came up alone. At the far end of the kitchen
wing, independent of every other part, it is self-sufficient and
sui generis, as was the woman whose name it bears.

Those twenty months were a new life that I never tired of
contemplating even while I lived it. The change I had made
was in the interest of less change—that, I told myself, was the
best thing about it. It simplified the year. There was more
monotony, and that was what I wanted.

> Of breakfast, then of walking to the pond;
> Of wind, work, rain, and sleep I never tire.
> God of monotony, may you be fond
> Of me and these forever, and wood fire.

So I wrote after three years of a routine I had tested and found
good. A satisfactory life cannot repeat itself too often; the same
old things, if they are the right things, give joy when they return—silently, too, as if they knew they would be welcome and
so had anticipated no greeting upon arrival. I can do with long
silences; and so can Dorothy, for hours pass between us with-

321

out a word. When I wrote "Country Boredom" in the second year of our exile I hoped it would be understood that the title was ironic. What it referred to exactly suited me.

> Whole days are city minutes if you measure
> Time by persons. Less. For no one comes.
> Ticktock is not a footstep, nor does wind
> Wear clothes. Nor does sunset speak to sunrise;
> They are not even strangers to each other,
> Here in this waste of purpose, in this faceless
> Forum where the atoms never argue:
> Equal and indivisible; content
> With the vast void between them. If you count
> By voices, music fails; and if you listen
> Only for wit there is no need of ears.
> What then? Why stay? What is the good of stillness,
> Had at so huge a cost? I will not tell you.
> I do not know. Except, with stillness itself
> For standard, I could be satisfied, and am.
> Listen. No one comes. That wasn't the wind.
> Even the clock is holding its breath; and the stars
> Have stopped. Or I think they have. Be quiet. Thinking
> Itself is sound. We shouldn't be here. Or if so,
> We shouldn't be disagreeing. Even agreeing.

One illusion I had, however, was quickly exposed as such, and Dorothy amused herself by reminding me that she had prophesied it would be. I never learned to get up early in the morning. Joe Krutch and Emery Neff rise with the sun—Joe to examine his animals and plants and Emery to go on with his Chinese painting—but I cannot manage it. I believe with all my heart that it is the best time to be awake. Thoreau's recommendation of the dawn converted me in theory as far back as 1915 when I was reading him for my first book; and whenever circumstances have got me up at that hour I have exclaimed about its beauty. But I keep city hours. I cannot go to bed without reading something, then reading something else; or writing letters, or straightening my desk, or eating, or simply strolling about; and of course if there are callers I never want them to go home. Once or twice every summer I wake up as early as six and look out at the sun as it gilds the great hanging branches of our crabapple tree west of the garden; it is the biggest tree of its kind I know, and the early light performs wonders among its leaves. I even wrote a story about a man (I pretended he was somebody else) who awoke just so and turned his head to admire just such a tree. But he never did anything about it either; nor has the story, which I called simply "The Tree," ever been printed, since nothing happens in it. Which does not mean that I took no pleasure in writing it. Or in writing "Get Up, I Say":

> Get up, I say, and see them,
> The green streaks of morning;
> Long and low, with white gold
> Alternating, adorning—
>
> Get up, I say; and sometimes,
> Just as they are striking,
> Obedient I do—ah, those
> Lances, so to my liking,
>
> That reach here so straightly,
> Unswerving, swinging,
> And pierce me—ah, little birds,
> Almost to singing.

But the poem is pure fiction. Perhaps it says for me that early morning is too sacred a time to be profaned by frequent visits. If it says this, it conceals the damaging fact that I am without capacity to pay them.

I freely admit, in other words, that I do not belong where I am in the same sense that the beasts and trees do, and the native people whom I so deeply respect for a kind of knowledge I shall never possess. The city remains necessary for me as I realize it has always been necessary for consciousness and civilization. As I have said on another occasion, I love New York because of its faults, chief among these being that it has too many people. But when I go there I am delighted by the throng, as I am by the vistas of purely artificial, man-made caverns and façades. Strangers, as Seth Golliday says to himself in *The Mayfield Deer,* are the spring of the world that winds it up and keeps it wound. The oldest human illusion is that cities can be dispensed with. They have always been hated, yet they have always been crowded. Men want to be where other men are, and the more of them the merrier—up to some limit when they cease to seem tolerable, and then the country dream is dreamed. Shakespeare understood this perfectly: witness *As You Like It,* where both the country and the court are dreams, bad or good as you like it. I dream the country dream two thirds of the year, then try the other. The only change in my life has been the fraction. That is important, but still I lay no claim to the whole number.

Meanwhile, for as many months as I desire, Cornwall presents itself as picture and makes itself heard as music, and both are clear and sweet. The "side hill," as Allyn Hurlburt calls the small tilted field, entirely surrounded by tall trees, which overlooks the Sedgwick cemetery; the old road, black with the shade of enormous pines, between it and the cemetery; the pasture east of that, where on misty days the boulders and juniper bushes appear to move downhill like floating islands never to reach the river or the sea because upon closer inspection they do not change position after all (they are the protagonists in my story "The Pasture"); the paddock by the garden where plum and pear and cherry trees have grown so well that some day there will be no grass beneath them; the brook in all of its reaches; the pond, the picnic place; the field where my study is—I must pass on the way a rock as big as a small house, covered with moss, wild columbine, and miniature ferns; the road, now closed, that used to go on up over Sedgwick Mountain to Goshen, but now is overarched with oak, maple, birch, witch hazel, hemlock, pine, beech, viburnum, and moosewood all the way to Macklin Cunningham's gate; the house we live in now, and the other house, the little one downhill by the brook where we may live some day— these and a hundred places like them are for me a harmony I cannot do without. They compose and blend; they are a world by themselves in which I know there is danger of being lost.

New England is almost too beautiful to live in long. The mind, accepting it too hungrily, and forgetting all things else, can in time grow queer. The silence it enjoins may not be the best thing for a man. For more than half a year, however, it is a blessed thing, and I have learned how to count the blessing even while I remember that:

> The hills of little Cornwall
> Themselves are dreams.
> The mind lies down among them,
> Even by day, and snores,
> Snug in the perilous knowledge
> That nothing more inward pleasing,
> More like itself,
> Sleeps anywhere beyond them
> Even by night
> In the great land it cares two pins about,
> Possibly; not more.
>
> The mind, eager for caresses,
> Lies down at its own risk in Cornwall;
> Whose hills,
> Whose cunning streams,
> Whose mazes where a thought,
> Doubling upon itself,
> Considers the way, lazily, well lost,
> Indulge it to the nick of death—
> Not quite, for where it curls it still can feel,
> Like feathers,
> Like affectionate mouse whiskers,
> The flattery, the trap.

So I recently began a tale in verse, "Anger in the Room," concerning an all too familiar New England phenomenon: the soul that takes too much satisfaction in silence, and so turns sour instead of sweet. The country, like the city, is pure idea. And both are perilous. But either one of them alone is more perilous still. In my new life I remember that.

Mark Van Doren

II

Nor do I forget that it is good sometimes to shift the scene at which one gazes. Dorothy and I are fond of what she calls "little trips" by car to Vermont, New Hampshire, or places closer by. It does not matter where they are, so they be strange. For one thing, I find it delicious to fly past houses and farms for whose care I have no responsibility. These people are neat and those are sluttish, but it makes no difference to the man behind the wheel or to the woman at his side; soon there will be other places, and then good-by to them as well.

> Let's go. Let's be somewhere awhile
> We haven't ever been before;
> And strangers cut the random grass
> Or leave it ragged.

Yet that is only one feature of the experience, and it may not be the salient one for my companion. I do not know, for on the way we do not speak much of such matters, or of anything else. I suspect, though, that Dorothy likes to eat meals she has not had to cook, and to sleep in motel beds—sometimes we stay away that long—which she does not have to make in the morning; though she enjoys planning the lunches we stop and eat on some hill (unless we passed it by mistake a few minutes back) where there is a handsome view of country never seen until this minute.

In any case we give ourselves completely to strangeness, and then return home with a fresh love for the sameness we had left, and the unchanging chores. The chore of mine that I like best is burning rubbish in the stone incinerator George Crosby built for me in 1924. Carl used to apostrophize fire as "the great cleanser," and so it is. I really wrote "Incinerator" for him, though he was no longer here to read it:

> Mornings, in a stone place,
> I worship fire the cleanser.

The Final Miracle: 1953–1957

I go there; he meets me;
And one scratch does it all.

The paper, the wet bones;
Last evening's greenstuff:
I bring them; he knows me;
And smoke is our word.

And then I am silent.
But he the undoer—
Ah, the fierce laughings
Of flame to itself.

The eggshells, the cardboard—
Matter into spirit—
No wonder he adores me,
And comes there every day.

There are countless other appointments I keep with order, and Dorothy has as many of her own. The routine that resumes has willing slaves in us, just as it has in the animals, wild or tame, that inhabit the place, or in the weather that obeys its own laws overhead. Weather is always the same and always different. I like every one of its varieties, though I can tire of windless days and long for inclemency—any kind of disturbance except hurricanes, though we have been lucky (I cross my fingers) as to those. I like clear days and thick; I disappear into heavy rains and do not come back till I am soaked; but then I can bask in warm sun, too, and feel it like a touch of love on my shoulders.

As for the animals, there are of course Walter and Blackie who share with us every foot of the place indoors and out; they walk with us in any kind of weather. But then there are wild visitors who sometimes seem to me to have been sent. A bittern haunted the pond all of one summer; herons come there, and kingfishers, and a water snake that devours I know not how many tadpoles and minnows. One fall a fox appeared every day in the field across from the house and looked at us between his pounces at grasshoppers and mice; I almost took him for supernatural until I learned that he had formerly been the pet of Mrs. Roberts across the Hollow; she decided to let him go, and here he was. Great horned owls in the evening, and golden eagles by day; weasels and wildcats; deer, as I have said, and pheasants and grouse—we have our fauna, as we have our small birds in winter, feeders at the tray I contrived at the top of a tall pipe the squirrels are unable to climb. Chickadees, nuthatches, juncos, downy woodpeckers, and evening grosbeaks —we do not see those at any other season. In this season they use us as the wrens and catbirds do in summer, and the song sparrows whose voices I can never hear too often. What they all did before there were houses and barns of course I know, but I continue to consider it as one of the unimaginables that make time interesting. Once I asked Edwin Way Teale, the naturalist whom I occasionally meet with Joe Krutch, how long—just at a guess—birds were here before our species was. He said it might have been much more than a hundred million years; and, stunned by the figure (which I do not hold him to), I wrote "Too Old to Read":

> The quickest movement of the quickest bird
> That comes in winter, then is gone again
> (But comes again, finding our suet good;
> Then off; then back; and now he wipes his bill)—
>
> That quickest movement marks the flick of time
> Mankind has been here (now he brings his mate:
> Less gay, more greedy; and the two contest;
> Not with each other; no, the stranger there)—
>
> Has been in houses that the wildest dream
> Of the first wing, before the world was cool,
> Could never have imagined standing (six
> More strangers: they descend; they have it all)—
>
> Standing here this moment, this ticktock
> Of cozy time; then gone again (Oh, God,
> Oh, history. These little darting eyes:
> Too old to read. Nor mind, mind to remember).

III

But in the spring of 1954, when ten of our twenty months had passed, we took a big trip in the car, a long one, to far places and to distant friends. Leaving the cats with Charlie in New York, we drove first to Fort Meade in Maryland, where Johnny was serving his two years in the army. He had been permitted to postpone this until April, 1953, when he finished his Columbia dissertation on certain American travelers in England. Earlier he had been stationed in Louisiana and Texas; he was soon to leave Fort Meade for Wilmington, Delaware, his last stop. He took us into Washington for dinner, and the next morning we went on west and south to see some battlefields of the Civil War which I knew only from my reading. I was to do the same thing with Charlie in the summer of 1956, but on a smaller scale. Having written (with Ralph Roske) a life of Lt. William B. Cushing, the naval hero who sank the *Albemarle,* he particularly wanted to examine the spot of ground at Gettysburg where Cushing's brother Alonzo had fired the last Federal gun before he fell dead. I went with Charlie in his car as far as Gettysburg and Antietam, and at Harpers Ferry we stopped at the hotel where Dorothy and I had stopped in 1923. The present tour was more extensive. Gettysburg, Antietam, Fredricksburg, Chancellorsville, The Wilderness, Spottsylvania, Petersburg, City Point, Richmond, Appomattox, Chickamauga, Chattanooga—we made the rounds, often in heavy rain which reminded me of the weather that had cursed Grant and Lee, miring their vehicles and soaking their rations.

The view I took of these fields was through the mind of Lincoln, whose anxieties were only intermittently relieved by what he heard from the front. My concern with him had long since narrowed down to the last years, indeed the last months, of the terrible war over which, by an irony almost unique, this rational, good man was called upon to preside; and I had begun to think, because of the way his story shrank into one drop of bitter and sweet pain, that a play was indicated rather than a narrative poem. The end of his life was what mattered. So I was relatively unmoved by his birthplace when we visited it at Hodgenville, Kentucky. The marble temple encasing a reconstructed log cabin seemed absurd to me in any case.

Gethsemani, where Thomas Merton lived, was only a few miles away from Hodgenville, and I had written him to ask if we might stop. We must, he said; he would be looking for us on the 5th of March—which was in Lent, but he had the permission. That morning, then, I jangled the monastery bell and was informed by a young bearded monk at the small window which opened that we could wait in the guest rooms for Father Louis. When Merton came, grinning, to shake our hands and make us welcome, I was stupid enough to be startled because he had altered in no respect from the mirthful student I once knew. Thirteen years had passed, and of course he looked a little older; but as we sat and talked I could see no important difference in him, and once I interrupted a reminiscence of his by laughing. "Tom," I said, "you haven't changed at all." "Why should I? Here," he said, "our duty is to be more ourselves, not less." It was a searching remark, and I stood happily corrected. Then he conducted me through the monastery while Dorothy waited among the books and pictures in the visitors' quarters. He showed me the church, the refectory, the classrooms where he instructed novices, and the library whose books and manuscripts he had in charge. Later he proposed that all three of us drive to inspect the new tobacco barn that the monks had built out of oak trees cut on the premises. After lunch, which we had by ourselves in a guest house overlooking the roofs of Gethsemani, we came back to meet another man, a lay brother who had known Carl in New York—indeed he looked like Carl—and who in his time had been a figure among the theaters of Broadway: he had even written dialogue for Beatrice Lillie, who only a few weeks ago was here to see him. He too had permission to talk—and to laugh, for there were many stories.

When we left at last, Merton took us to the car and sent special messages to Krutch and Thurber, whom he knew I liked; they were both good men, he said; he would pray for them when he prayed for us. My final thought as I looked back and waved was about how wrong anyone would be who considered him a prisoner in that place. He seemed a happy man if I ever saw one: serene and certain, grave and smiling, utterly serious and utterly free. The poem, "Once in Kentucky," which I eventually wrote and sent him was acknowledged by the statement, made of course in another world than mine, that it is always interesting to learn what one looks like from the outside.

In our fat times, a monk:
I had not thought to see one;
Nor, even with my own poor lean concerns,
Ever to be one.

No. But in Kentucky,
Midway of sweet hills,
When housewives swept their porches, and March light
Lapped windowsills,

He, once my merry friend,
Came to the stone door,
And the only difference in his smiling was,
It sorrowed more.

No change in him, except
His merriment was graver.
As if he knew now where it started from;
And what the flavor.

He tasted it, the joy,
Then gave it all to me:
As much, I mean, as I could carry home
To this country,

To this country whose laughter
Is a fat thing, and dies.

> I step across its body and consider,
> Still, those eyes.

From Gethsemani we went northwest across Kentucky and Illinois to Tuscola, where Frank and Grace expected us; there is no house at which I would rather arrive. Evenings we played Scrabble, a new word-game of which none of us could have enough, and by day we drove to places in Illinois where Lincoln had lived. But soon enough we were off to our ultimate destination, Arizona and the Krutches. It was a long drive, through states suffering from drought; there was even a dust storm in New Mexico which would have prevented us from going on had we not started shortly after midnight the last morning. Roswell, where I searched in vain for traces of my Uncle Frank—there were plenty of Van Dorens, but they took little interest in my questions—was itself a dust bowl, hot and hopeless. The weather was not right in Arizona, either; the little rain they were justified in expecting had not fallen, and the days were cloudy and cool, so that desert flowers were holding back—a disappointment to Dorothy as we approached Tucson.

But the Krutches were all that mattered, and there was no disappointment when we got to them. As guests for a week in their new house on the edge of town, solitary among cactuses and creosote bushes, we resumed the old conversation as if it had never ceased. The first night Joe followed us into our bedroom, still talking, and paced the floor in his customary style while we lay with our hands beneath our heads, nodding and talking too until Marcelle decided that tomorrow, being pretty sure to come, would be a better time to go on with the business. We took trips here and there; we visited a museum of which Joe was secretary—Georgie the mountain lion, lying on a ledge, roared blissfully in his sleep when he heard Joe's familiar endearments—and one whole day we spent on Mt. Lemmon, to the north of Tucson, where as we climbed in the station wagon a gathering rain, unprecedented in its volume,

washed boulders down and drove us home again. It was in fact
a disastrous rain, a flood before it finished. And doubtless it
brought millions of flowers into being.

But before that happened we were gone, with a week's words
in our minds and ears and with a new image of Joe to place
among the many he had made through forty years: the image
of a mystic, I told him. He had penetrated to the ultimate
equality of things animate and inanimate, but particularly, if
there was any choice at all, of things animate. Life was now
his religion: the single, ever-present, multiform, subvocal thing
which nevertheless he teased until it offered up some sort of
testimony that he took down and entered in his books. Yet he
was the same person too that he had ever been: changed, un-
changed, he still was Krutch. More than a year later I sent him
this poem, "And Still the Same." I was not surprised to have
him protest that he had no notion what two characters it was
about.

> He differs day by day,
> Or else I do.
> Yet it is not my way
> Thus to be ever new
> And still the same:
> Both wild and tame;
> Both added to and one
> When that is done.
>
> It seems no more than chance
> That changes him.
> And molecules do dance,
> I know, and atoms swim.
> With this man, though,
> It is not so.
> Surprising to the end,
> He is my friend.
>
> Not that his wit consents.
> He hides his heart.
> So it is my pretense,
> And both of ours the art,
> Thus to despise

Mark Van Doren

What never dies;
What never will be done
Till many is one.

We drove home a different way: through San Antonio and Fort Sam Houston, to see where Johnny had been stationed; to Texas City, where Martha, Frank's daughter, lived with her children; to New Orleans, where of course we ate an excellent French dinner; up through Mississippi, Tennessee, Arkansas, and southern Illinois to Frank and Grace again; then on to Clinton, after which we picked up Walter and Blackie in New York—they were in good condition—and took them with us to Cornwall.

Charlie, their bachelor host for a month, would not be married until after Johnny was. In 1955 he was best man when Mira Jedwabnik, who at ten had escaped to America with her parents from Vilna, became Johnny's wife and our daughter; the two of them went to Europe in the summer of 1956, for a fling before Johnny began teaching history at Brandeis University. A year before this Charlie had started teaching English in Hamilton Hall as one of my colleagues, though in the fall term, his first, I was naturally not on hand. His utter lack of self-consciousness when I returned was a pleasure to me which I still cannot overstate: he might have been any other of the dozen young instructors who met their classes and chatted with their elders in the corridor.

I suspect it was a like composure that made Charlie successful and famous on television when in the winter of 1956–1957 he took part, simply for fun at first, in a quiz program called "Twenty-One." He answered endless questions and made (for a teacher) fantastic sums of money; but the notable thing was that something like thirty million listeners fell in love with him. Nuns in convents prayed for him: little girls and United States senators competed to see which of them could praise him more; teachers wrote to thank him for having made the intellect respectable again; and all of my relatives, not to speak of old friends unheard from for as many as fifty years, wrote me

334

about our tall, modest son whom they were gathering in houses to watch on Monday nights. Guy was a center for the same attention in Michigan, Frank in Illinois, and Paul in Wall Street. The whole world seemed to wake and stir. Lieutenant Muse, my friend at Camp Pike, wrote me from his retirement in South Carolina, quoting in the course of a long letter two priceless lines from a Southern folk poem whose origin I am still curious about:

> Here comes Pa a-stepping high,
> Which is of his walk the way.

But no letter moved me more than one that came to Charlie from Otto Henry, my cousin in Illinois, now seventy; it was his sister Gladys with whom Frank and I had played doctor at Hope. After identifying himself and saying that if asked I could identify him still further, he went on to speak of my father, who had been his family's physician when he was young. "We thought the world of him," he said: "but you may be particularly interested to learn that last Monday night when the show was on I shut my eyes and could hear Dr. Van Doren talking."

Charlie's marriage in April to Geraldine Bernstein, a friend for more than a year who recently had quit her own work to help him with his correspondence, took place on St. Thomas in the Virgin Islands, where the two of them were visiting Geraldine's uncle as guests in his hotel. The cablegram Charlie sent us seemed wrong to those who dispatched it, for the first word arrived with a penciled correction. But we had no difficulty in making out what Charlie had written on the blank. It was: "Worried today. Love."

IV

I did not return from Arizona to an altogether lazy life in Cornwall. Columbia was two hundred years old that year, and I had been asked to assist in celebrating the fact. One such duty involved convocations in distant places at which I spoke. In May I went to Raleigh, North Carolina, to Fayetteville, Arkansas, and to Detroit: a round trip that took a week's time, and in that time I wrote my Lincoln play.

It began in Raleigh, when I had an idle day in the hotel and wondered how I should spend it. I had not planned to begin the play yet; I had no books or notes with me, and I had scarcely settled upon the whereabouts of the opening scene. Nor had I made any attempt to discover whether I could write dialogue. Then suddenly I was doing it. Lincoln walked into his office at the White House where John Hay and William Stoddard were sorting letters for him to see, and I could hear what he said to them. From then on there was no insoluble problem. I wrote all day, and part of the next day on a train to Memphis. In Fayetteville I kept it up between engagements, and on the train between St. Louis and Detroit I scribbled without stopping in the bound black notebook I always take with me just in case. Across Indiana I was alone in the club car with a little man of great age who without my knowing it must have been watching me, for when the lead in my mechanical pencil gave out, and I shook it in vain for further ammunition, he bent over his briefcase, removed from it a wooden pencil nicely sharpened, and as the train slowed down for Fort Wayne brought it to me, saying: "Permit me to make this small contribution to art." Before I could even say thank you he tottered back to his end of the car, gathered his belongings, and got out. I was therefore unable to ask him how he knew I had not been writing a report of sales or checking an inventory. I could only bless him for what he had done: with his pencil I finished the last scene before I was in Cornwall again.

Nothing about the play as I wrote it interested me more than the difference between Lincoln's voice and that of any person with whom he spoke; and he spoke a lot, for I knew he had never been a laconic man—he was brilliant, and delighted in conversation. The uncanny thing was that I not only could hear his voice but could anticipate what he would say. He talked in prose, whereas the others used blank verse. But that was not it: I had previously made the decision to differentiate him thus, and had resolved that if I could manage it his prose would contain more poetry than their verse. No, the startling revelation was that I had really, in the course of reading several million words by and about him, come to clear conclusions as to his genius; they might be wrong, but they were distinct.

I took certain liberties with the record: I kept Joshua Speed, Lincoln's old Springfield friend, more closely on hand in Washington than he could have been during the last weeks of the war; but he had to be there as Horatio has to be in *Hamlet,* so I brought him on from Louisville and never let him go. The scenes themselves were the natural ones that had stood out in my reading: at City Point, where Lincoln and Grant discussed the terms Lee would be given when he surrendered; in Richmond after its fall; then back in the White House where Lincoln maneuvered daily against senators who would have him consider another policy toward the beaten South than the one he had determined to pursue. The entire reference of the play was to the time after the war, the time Lincoln did not live to see. The irony and the pity were in that. And all the while, if I may say so again, I could hear Lincoln talking. I could almost hear him thinking. And this was just as true in subsequent months or years when with Johnny's help I revised the play. Opened at any seam, it contained the same man, the common man whom no other man resembles.

In that same year I published a volume of *Selected Poems.* I had considered doing this for years, but had not known how: I could not make the selection. Nor was it easy now. During many months I alternated between reading Lincoln and re-reading myself, and sometimes the second exercise seemed to lead nowhere, for I kept putting poems in and taking them out until I feared I was deaf to whatever in them was better or worse. But Cecil Hemley had urged me to try, and José Villa added his voice—a soft one, as I have said, but so authoritative with me as to amount to something like the distant thunder of command. Allen Tate also agreed; though what he had in mind was a smaller volume than finally appeared. If that volume was too large, the moral perhaps is that a poet should not pass upon his own work. In the long run, supposing that the work survives, no opinion of it is less important than his, or more rudely disregarded. His readers, right or wrong, are the only judges.

Yet, having decided to try, I could only do my best; and in the process I came to certain conclusions about the hundreds of poems I had written over more than thirty years. Furthermore, I produced a book which I could mine in various directions, following distinct veins, whenever I was asked to read my poems and discuss them. They all may have one subject in the end, but on the surface they have several; and these can surprise me by the clarity with which they appear when I pursue them through the volume.

At St. John's, for example, I discovered how often I had chosen, when faced with the oldest of philosophical alternatives, the Many over the One. Happening upon "How Deep To Go," with its suggestion that the sphere of existence is best explored from the outside, not the inside, the center, where a mind may well be lost—

> How deep to go, how dark,
> O you that made all things in number,
> How deep, how dark shall my desire descend?
> And is there any happy coming
> Home from that cold end?
>
> There have been those that dived,
> O you that made all things in weight,
> Until solidity, that locks things in,
> Suspending mind and body both—
> Where did that death begin?
>
> Why should it not be good,
> O you that made all things in measure,

The Final Miracle: 1953–1957

Not to sink deeper than the nether side
Of this we see, this film of world
Spread now so fine, so wide?

How near, and yet how changed,
O you whose glass stands always full,
How bright might this reality then be,
By undermirror watched; how warm,
And how quicksilver free—

and turning to "Praise Doubt," which prefers the sun upon the
whitecaps to the "deep waters of this world," I wondered how
many poems of mine had made a similar election. I found
that dozens had, including "Axle Song," "The Little Wars,"
and "Why, Lord." But the chief of them was "No Faith," the
pertinence of which amazed me as I read it in this company:

What held the bones together? Not belief,
Not anything he could probe, no ligament god.
Why was the world so one for him yet many,
So woman and yet so speechless? Then the odd,
The furtive, ashamed security. We wondered.
But there was no faith in him that sang or thundered.

There was no understanding in this man
Of his own simplest secret: of the way
Earth's air kept warm for him, and how there shone
Always another light outdoors of day.
He would have chosen darkness; he denied
What was so strange, so palpable, inside;

He said he could be unhappy. But we knew.
There was this sweet continuum, this flesh;
There were these bones, articulated so:
A web they were, with music up the mesh,
A frame of hidden wires too deep for tone,
A skeleton wholeness, humming to him alone.

He must have heard the harmony, but he swore
Time talked to him in separated sounds.
He took them as they came and loved them singly:
Each one, he parried, perfect within its bounds.
As for the burden's end, the tune's direction—
He smiled; he was content with disconnection.

Mark Van Doren

Yet who could smile and mean it? Who could rest,
As this man did, midway the million things?
Who else could be serene at truth's circumference
When only the known center of it sings?
Who else but he?—submissive to each part
Till it became the all, the homeless heart.

The person in that poem, published twenty years before, was of course myself, and there had been no change in him. He still refused to say that the world had one meaning and no other; he still inclined to take as it came, in numerous guises which he would not question as to the order of their importance and truth. All things continued acceptable to him; he was happy, and he insisted he did not know why; there was no single secret he had discovered.

But other themes have emerged on other occasions. They do not contradict this one, yet they are not the same. Scott Buchanan told me once that my poems had knowledge in them, though he could not say of what. Joe Krutch once said they were all love poems. Each time I was pleased, as of course I was pleased when a third man, an editor, wrote me that my lyrics were both intense and geometrical. In that case I was pleased because somebody had noticed the geometry. I have never ceased to be fascinated by form. I like the challenge of a complicated stanza, Spenser's, Dante's, Herbert's, or Donne's, that I have never tried before. Yet all the while I have been principally concerned with what I want to say; as latterly I have wanted to describe and celebrate my friends, to reassert the terrible power of love, to note the ways of sun and shadow on the ground, to muse upon the minds of animals and children, and to testify, as only time makes possible, concerning the all but incommunicable insights, or is it hindsights, of old age, as well as the force with which it feels them.

Old men's intensities are not to be believed.
Their pities and their rages, humorous, unterrible,
Return and burn again, building a whiter ash
About a hotter fire: some day, some day, unbearable.

340

Some day then it is clear: soul must consume itself.
After so many trials, nothing but ache, but error.
So with no world to watch, and neither with smoke nor flame,
Simply it burns and burns; and no tale of the terror.

In that poem, "Some Day Then," I have imagined men much
older than myself—old, indeed, to the point of utter defeat
when they think to express their passion—but not enough
older to be ignored as, doubtless quite properly, absolute
ancients are by the very young.

V

On August 19, 1955, Dorothy and I sailed for Europe, which
we had not seen since 1924. We planned to drive by car
through England, Scotland, Ireland, and France, then go by
train to Greece. The night before we sailed we spent in New
York with the boys and Mira, never suspecting that a heavy
rain at the windows was more than matched by hurricane
downpours farther north. Not until we read the ship's news
did we learn of a "disaster in Connecticut." Nor could we
get any details until we landed at Plymouth and found letters
from the boys. Towns near Cornwall had been torn to pieces
by mad rivers that very night. The bridge by Paul's house had
disappeared; our own bridge that led to the maple grove where
Will Bailey cut stove wood for us in 1932 was simply nowhere
to be seen—not a stick or stone of it remained. And the
brook, its bed fantastically ripped and littered with boulders
rolled the entire length of Sedgwick Mountain, would never
be the same again. The pond, except for some damage that
Johnny repaired, had escaped; and the house still stood. Hearing this, we went on about our business; we had come to see
the Old World again, and see it we would.

We renewed our acquaintance with London, still beautiful,
still mighty, then after a week drove north through Cambridge,
Olney, York, and Durham to the country I had once missed

seeing by the toss of a sixpence. There we kept on going, north by west, until the roads became difficult and the moors and glens began to seem infinite in number, so that it clearly would be impossible to trespass upon them all. Any trip by car is especially interesting to me when the road leads into barren, bleak places and the mountains, if there are mountains, strike me as grand in their inaccessible, inhuman solitude. Scotland was supreme in that respect. Glencoe, even if there had never been a massacre in it, would have been all my imagination desired. But there must be a companion in the wilderness; the minimum population of a paradise is two. Dorothy responds as I do to spaces that promise to be dreary and are not; or so I have assumed in "I Am Not Ever":

> The desert moor, the empty glen:
> I am not ever, travelling at your side, so much at home
> As then.
>
> The swept road, the swift car,
> Flying, flying on the wings of those forsaken worlds,
> As far
>
> As God's body, death's end:
> I am not ever, dear, so deep in love with you; nor you
> With wind.

In Ireland, for all the charms of Dublin and the towns beyond it, the desolation of the extreme west supplied for me the most delectable details: the scoured summits of the Aran Islands, the stony hillsides of Connemara, and above Westport the endless peat bogs—on and on, until we turned and came south again, the whole world seemed one vast rolling plain of peat, and I was reluctant to escape from it into the center of the island where donkeys trotted and white cottages lined the roads. Even there, however, by the River Shannon, Clonmacnoise, a thousand years ago the intellectual capital of Europe, huddled the ruins of its seven churches on a windy hill so utterly barren and alone that I was in my element once more.

On the way back to London I took a sudden notion to de-

tour southwest into Devon and find if I could the village of
Dean Prior where Robert Herrick was once vicar. To Herrick,
a London poet and wit of exquisite refinement, Devon itself
had been a desolation; but only, of course, in the sense that
it was not London. It was full of people, and he learned to
love some of them; yet it was a land of exile as any reader of
him knows. To be sure his church was there; a small one, in
which a young woman was practicing on the organ. She told us
that in the vicar's house—the vicar was away—were the two
rooms whose littleness the poet had been so amusing about;
there was scarcely space in them for him and his servant Prue.
We saw the rooms, and walked for a while under some neighboring trees. But of course Herrick was not there, nor indeed
had I expected him to be. Only, of all English poets he was the
one I wanted to call on in this fashion. For in Cornwall I had
read him over and over, and even spoken to him in his kind of
verse:

> Herrick, hello.
> You cannot be asleep; and yet if so,
> Kinsman, your book is not: the lyric
> Spring, unquenchable, of him I know,
> Robert, as my Herrick.
>
> And I am his,
> And therefore yours, like those nine mistresses
> Who never spoke one word, yet wore
> The crimson ribands and the stomachers
> You still I think adore.
>
> I do but read,
> Herrick, I do but listen; yet indeed
> All that you asked was eyes and ears.
> Well, mine are thine, and I shall intercede
> With others to give theirs.
>
> Herrick, be sure
> Your maids, your meadows, and your verse endure,
> And your delicious lewdness, drawn
> By the same sun, that loves impure with pure,
> From him I dote upon.

Cornwall was not to me as Devon was to him; if I was an exile there, I was a willing one; yet both the poet and the man—doubtless two very different creatures—had begun to seem my kin, and I addressed them as familiars.

In France we made a great circle: out from Paris, which now we saw through Charlie's eyes, to Mont-St.-Michel, then down through the château country and the caves of Lascaux to Cannes, where we lay a week in the sun, and finally north again over the French Alps through Burgundy to Paris. At Corps, in the southeastern mountains, we looked up Robert Lax, who had been writing me from St. Joseph's Seminary; he vaguely described himself as a poet in residence. I still do not know what he was or did there, but I shall not forget the delight in his long face as it looked out from a window where he was waiting; I had called from Serres the evening before, and he had told us when to come. He gave us bowls of coffee and plates of bread and butter in a room near the entrance, and after that he walked with us up and down the paths of the orchard and garden. He did not know the name of any plant or tree, but he knew how beautiful each one of them was, and he still knew—but without speech—how unspeakably fair the whole of creation looks when nothing is permitted to stand in its way. He took pictures of us, and we of him; then we were off, waving, to ascend next day, over chasms and past savage waterfalls, the height on which the Grande Chartreuse keeps its contemplatives forever out of view. Then there was Burgundy, the country of great wines, as climax to a tour through what had sometimes seemed a world of nothing whatever but wine. It was early October, and all France reeked with the pressing of grapes. The odor was still with us when we reached Paris in time to take the Orient Express to Athens.

Greece, which I almost dared not visit because its past had come to mean for me so many rare and special things, reassured me even while it awed me. It was too beautiful not to be somehow good as a country to go through in the simple way we did, marveling at the names on every side: Helicon, Par-

The Final Miracle: 1953–1957

nassus, Delphi, Cithaeron, Thebes, Athens, Olympia, Ithaca, Sparta, Arcadia, Argos, Mycenae, Corinth, Delos, Crete. And with each name went in every case an appropriate landscape: Earth herself had collaborated with the poets who left this peninsula and the islands around it a truly created piece of ground, for no other mountains, valleys, plains, and sites of cities live on as these do, whether or not the present inhabitants resemble those who were famous before them. In a sense they do resemble them: the Greeks are still a hospitable, mentally active, and talkative people. Fivos Delfis, a poet with whom I had long corresponded, took time off from his work to show us his house, his wife, his children, his old wrinkled mother from Delphi, and as much of Athens as he could.

Fivos (Phoebus) Delfis is the pen name of George Canellos, who took it in honor of the town where he was born; and no wonder, for the fame of Delphi is a continuing and indeed a limitless thing. It was the sacred center and holy ground of ancient Greece; halfway up Parnassus, it overlooked the most beautiful world men have ever been given to see. The poet's mother, when she understood we were going there the next day, kept coming up to me in her son's house and putting her hand in mine as she said, so softly that I had to lean and hear the word: "Delphi." She impressed me, as most of the women in Greece did, by her sadness and sweetness, both of which qualities carried in her case an overtone of strength. The great thing about any country is its women, but that is nowhere truer than in Greece, and there was no better instance of it than this old lady. I wrote a poem about her a year after our return and sent it to Fivos Delfis:

> In little Greece, great mountains:
> Walls of an old world that only eagles and the ghosts
> Of heroes (Agamemnon in his shroud)
> Remember, and that only
> Women such as walk there now can wear
> Like sadness on their shoulders, in their eyes.
> Their smile assumes sobriety
> In strangers too; the wind

Is one to them and these; the hard,
High, marvellous brown mountains are a wingèd
Weight they share with who comes up,
Comes down the stony passes, and is nightly
Glad for olives, ancient on the plain.

In Athens, though, a honey-sweet
Old wrinkled woman, captive of the suburbs,
Beamed when her son said "Delphi";
Beamed, holding my hand in hers, and said it after him
As a girl says a lesson; said it softly,
"Delphi, Delphi," twice, for then, for now:
Her birthplace, and her second childhood's
Innermost clandestine pleasure
Hugged here in this faraway new house
Where lights mean other houses, not the stars.
"Delphi." And I saw her halfway up
Parnassus, gathering thyme, the flowery food
Of old ancestor bees long since
In Hades, mourning the hot sun.
I saw her, not in shadow, bearing
Both of those huge tawny summits,
Desolate, for burden, smiling
Ruefully, remembering,
Remembering,
Not here but there,
Not now but then and then,
The cries of heroes (Laius in his car).

He translated it and published it, and because of it, and because of an article on Greece I had written for the *Reporter*, the Demos of Delphi proclaimed me an honorary member of the holy city. I was proud of that. Yet I shall always remember too how our driver in Greece, for we went over it by car (with William and Lois Kugeman of Cornwall), curdled my blood at a point in the mountains between Thebes and Delphi. The road forked suddenly—three roads met—and the man at my side said: "This is the place where Oedipus killed his father."

I nowhere had the illusion that I was seeing what any Greek saw in the time of Homer or Pericles. Nor did I mind too much that our train, after a long, wild trip through Yugoslavia, had entered the north of Greece by night so that we could not see Olympus. Perhaps no ancient Greek could see it either; it was too great a thing to stare at, and anyway it was the creation of a poet who had no eyes with which to stare. I comforted myself with an epigram, called "Tourist," which put the mountain and me, I hoped, in the right place and relation:

> I passed Olympus in the night,
> But had I passed by day
> I still could tell you less of it
> Than blind Homer may.

Then in November we came home by plane to Rome, by train to Naples, and by ship through the pillars of Hercules to the North Atlantic and New York, where Walter and Blackie, indifferent to where we had been, waited to ride with us to Cornwall.

VI

The winter that was coming on would be, I knew, both wild and tame in the good way of country winters, one of which I had set down in the *Diary* of nearly a quarter-century ago. It turned out to be a time, identical for that matter with the time that followed twelve months later, and with other times, I trust, that are to come, when I reflected at leisure upon the world as now at last it looked and felt to me. That world is full of people who announce daily, after consulting graphs, that it is such and such a place, with this or that future concerning which for the most part they are uneasy. Without the graphs, and certain convenient statistics, and random interviews with other people on street corners or with important citizens at their desks, it would appear that no such prophet has any way of judging for himself what lies around him. He does not know where he is. It seems that he has been dropped here, as on a strange planet, and now he must get out his apparatus so that he may study the quaint phenomena that come his way. I like to think that my own mind has been made up in a different fashion: less professional, I grant, but more natural and free, and with due, affectionate regard for countless accidents, of time, place, and character, that have made things seem for me what they do seem.

The world, I am certain, is a terrible place, but I am just as certain that I love it. How this can be I do not know, for in any rational view it does not deserve to be loved. It changes too often and too much; it harbors, even helps, a multitude of persons who misuse their minds, by stupidity or false witness, to the end that justice and joy shall everywhere decrease; it is neither plainly good nor plainly bad; it is not even, I suppose, intelligible at all. Yet I love it. And my reason, if any, seems to be better than the lame one that it is the only world I have. That is true, but then there might be other conclusions, such for example as that I should be glad to leave it. I have not come to that conclusion, though I did not logically escape it in "All Seasons":

> All months, all days, all hours,
> All sister seconds even, oh, all seasons
> Beautify the world and bless
> The walkers on it.
>
> Some of whom they drown,
> And some make die of thirst; they burn, they freeze,
> They kill us every minute; yet
> We must adore them.
>
> Supposing them gone out:
> Time's candles. Then no joy or darkness either.
> No bitter, sweet; beginning, end.
> Oh, mercy on us.

Nor did I in "Wish for the World":

> Wish for the world that it will never change,
> Even if terrible, to total strange.
> Even if good, may there be no excess
> Beyond this power to think of more, of less,

The Final Miracle: 1953–1957

That is our lone reward for living here.
May only what is missing still be clear
On any earth to come, that so can teach
Hell's difference, and heaven's—each from each,
And both from its dear self: the single place
Than which all others have exacter grace,
And yet it is the measure. Be it thus
Forever, little world that lengthens us.

Those poems make the best of something bad: a poor thing, but our own. But what if the world is good? An indefensible position, but what if it is?

The whole truth for me is no longer content with half-statements, lame praises. In the summer of 1956 I sat down to make a list of things whose existence I would celebrate if time and strength were left to me. The list grew longer and longer, until it seemed an idiot enterprise, a vain attempt at what no single mind can do. Did I think I was Adam, naming all nature? Then, quite suddenly, I imagined myself dead, and these things gone; and I wrote "Morning Worship," which Robert Lax, then back in New York, printed for me in his magazine *Pax*, which comes out only now and then and never has more than one page, so that every word of it will be read:

I wake and hear it raining.
Were I dead, what would I give
Lazily to lie here,
Like this, and live?

Or better yet: birdsong,
Brightening and spreading—
How far would I come then
To be at the world's wedding?

Now that I lie, though,
Listening, living,
(Oh, but not forever,
Oh, end arriving)

How shall I praise them:
All the sweet beings

349

Mark Van Doren

Eternally that outlive
Me and my dying?

Mountains, I mean; wind, water, air;
Grass, and huge trees; clouds, flowers,
And thunder, and night.

Turtles, I mean, and toads; hawks, herons, owls;
Graveyards, and towns, and trout; roads, gardens,
Red berries, and deer.

Lightning, I mean, and eagles; fences; snow;
Sunrise, and ferns; waterfalls, serpents,
Green islands, and sleep.

Horses, I mean; butterflies, whales;
Mosses, and stars; and gravelly
Rivers, and fruit.

Oceans, I mean; black valleys; corn;
Brambles, and cliffs; rock, dirt, dust, ice;
And warnings of flood.

How shall I name them?
And in what order?
Each would be first.
Omission is murder.

Maidens, I mean, and apples; needles; leaves;
Worms, and planets, and clover; whirlwinds; dew;
Bulls; geese—

Stop. Lie still.
You will never be done.
Leave them all there,
Old lover. Live on.

The poem is the list; and breaks off when there is no point in voyaging any further towards infinity. It could have gone on, of course, and mentioned all sorts of things that for me are just as precious as these are. My family and my friends, for instance; and the good people I know—miracles not to be explained any more than they could have been expected, for the problem of good is tougher than the problem, more often and more eloquently attacked, of evil. And the good books, the really good ones—they are few—that depend on no ingenious theories about life which life will disprove. I have come to think of their heroes as my friends, though I am none of theirs:

> My great friends do not know me.
> Hamlet in the halls,
> Achilles by the river, and Don Quixote
> Feasting with the Duke see no one there
> Like me, like Mark Van Doren, who grows daily
> Older while they look not, change not,
> Die not save the deaths their masters made.
>
> Those, yes, over and over.
> And Bottom stands tremendous,
> And Sancho rubs his head, half comprehending
> Knighthood, and Malvolio's cold voice
> Invites the madhouse hour. These neither die
> Nor rise again. They look not, change not,
> Only as folly, wonderful, lasts on.
>
> Still my great friends ignore me,
> Momently grown older
> And dying in the west. They will be there
> Forever, gods of the world, my own immortals
> Who will not go along. Nor do I ask them.
> Let them forever look not, change not,
> Die not save as mortals may behold.

But no matter; their world is as familiar to me as that of Hope and Urbana, of Cornwall and New York. It is of course the same world, terrible and wonderful, and it never becomes unrecognizable.

I should not like to think I am complacent, or lucky, or deluded, or merely pleased. It is more positive than that. By some odd chance and for no good reason I am happy. And there I rest—with side glances toward Solon, who according to Herodotus told Croesus that no man can be called happy until he is dead. Of course that is true, and I hope I do not tempt fate when I say I am happy now. Anything can occur, and the worst things have a way of occurring last. I leave them to be what they will. I speak only of time gone. It went well, and I would be unfair to fate if I denied it.

Between tragedy and comedy I have elected comedy for my mask; or if not that, for my muse. I have learned how to live with contradiction: to accept the unacceptable. I think I understand all that Kazantzakis, the modern Greek, once put in a dozen words: "Life has performed its final miracle. It has become a fairy tale." Fairy tales are full of evil, and of crazy good. The world is a funny place that nevertheless makes sense to those who love it. Without love it cannot be comprehended in any of its corners, let alone its roof and floor. Some years ago I wrote an epitaph for myself:

> Let this be true, that I have loved
> All men and things both here and gone;
> But most the men whose love surpassed
> My love, and so lives on and on.

More recently, in "Undersong," a poem whose stanza I borrowed from Spenser, I said of the world that it was one for me as only music makes things one. Not faith, not reason; merely music, which I claimed I heard. Literally I do not, but nothing is more clear to me than this harmony that yields no sound and thereby does not force a single note:

i

> In wonderment I walk to music pouring
> Out of so dark a source it makes no sound:
> Not waterfalls, not wind, not eagles soaring
> On wings that whistle insult to the ground;
> Not insect whine at which the flower rejoices;
> Not instruments, not voices;
> Not, taciturn, those numbers where they wheel
> While the fixed stars, creation's counterpoises,
> Sing in deep throats a song of commonweal
> More ancient than mankind, than beast or bird
> Coeval with the Word:
> No, none of these is what I overhear
> In wonderment, in walking every day.
> A harmony more hidden, as midway

352

The Final Miracle: 1953–1957

Of the whole world it hums, and yet more near,
More secret in my ear,
Keeps coming to me, coming, and I know
As long as I go forth it shall be so.

ii

Each day I walk in is made slyly one
By symmetries whose names I never seek.
For if I did, and found them, and were done
With listening, with looking, and could speak
Love's language with the subtlety they do,
It might no more be true.
For it is music's language, meant to please
No mind except its own, and if I too
Attempted it the melody would cease;
As birds do in the forest if a foot
Too suddenly is put
On pathways saved for silence, or for such
Plumed echoes as are proper to the place.
The music is not mine in any case;
I only let it come, by sight, by touch,
As often as by hearing; though the ghost
Of sound is innermost;
And mightiest, as if the great one there
Had burst his heart and scattered it in air.

iii

Down it falls, that wild unfigured tune
Which nevertheless reorders all my earth.
I walk, and every acre is bestrewn
With witnesses of morning in slow birth,
And of the sky's contentment that things be
Just as they are to see.
Different were deadly, something sings
In a low voice as of a leafy tree
Preoccupied with shade, and two sure wings
That aim at it to enter by and by
When the half-day shall die,
And perfect sunlight shall hang due above
Like a dark lantern swinging. Something says,
Barely aloud, in less than sentences:
Just as they are, together in their love,
The whirlwind, the dove,

353

Mark Van Doren

The contraries. Listen. That rough chord:
It is his breathing, it is our overlord.

iv

In times of tempest when disorder seems
Order itself, the very rule of motion,
And moaning as they bend, the trees and streams,
In horror at their own perverse devotion
To chaos come alive, strain not to shatter
Form, and the first matter
Of which all possibility was made;
But then the roar increases, and winds batter
Winds above the world as fields are flayed
And savage grasses, blowing, strip the bones
Even of sunk stones;
In times of tumult when the lines should snap
That lead like silk from note to kissing note,
And the sweet song should strangle in the throat,
There it still is, miles above thunderclap,
As audible as when on halcyon days
It mastered the same ways;
Compounded of all tones, including these
Of stricken ground and hideous green seas.

v

And if there be those who would mock me, saying:
Music? None is here save in your head;
Noises, yes, delectable, dismaying,
But not in measure, as if more were said
Than owls and larks will tell you, or mad crows,
Or the wind-ravished rose,
Or human chatter, changeless year by year;
Then soberly I say to such as those:
The sound is one, and is not sinister.
It is an honest music through and through.
And so the chatter, too,
And so the silences that wait sometimes
Like a tired giant thinking, so they all
Return and go, then come again and fall,
Evenly, unevenly, as rhymes
Rival the pure chimes
Of never-ending truth, that for so long
Has sung to such as me this undersong.

Index

Index

Index

Index

Index

Index

Index

Index

Index

Index

Man and Superman (Shaw), 75
Manistee, Mich., 151
Mann, Thomas, 262
Manuscript Committee, 262
Marguerite the mare, 28, 39, 55
Marines, U.S., 90, 100–01, 116, 251
Marlboro, N. H., 218
Marsh, Emily, 280
Martha's Vineyard, Mass., 255
Martin, Everett Dean, 158–59
Marvell, Andrew, 209
Maryland, 216, 223, 266, 275, 282, 291–92, 329; *see* St. John's College
Masefield, John, 66
Massachusetts, 127, 159, 164, 227, 269, 291, 296, 298, 300, 304
Mather, Frank Jewett, 109
"Matins," 267–68
Matthews, Brander, 125–26, 128
Mattis, Mr., 71
Maulick, Charles, 238
Mawanda (honor society), 67
Mayfield Deer, The, 56, 85, 167, 236–41, 248, 295, 324
Mazzeo, Joseph, 302
McCray, Verla, 69
McKeon, Richard, 214
McLean, Kenneth, 291
Mead, Gilbert, 72
Mediterranean, 295; *see* Italy *and* Greece
Meiklejohn, Alexander, 265
Meisel, Frederic Howard, 208
Melville, Herman, 123
Memphis, Tenn., 96, 336
Mencken, H. L., 67
Menorah Journal, 130
"Merry Trainman, The," 314
Merton, Thomas, 211–13, 268–69, 275, 298–300, 330–31
Metropolitan Life Insurance Company, 139
Mexico, 188
Miami, Fla., 271
"Michael" (Wordsworth), 102
Michael (Archangel), 295
Michigan, 54, 69, 78, 96, 116, 137, 185, 231, 335–36
Middle West, 179, 219; *see* Illinois
"Midland," 315
Midsummer Night's Dream, 63
"Midwife Cat," 117

Mike the dog, 233
Miles, Fiske, 32
Mill, John Stuart, 75, 123
Millburn, N. J., 196
Millington, Ralph, 260
Milton, John, 76, 126, 134, 207, 209–11, 217, 226, 250, 285, 290, 305–06
Minnesota, 87, 137
Minou the cat, 161
"Miss Swallow," 293–94
Mississippi, 51, 95, 271, 334
Mississippi County, Ark., 91
Mississippi River, 70, 91, 179, 185
Missouri, 56–57, 79–80, 235, 336
"Mr. Flood's Party" (Edwin Arlington Robinson), 169
"Mr. Hasbrouck," 294
"Mr. Pope" (Allen Tate), 156
Mitty, Walter, 282–83
Modern Language Association, 209
Modern Temper, The (Joseph Wood Krutch), 177
Molière, 111, 132, 211
"Moments He Remembers, The," 30
Montaigne, 132, 211, 217
Montmartre, 111
Mont-Saint-Michel, 344
"Monument, The," 40
Moore, Marianne, 262
Morals (Seneca), 45
More, Paul Elmer, 67–68, 118
"Morning Worship," 349–50
Morningside (periodical), 128
Mortal Summer, 295
Moscow, 163
Moses, 318
Motteux, Peter Anthony, 284
Mt. Lemmon, 332
Mozart, 268
Muhlenberg Branch of New York Public Library, 159–60
Muir, John, 89, 151, 166
Mullin, Glen, 36, 72
Muncie, Ill., 3, 9, 48
Murray, A. T., 272
Muse, Lieutenant W. H., 95, 335
Muskogee, Okla., 47, 69, 95
Mutiny in January (Carl Van Doren), 259, 262
Mycenae, 345
My First Summer in the Sierra (John Muir), 89

Index

Index

Index

Index

Index

Index

247, 249, 260, 262, 271–73, 276–77, 304, 309–12, 326, 330
Van Doren, Charles, 154, 157, 174–75, 184, 188–89, 193, 198, 202, 228–30, 233, 245, 255, 264, 270–73, 275, 277, 278, 282, 285, 308, 312, 317, 329, 334–35, 341, 344
Van Doren, Charles Lucius (father), 12–20, 24–27, 35, 38–42, 49–50, 55, 57, 63, 71, 78–79, 83–90, 95, 116, 154–55, 161, 183, 195, 201–03, 215, 267, 335
Van Doren, David, 51
Van Doren, Dora Ann Butz (mother), 4–7, 11–17, 20, 24–25, 37–38, 42–43, 47, 57, 64, 67, 70, 83–88, 96, 116, 201–02, 214–15, 219, 312, 315–17
Van Doren, Dorothy, 115, 118–19, 128, 134–48, 151, 154, 157, 163–65, 170, 173, 184, 188–95, 197, 199, 202, 207, 218, 220–22, 227–34, 244–45, 254–55, 258–62, 270, 272–77, 279, 282, 294, 300, 303–04, 307–09, 312, 319–22, 326–32, 341–42
Van Doren, Earl, 51, 197
Van Doren, Esther, 51
Van Doren, Frank (uncle), 50, 332
Van Doren, Frank, 3–14, 23–39, 42, 44–48, 54–64, 67–69, 79–80, 83, 85, 88, 95, 117, 135, 138, 183–86, 214–16, 230, 234, 275, 292–93, 313–17, 332, 334–35
Van Doren, Geraldine, 335
Van Doren, Grace Gay, 68, 79–80, 85, 117, 137–38, 185, 214, 234, 238, 313, 315, 332, 334
Van Doren, Guy, 4–6, 10, 14, 25, 33, 57, 64, 67, 69, 71, 78, 83, 137, 184–85, 231, 247, 335
Van Doren, Hannah Chapman, 50
Van Doren, Irita, 69–70, 78, 80–81, 96–97, 115, 120, 140, 155, 163, 310
Van Doren, Jean Wright, 163
Van Doren, Jessie Hess, 138, 185, 196, 314
Van Doren, John, 154–55, 165, 175, 184, 188–89, 193, 198, 202, 228–30, 233, 245, 255, 264, 270, 275, 282, 312, 317, 329, 334, 337, 341
Van Doren, Lena, 51
Van Doren, Margaret, 97, 310
Van Doren, Martha, 80, 214, 334

Van Doren, Mary Elizabeth, 78
Van Doren, Mira, 334, 341
Van Doren, Paul, 5, 8–9, 14, 25, 33–36, 46, 62, 64, 70, 71, 80, 83, 85, 89–90, 100–01, 116–17, 119–20, 138, 145, 150, 185, 196–97, 311, 314, 316, 321, 335, 341
Van Doren, Paula, 196
Van Doren, Peter, 185
Van Doren, Silas, 17
Van Doren, Verla McCray, 69
Van Doren, Walter, 50–51, 95, 144, 162, 197
Van Doren, William Henry, 16, 50–51
Vassar College, 255
Vermeer, 109
Vermilion County, Ill., 43, 48–49
Vermont, 159, 170, 326
Vernon, France, 111
Versailles, 111, 146
Vienna, 163
Villa, Jose Garcia, 252–53, 313, 337–38
Villa, Randy, 253
Villa Grove, Ill., 38, 55–56, 59, 67–68, 79–80, 84–85, 96, 117, 135, 138, 158, 161, 185, 186, 194, 238
Villard, Oswald Garrison, 115, 117, 156, 165
Vilna, Russia, 334
Virgil, 210–11, 217, 285
Virgin Islands, 335
Virginia, 100, 116, 138, 158, 209, 237, 302–03
Virginia, University of, 176, 214
"Visitor, The," 317
Voltaire, 104, 132, 211
Vyvyans, the, 63

Wabash Railroad, 54
Wabash River, 57, 237
Walker, Dr. Bradford, 282, 310
Wall Street, 173, 197, 335
Walter the cat, 282–83, 327, 347
Walton, Izaak, 45
"Wander's World," 294
Wapanucka, Okla,, 229, 231
"War Aims," 123
War Department, 95, 254
Warner, Arthur, 115, 117, 15
"War's Distance," 271
Washington, D. C., 95, 253–54, 260–61, 273, 304, 329, 337

370

Index